PROBLEMS IN MODERN GEOGRAPHY

British Regional Development Since World War 1

Series Editor	Richard Lawton, *Professor of Geography, University of Liverpool*
Andrew W. Gilg	*Countryside Planning: The First Three Decades 1945–76*
David Herbert	*Urban Geography*
Andrew Learmouth	*Patterns of Disease and Hunger*
G.J. Lewis	*Rural Communities*
J.V.R. Prescott	*Political Geography of the Oceans*
David M. Smith	*Patterns in Human Geography*
John R. Tarrant	*Agricultural Geography*
Kenneth Warren	*World Steel*

PROBLEMS IN MODERN GEOGRAPHY

CHRISTOPHER M. LAW

British Regional Development Since World War 1

David & Charles

Newton Abbot London North Pomfret (Vt)

for Elizabeth

British Library Cataloguing in Publication Data

Law, Christopher M
British regional development since World War I. – (Problems in modern geography).
1. Regional planning – Great Britain – History
2. Great Britain – Economic policy
I. Title II. Series
330.9'41'082 HT395.G7

ISBN 0 7153 7974 7

Photoset and printed in Great Britain by Redwood Burn Limited, Trowbridge and Esher for David & Charles (Publishers) Limited Brunel House Newton Abbot Devon

Published in the United States of America by David & Charles Inc North Pomfret Vermont 05053 USA

Contents

List of Figures

List of Tables

Preface

The topic of British regional development and regional problems has received a great deal of attention in the last twenty years. A whole industry has developed consisting of research centres, learned organisations and a veritable flood of publications. In universities and polytechnics students in economics, geography, planning and allied subjects are provided with courses involving lengthy discussions on Britain's regional problems. For the last twelve years the author has provided such a course, and it is out of such an experience that the idea for this book has arisen. Although there is a vast literature on the subject, most of the works are of a specialised nature dealing with particular regions, limited periods or selected aspects of the topic such as manufacturing industry or offices. However, the intending student of the subject requires a broad introduction to the subject to enable him to move from the general to the particular. The aim in writing this book has been to provide a comprehensive and balanced introduction to the problems of regional development in Britain. In order to give sufficient historical perspective to these problems, the study has been taken back to the end of World War I which to a certain extent was a turning point for regional development. It will be obvious to the reader that the topic thus defined is vast and worthy not of one but several books. The only limitation which has been imposed on the work is to concentrate attention on inter-regional as opposed to intra-regional development. Thus we are concerned with the differences in growth between say the South East and Scotland rather than the pattern of change within these regions. Even with this limitation the topic is still vast, and it will be easy for specialists to say that there is not enough on this or that aspect. However, I hope that the overall impression is one of balanced coverage with sufficient references to enable specialist interests to be pursued.

The idea for this book has matured over several years and its writing would not have been possible without study leave from the University of Salford, to whom grateful acknowledgement is made. I am also grateful to the editor of the series, Professor Dick Lawton for his helpful comments. Acknowledgement is also made to the editor of 'Social Trends' for permission to reproduce the diagram in Figure 2. I should also like to thank Janet Richardson, Marie Partington and Julie Jones for typing the manuscript and Christine Minister and Gustav Dobrzynski for drawing the maps. Finally to my wife, Elizabeth, and children, Katherine and Nicholas, my thanks for their tolerance of my work which so often transforms holidays into field trips.

CHAPTER ONE

An Approach to Regional Development

The contrast between regional development in Britain in the nineteenth and twentieth centuries is well known: in the nineteenth century economic activity was strongly attracted towards the coalfields found mainly in the northern and western parts of the country, although London as national and empire capital continued to grow; whilst in the twentieth century spontaneous economic growth has mainly occurred in the South East and Midlands. The reasons often given for this change include the lessening importance of coal consequent upon the growth of new forms of energy such as electricity and oil, and the decline in the relative cost of transport, encouraging market as opposed to material orientation of industries. However, whilst these factors explain the reduction in the restraints upon location, they hardly account for the new patterns of growth and its absence in the important nineteenth-century industrial areas. Accordingly further factors have been suggested for the twentieth-century importance of the South East and Midlands including the availability of requisite skills, ancillary industries, the growth of government spending and employment, the location of the wealthy and affluent requiring new products, the concentration of financial institutions in London, and so on. To explain the absence of spontaneous growth in other parts of the country, other factors have been alluded to such as the over-dependence on declining industries, poor economic structure, lack of entreprenurial initiative and poor physical environment. With such a long list of factors it could hardly be suggested that they are not relevant; but how important, and at what time? It is the aim of this book to describe more fully the process of regional development in the United Kingdom and make a more precise evaluation of the factors involved. The main theme is the difference in economic prosperity between the major regions of the United Kingdom, and differences within regions will be largely but not completely ignored.

The period chosen for the study is from the end of World War I to the early 1970s and some words of justification for this period may be appropriate. The main reason for choosing this period has already been alluded to in the contrast between regional economic development in the nineteenth and twentieth centuries. Clearly there are no complete breaks in economic development, and any limits chosen are to some extent arbitrary and involve the continuation of some trends across the limits chosen. In this pattern of regional development World War I does appear to mark a turning point in the UK. Up to that time nineteenth-century patterns of prosperity and growth based on the coalfields still seemed to operate. The output of coal for this country reached its peak in 1913 and has since, except for brief periods, been in decline. The other great nineteenth-century industry, textiles, also reached its peak just prior to World War I. In both cases the loss of exports, initially caused by the disruption of the war but in the long term caused by a lack of competitiveness, was a major factor in their decline. Inevitably the change in fortune for these industries seriously affected the prosperity of the regions in which they were dominant and has been a major factor in post World War I regional development. Thereafter the growth of the so-called 'new industries', such as mechanical and electrical engineering, motor vehicles and aircraft, all of which had their roots in the period before the war, became significant for regional development.

Up to 1914 UK policy was largely dominated by free trade and, although this was expected to continue after the war, gradually during the 1920s and particularly from 1931, tariffs were introduced with important consequences for industrial development. This was evident in the country's relations with southern Ireland which shortly after the war became a separate republic and so could no longer be regarded as one of the regions of the United Kingdom. More recently protectionism has been eroded both by general agreements between industrialised countries to reduce tariffs (GATT) and by the entry of the United Kingdom into the European Economic Community. Over a period of ten years from the late 1960s patterns of trade have changed with varied consequences for British industries. Increasingly these are being integrated with activities on the continent, and the policies of the EEC, including its regional policies, can be expected to affect the fortunes of the regions of Britain.

The 1970s have also witnessed other significant changes. Discoveries of natural gas and oil in the British sector of the North Sea have transformed the energy position of the country, whilst the rise of world oil prices in late 1973 had given renewed importance to the country's coal resources. Other changes include the falling birth rate, giving rise to the possibility of a static population in the future reminiscent of the perceived situation in the 1930s, and the move towards regional devolution in Scotland and Wales. It is too early to assess the significance of these changes for regional development, or even whether they are permanent, but it could be that the mid-1970s will mark another turning point in regional development.

Theories of Regional Development

It is impossible to evaluate regional development without having norms against which comparisons can be made. One way of doing this is to interpret regional development against a model of what could have been expected. In the field of regional development there is no universally accepted model, but only a collection of ill-fitting ideas (Richardson, 1973). Nevertheless it is useful to begin by briefly describing these and the underlying ideas against which the British case will be examined. We shall assume that a region is a subnational area of a country which cannot devalue its currency.

In the past it has been suggested that economic activities

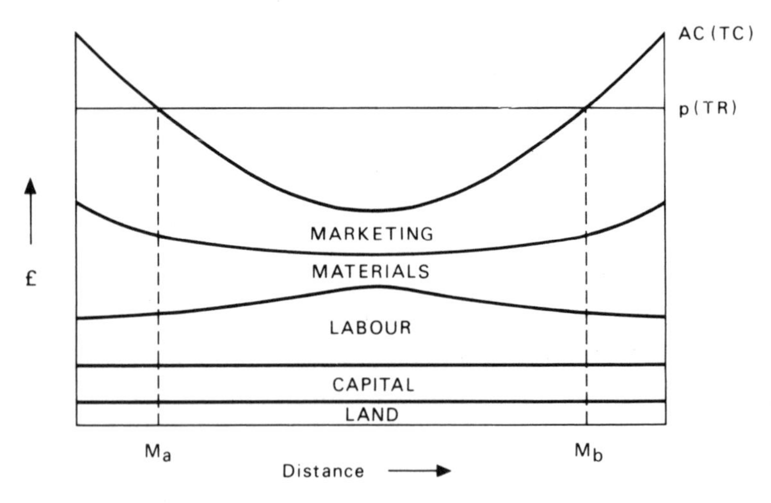

Fig. 1 D.M. Smith's Framework of Industrial Location (1966)

will be located where they can most efficiently be carried out, where profits are greatest, and usually where costs are least. The efficient entrepreneur will seek out these optimum locations whilst the inefficient one will find that if he has not accidentally chosen such a location, it will be unprofitable to continue in business. If all this were true then it might be possible to explain regional development on the basis of the economic advantages or disadvantages of particular areas for industrial or other economic activities. Unfortunately such a simple view cannot be accepted since similar activities are often found to exist successfully in a wide range of locations. An understanding of how this situation occurs can be gained by referring to D. M. Smith's framework of industrial location (1966). In this model (Figure 1) costs (AC) and revenue (p) are represented on a vertical axis and space on the horizontal axis. For simplicity revenue is assumed to be the same wherever the activity is located, although this assumption could be relaxed without altering the interpretation. In reality the price obtained by a firm for its product is often fixed by the competition prevailing between firms, and so by altering its location a firm cannot affect the revenue obtained. Obviously the firm can only operate in space where the revenue is greater than the costs, and this area is shown by the lines M_a

and M_b. These are referred to as the spatial margins of profitability, and although shown here as a continuous zone they could be discontinuous areas, such as port districts. The traditional cost components have been added to the diagram and they cover marketing, including the cost of transport to the market, and materials, again including the cost of transport to the plant. In the past when transport costs were relatively greater than today, the spatial margins of profitability were often narrow with a clear optimum point. In the twentieth century spatial variations in these basic costs have been reduced whilst at the same time there has been an increase in costs such as research and development, and advertising which vary little in space. The result is that today the spatial margins in many industries are wide and there is no optimum point, so that the oft-called 'economic' explanations alone are rarely able to explain regional development, certainly not within a country the size of the United Kingdom. Moreover these factors are not necessarily autonomous and may vary according to other factors so that a wider approach to the system is necessary.

The simplest model of regional development, 'Development Stages' theory, provides a description of what often happens rather than an explanation. In the early stages of regional development most employment will be in the primary sector—agriculture, forestry, fishing and mining —but as economic development proceeds there will be an increase in the secondary and tertiary sectors whilst the primary sector declines in terms of its employment share (Figure 2). In the mature economy employment in the secondary or manufacturing sector will also decline as automation reduces the number of jobs, so that the service sector will come to have the largest share of employment. Unfortunately this theory does not explain how the regional economy proceeds from one phase to the next, or how some regions are able to jump stages. In its simple three-fold division of the economy it ignores many other differences in economic structure, such as types of industries. More importantly it does not describe the relationships of regions within a country to one another,

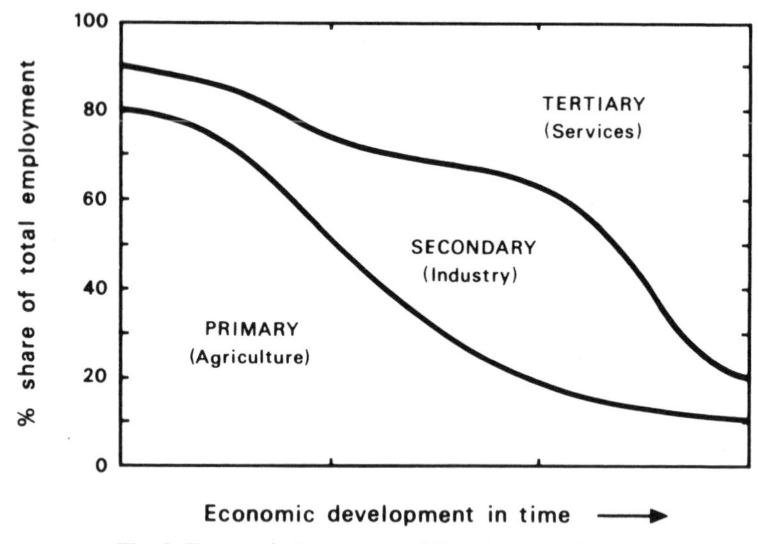

Fig. 2 Economic Structure and Development in Time

particularly as these regions may be at different stages.

The 'export base' theory of regional development (North, 1955) suggests a similar cycle of development, but attempts to suggest a mechanism for the progression. The mechanism is the role of exports which bring income into the region and pay for further development. Most regions, but not all, will begin by exporting primary commodities and the income thus generated will enable home-serving industries to grow which may later become exporting. The larger and maturer the economy, the less important will be the role of exports. The analysis of exporting industries has resulted in the basic/non-basic technique which seeks to identify the exporting or basic industries of a region. Whilst it is usually suggested that the export of primary commodities will begin the cycle, this is not strictly necessary and it may start with industrial or even service activities (e.g. tourism). It may also be possible for a region to develop a high standard of living based on primary activities. Once again the weakness of the theory is in not relating regions together in a system of regions.

So far the activities or industries causing economic growth have not been distinguished in any way, but according to Perroux's 'Growth Pole' theory (1950) only certain activities are suitable. These are termed 'propulsive' industries which are capable of growing rapidly, reaching a large size and, most important of all, which are interlinked with other sectors of the economy. The theory was put forward to explain national economic growth, but its applicability to regional growth was quickly seen (Darwent, 1969). Thus the cotton industry may be seen as a propulsive industry in the growth of north-west England, linking up with the development of communications and the development of chemical and engineering industries. However, in the twentieth century it is by no means clear that such propulsive industries will be necessarily concentrated in one region or only have linkages in one region (Lausen, 1969). Today industrial development is diffuse with a wide range of products manufactured, often giving rise to only small industries, and with considerable international links. In so far as growth pole theory can be applied to regions, however, it does not relate the growth of regions to one another.

Borrowing from neo-classical international trade theory, economists have put forward a spatial equilibrium theory of regional development which suggests that inequalities between regions will be self-correcting. Should one or a group of regions in a country develop higher levels of income and employment than the remainder of the regions, then either capital will move from the former or labour from the latter to correct the imbalance. The poorer regions will have higher unemployment and therefore lower wages, and this will attract industries to these regions so that capital will earn a higher return on investment. In particular it could be expected that labour-intensive industries requiring unskilled labour would filter down to these regions. New industries often require skilled labour, but once production becomes routine less skill is necessary, and they may seek out labour resources (Thomson, 1969). On the other hand the wage differentials between the poorer and richer regions will encourage migration from the former to the latter. Thus the twin movements of labour and capital will cause a reduction in inequalities and eventual equilibrium, although different regions may have differing quantities of economic activity.

Myrdal (1957) and Hirschman (1958) have attacked these ideas, suggesting that multiplier effects will produce the opposite result with inequalities being perpetuated. If the outward movement of population causes an actual population decrease, this will tend to lower the demand for locally produced goods and services, resulting in more people being put out of work. If they in turn move out, the region will begin a vicious circle of decline. Outward migration is usually selective, with the young worker, for whom the physical and social costs of moving are less, forming the main vanguard. This leaves an ageing population unattractive to potential incoming industrialists and which is often resistant to the industrial change that may be necessary for the survival of the region. The filter down process of industrial location just described will in fact perpetuate regional differences with the poorer regions having low-paid unskilled work and the richer regions high-paid skilled work. Moreover, in a modern economy the operation of trade unions may prevent manufacturers gaining lower wages by moving to these regions and outdated work practices causing lower productivity may be a further disincentive. In some regions, or parts of regions, the industrial inheritance of a poor environment may be a further disincentive to inward movement.

In the prosperous regions the operation of multiplier effects consequent upon the inmovement of people will create more jobs and put the regions in the virtuous circle of growth. Increasing production and other economies of scale may negate any labour cost gains which could be had by moving to the poorer regions. The capital generated in these regions will therefore often be ploughed back in situ creating further advantages. Even where savings could be had by movement to a poorer region, industrialists could either not perceive them, or be content to stay put in what is considered to be a satisfactory location. The continuance of these tendencies could lead to increasing polarisation of economic development within a country, with a core region or regions having most of the growth and prosperity, and the rest being in a peripheral or colonial relationship to the core. The centre-periphery model put forward for developing countries (Friedmann, 1966) could be applicable on this basis to advanced countries as well.

However, whilst stressing the strength of these polarisation effects, Myrdal and Hirschman did acknowledge the strength of equilibrating and countervailing forces. The prosperity of flourishing regions would spread or trickle down to the other regions, either through the filter down of some industries such as those requiring cheap unskilled labour or from the demand for goods and services from them. The very absence of economic development might make at least parts of them attractive for tourism and recreation, and perhaps for other activities. In advanced countries good environments have become highly valued in recent years and the nineteenth-century centri-petal movements have been reversed in the twentieth century by centrifugal tendencies. In particular, the effects of direct and indirect government policies do not allow large differences in the standards of public services between regions, and to this end will subsidise to a larger extent local authorities in the poorer regions. The more public services there are and the higher the standards demanded, the greater will be this cross-subsidy between regions. Putting these two opposite tendencies in a historical perspective, it can be suggested that in the early stages of economic development inequalities between regions will tend to increase, but in the latter stages, as wealth and government activity increase, there will be a reduction in these inequalities. Whilst the scale of differences may be reduced, basic differences between the regions could remain.

Whereas economists have discussed regional development without defining regions, geographers have created sophisticated theories involving regional delineation. The most important of these have evolved from Christaller's central place theory (1966). Put briefly this theory suggests that space is organised around urban centres from whence goods and services are distributed. These centres can be arranged in a hierarchy according to the types of goods and service offered and the distance over which consumers will travel to them. At the lowest level are small centres providing a narrow range of goods and services which customers need regularly and for which they will only travel a short distance. These will be grouped under higher order centres providing a wider range of services, and these likewise under the next order of the hierarchy until the top of the pyramid is reached in the national capital. This performs very specialised services for the whole country, and also relates the national system to external systems. Within the national system nodal regions can be defined on the basis of relating areas to the centres to which they look for services, and this can be done for different levels in the hierarchy. The national capital will be a central place for every level in the hierarchy, whilst the regional capitals for every level except the highest. From this it will be seen that not all regions can be equal for there will always be one regional capital which has a national function as well, and therefore gives its region, through proximity, an advantage over all others. This of course will only apply where the national functions are concentrated in one centre as in Britain and have not been divided as occurs in some countries.

Stated as such, central place theory provides no clue to the growth of regions, although it does suggest important relationships between them. To be of further use it needs to be allied with a theory of innovation diffusion. Growth takes place as a result of innovation which reduces costs and introduces new products. Some of these innovations are introduced first at the national or largest centre and then filter down the urban hierarchy. In an interesting study, Robson (1973) has suggested how hierarchical diffusion in conjunction with neighbourhood diffusion operated with regard to gas works, telephone exchanges and building societies during the nineteenth century. These are all infrastructural phenomena in which initially high threshold populations are desirable for the innovators. Such infrastructural innovation can be important in maintaining the economic advantages of the large city and particularly of the national capital. Nevertheless many other innovations diffuse in different ways, and are not related to central place hierarchy. Consideration of these ideas about central place functions and the urban hierarchy suggests further evidence for the working of a centre-periphery model in advanced countries. The centre or core region of the country retains its dominant position by having the nation's highest order centre which attracts new infrastructural innovations. More importantly it attracts the decision-making functions of the country which not only enrich the region itself but give control over other regions.

A summation of these ideas does not produce a very convincing theory of regional development. There are clear tendencies towards centralisation in regional development, most likely centred on the national capital, but extreme inequalities are likely to be reduced by the various spread and trickling down effects mentioned above. Such ideas do not take account of historical development and the inherited resources a region may possess. Each region enters a given period with a different potential for growth or decline determined largely by its industrial and occupational structure. The role played by industrial structure has been an important theme in the study of British regional development in the twentieth century. These theories also say little about the process of economic growth and the role played by research and development and by different sized firms (Leigh and North, 1978b). Traditional economic theories have assumed the existence of a large number of competing small firms with the possibility of easy entry for new enterprises. In the mid-twentieth century this framework appears increasingly unreal as the economy becomes dominated by large companies and the small firm is squeezed out. Finally these theories say little about the role of government. Since the 1930s British governments have not been prepared to let regional development happen of its own accord, but have sought to direct economic growth towards the regions they considered appropriate. In general they have been motivated by ideas of equality to ensure that prosperity is spread evenly around and poverty is abolished or, at least, ameliorated. It would be impossible to make an interpretation of regional development since World War I without examining and evaluating the direct interventions of British governments, which have evolved sophisticated if not consistent policies. The government's aims are equality and balance between the regions, expressed in terms of job opportunities, employment growth, availability of services and incomes.

To summarise this section so far, it can be suggested that there are a number of important themes in the study of regional development. These include the role of the traditional location factors such as materials, labour, and markets, in attracting economic growth; the role of the national system including equilibrating and disequilibrating forces as well as the effect of the urban hierarchy; the role of inherited industrial structure; the role of corporate change in the economy; and finally the effect of government policies.

The method of study adopted in this book follows on from the above discussion. Since the development of regions can only be understood by reference to the wider system, Chapter 2 describes the evolution of the national system including the growing role of government. Chapter 3 provides an outline of regional development examining how the regions have evolved from their positions in 1914 to their present situation in the 1970s. The role of inherited industrial structure in regional employment change is examined in Chapter 4 while in Chapters 5, 6 and 7 the study of structure is continued through a discussion of spatial economic change in the three sectors, primary, secondary and tertiary. Chapter 8 explores the role of firms in regional growth including the increasing importance of the large corporation. In Chapter 9 the influence of equilibrating forces and of government policies is examined with respect to the movement of economic activities, whilst in Chapter 10 the role of the traditional location factors is considered. In Chapter 11 an attempt is made to bring all these factors together in a synthesis of the British experience. Finally in Chapter 12, using past experience and expected changes, some speculation is made about the future of regional development in Britain. However, before all this it is necessary to discuss the regions which are to be used.

Regional Definitions

The United Kingdom, although small on a world scale, is large enough to have significant regional differences. The people of Scotland, Wales, Ulster, the North, Midlands and the South feel themselves to be different. These differences are a reflection of past economic and political history, of culture and the role that space still plays in separating peoples. Such differences provide some clues as to how the United Kingdom may be divided on a regional basis. In order to describe and interpret regional development over the period since World War I, it is necessary to have a set of regions which can be used throughout the period. This is a tall order since government statistics have been given for many different regions, although regrouping is possible in some cases. Inevitably a set of regions will be a compromise between what is desirable and what is practicable.

Traditionally, geographers have defined regions either on the basis of homogeneity or nodality depending on what is considered most significant in the context. For an advanced and urbanised country like Britain nodal regions are usually considered most appropriate. These are centred on conurbations and metropolitan centres and are to a certain extent self-contained. Such regions will have at their cores the main centres of population and the boundaries will pass through less populated regions, where cross-boundary movements will be lower (Fawcett, 1960).

However, nodality is not the only criterion and culture, tradition and local patriotism must also be considered. On this basis there is a strong argument for the delimitation of Scotland, Wales and Northern Ireland as separate regions. It is within England that the nodality principle is most important for delimiting regions. Within the UK, London acts in certain higher order activities for the whole of the country and is described as a first order centre. Second order centres function at a slightly lower level serving major regions of the country, and it is this level which can be used to identify regional capitals and regional boundaries. London also functions as a second order centre and because of its size and importance has inhibited the development of other centres nearby. There is widespread agreement that the centres of the other conurbations—Birmingham, Leeds, Liverpool, Manchester and Newcastle—are also second order centres (Diamond, 1977). Other possible inclusions are Bristol, Nottingham, Bradford, Hull, Sheffield, Leicester, Norwich, Coventry, Southampton and Plymouth. To use all these cities for defining regions would produce a very large number and it is apparent that some are close to each other and, although important, subsidiary to another second order centre. Thus in the case of Yorkshire, Leeds is the outstanding centre and Bradford, Hull and even Sheffield look to it for some services. The situation in the North West is more difficult with two high second order centres in Liverpool and Manchester close to each other, but since the industrial revolution Manchester has performed the major regional role. In the West Midlands, Birmingham's major regional role is undisputed, notwithstanding the twentieth-century rise of Coventry. However, does Birmingham's sphere of influence extend into the eastern part of the Midlands? This area has several important towns with both Leicester and Nottingham often competing as second order centres. These central place functions clearly differentiate this part of the Midlands from the western area but make it difficult to find an outstanding capital. Usually Nottingham is slightly ahead of Leicester and performs a number of functions for the East Midlands. In the West Country, Bristol is a clear second order centre, but Plymouth is marginal to this category. The remoteness of the south-west peninsula enables Plymouth to perform many functions usually only found in larger cities, but even so it lacks the full status at this level. A region based on Plymouth would be small in population and dependent on Bristol for certain functions and accordingly it appears desir-

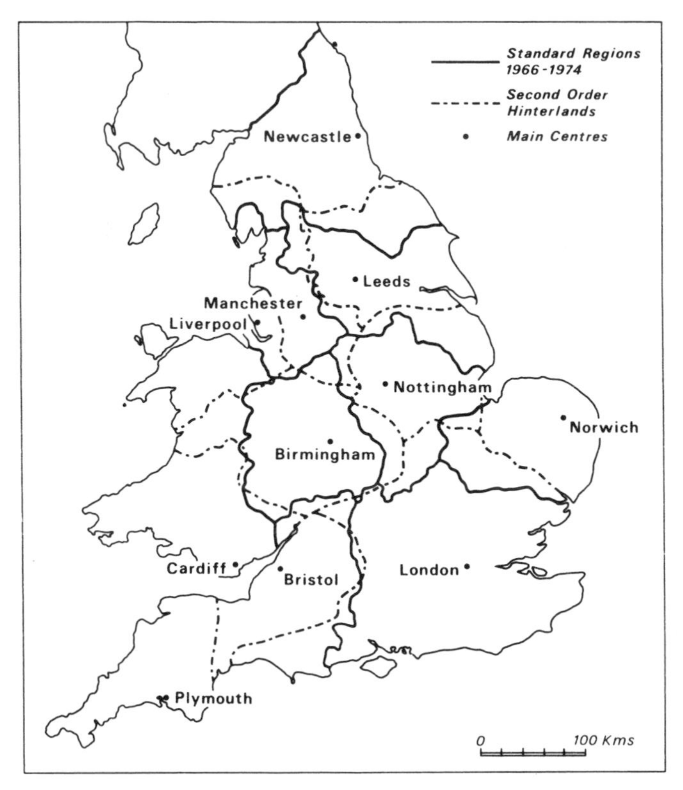

Fig. 3 Standard Regions and Second Order Hinterlands

able to include this area in a South-West region based on Bristol. Finally there is the similar problem of East Anglia which is a small region in terms of population and also has a marginal second order centre in Norwich. This region is in many ways subsidiary to London but to include it in a South-East region would be to enlarge an already large region so in this case it may be preferable to retain an East Anglia region.

The discussion so far has suggested eight English regions, the South East based on London, the South West centred on Bristol, the West Midlands based on Birmingham, the East Midlands centred on Nottingham, the North West based on Manchester, Yorkshire based on Leeds and the North based on Newcastle. Inevitably for statistical purposes the boundaries will have to follow county boundaries but should, as far as possible, reflect the hinterlands of the second order

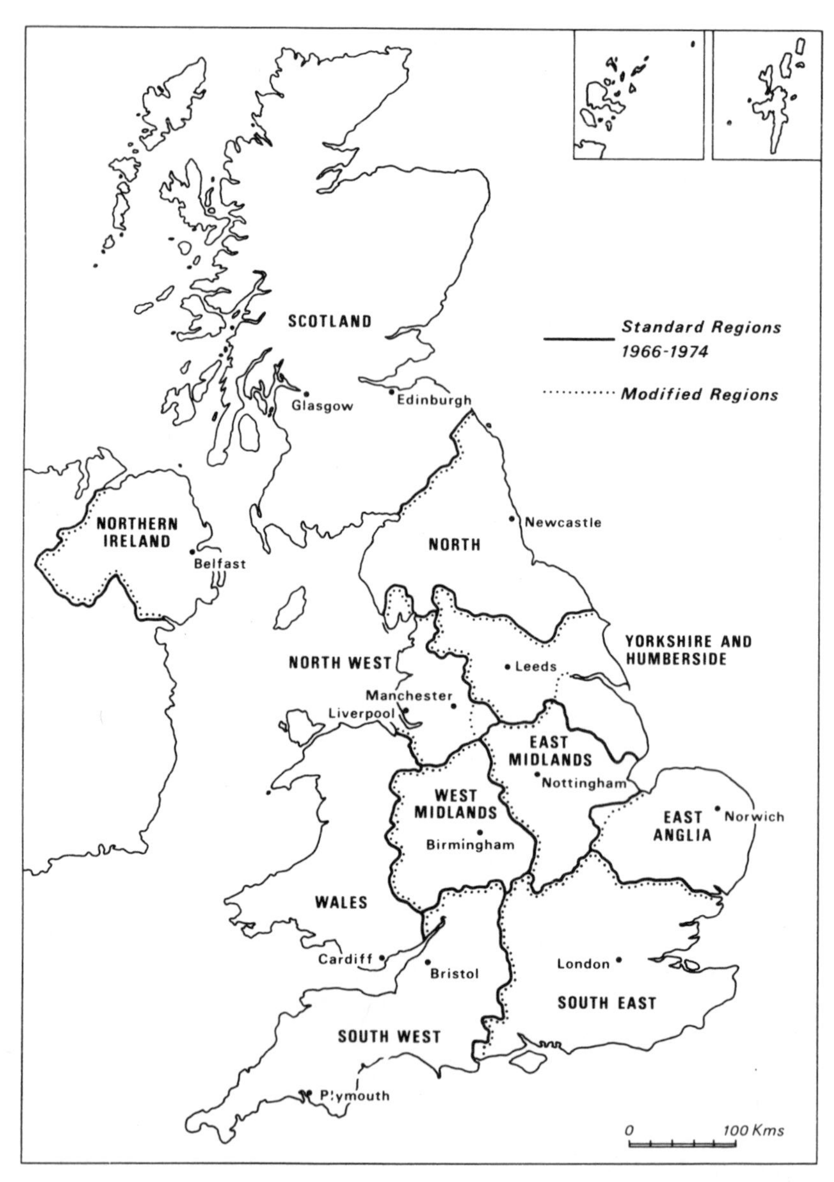

Fig. 4 Standard and Modified Regions

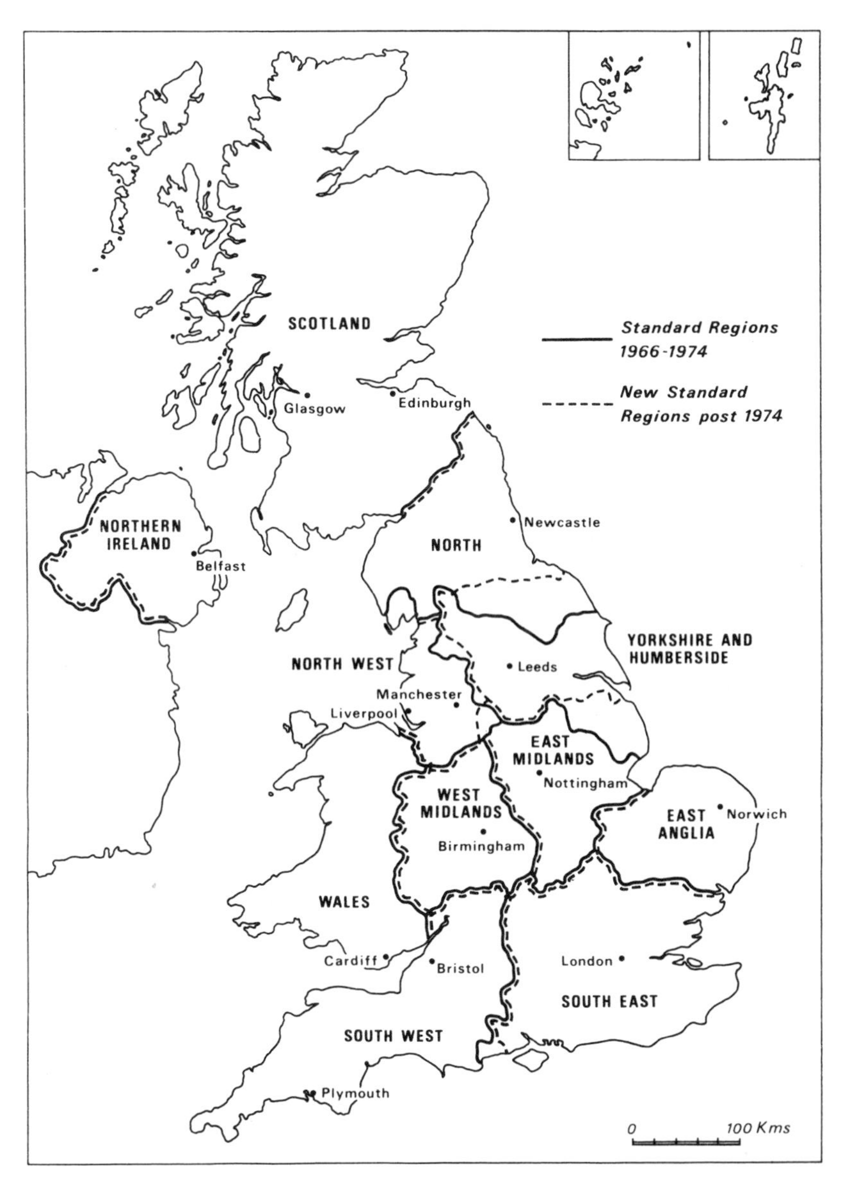

Fig. 5 Standard and New Standard Regions

TABLE 1 British Regions

Region	*Area 000 acres*	*Population 000 (1973)*	*Employees 000 (1973)*	*Unemployed 000 (1973)*	*Income £ per Person**
South East	6,773	17,316	7,565	114.0	18.14
East Anglia	3,105	1,739	663	12.5	15.13
South West	5,846	3,878	1,428	34.5	15.65
West Midlands	3,216	5,163	2,288	50.4	15.94
East Midlands	3,010	3,448	1,437	29.8	15.23
Yorkshire & Humberside	3,508	4,831	1,994	57.0	14.24
North West	1,975	6,755	2,848	102.4	15.41
North	4,781	3,295	1,331	62.1	14.48
Wales	5,131	2,749	1,032	36.4	14.44
Scotland	19,465	5,212	2,142	98.9	14.28
N. Ireland	3,489	1,547	510	32.4	11.59
UK	60,299	55,933	23,238	630.3	16.08

* 1972/3
Source: Regional Statistics 1973 and 1974
Standard Regions 1966–1974

centres. Carruthers (1957) attempted to delimit these hinterlands using coach service timetables for the winter of 1947–8. His map reproduced in Figure 3 provides some justification for the standard regions in operation from 1966 to 1974 which have been superimposed. These were evolved for government use over many years (Smith, B.C. 1965) and have gained increased status in recent years. Carruthers did delimit a Cardiff region covering south Wales, but allotted central Wales to Birmingham and north Wales to Liverpool, an example followed by some geographers (Manners et al, 1972). However, as discussed above, it does seem justifiable in this case to allow the cultural homogeneity of Wales to override the nodal principle. The overall result is an eleven region division of the United Kingdom with regions of varying size and character as shown in Table 1. In collecting statistics for this work, it was hoped to use these standard regions for the whole period under consideration, but census data which was preferred (see Appendix B) made this impossible. It was, therefore, necessary to slightly adjust these regions to produce modified regions which are shown in Figure 4. Finally the reorganisation of local government in 1974 altered county boundaries in some cases and necessitated central government adopting new standard regions as shown in Figure 5. As yet few time series statistics are available on this base and it is very difficult to recalculate earlier data for these boundaries so that at present it is not possible to use them in any historical study.

The resulting eleven-fold division has the advantage of producing a relatively small number of divisions enabling easy comparison between the macro-areas of the country. Any system is bound to have its weaknesses, which need to be remembered in using it. One of these may be that it overrides, deliberately, the division between the heavily urbanised areas of the country and truly rural areas. The latter may well be serving as residential areas and such dichotomies may well be an important facet of regional development in the latter part of the twentieth century. Whatever may be the future it is obviously true that in the period under review the country has been divided into two types of region which have been variously named. At one time it was popular to talk of the differences between north and south, although the dividing line between them runs from south west to north east and Wales can hardly be described as in the north. These regions of the north and west which have suffered from slower growth have been described by such terms as the lagging regions, the depressed areas, special areas, development areas and now the assisted areas, which is perhaps a more accurate term. The regions in the south and midlands have been called the prosperous or congested areas, although the latter term can only be correctly applied to the London and West Midland conurbations. More recently, with the popularity of the Friedman model, the terms centre or core have been applied to these regions and the term periphery to the other regions. Another phrase sometimes used is inner and outer Britain. All of these terms are suggestive rather than definitive and a full discussion of their use will be deferred until Chapter 11.

CHAPTER TWO

The Development of the National System

In the last chapter we saw that the growth of a region cannot be understood without reference to changes in the national system: since this regional system is very open, trends within the nation are bound to influence it in some way. Accordingly in this chapter we shall examine certain parameters of growth in the United Kingdom which have been important for regional development. Some of these will be discussed later more fully with respect to the regions.

Economic Growth

World War I led to an acceleration in the growth of the economy to cope with the demands of the war. For the first time the government was forced to take control of the economy and to intervene in a way that was later to become commonplace. Special attention was given to strategic industries: for example the government promoted a zinc smelter at Avonmouth, an ironworks at Port Talbot and a chemical works at Billingham. The war highlighted the weakness of certain British industries like chemicals where there was a dependence on imports, particularly from Germany. In the case of dyestuffs the government intervened to help establish a British industry so that within a few years Britain was almost self-sufficient (Richardson, 1962). The war also witnessed the beginning of the abandonment of free trade. In 1915 the McKenna duties were imposed on the import of luxury goods including cars with the aim of saving foreign exchange. These were retained after the war and in 1921 extended to cover certain key industries. After a brief abandonment in 1924–5 they were further extended in 1925 to include industries affected by unfair competition. Finally in 1931 duties were imposed on all imports with the exception of food and certain raw materials (Musson, 1978, 266).

Towards the end of the war output began to fall and this continued to 1921 only slightly affected by a short-lived, post-war boom (Figure 6). Already unemployment was beginning to appear in those parts of the country dependent on coal and textile exports. For the rest of the 1920s there was a steady if slow rate of growth interrupted by the 1926 General Strike.

The general world depression of 1929–32 affected Britain less than some other economically advanced countries mainly because the growth of output in the late 1920s had been much less here than in those countries. Nevertheless output fell and unemployment rose to reach a peak of 2,829,000 in the third quarter of 1932 representing 22.1 per cent of the insured population. This was most strongly felt in the northern and western regions dependent on exports and the manufacture of capital goods. Thereafter recovery began aided by currency devaluation and the introduction of tariffs. Many foreign firms previously importing into the country began to manufacture in Britain, whilst some British firms increased output as a result of the new protection for their goods. The low price of commodities on world markets helped the cost of living to fall so that for those in employment, who formed a higher proportion of the population in the South and Midlands, there was a rise in the standard of

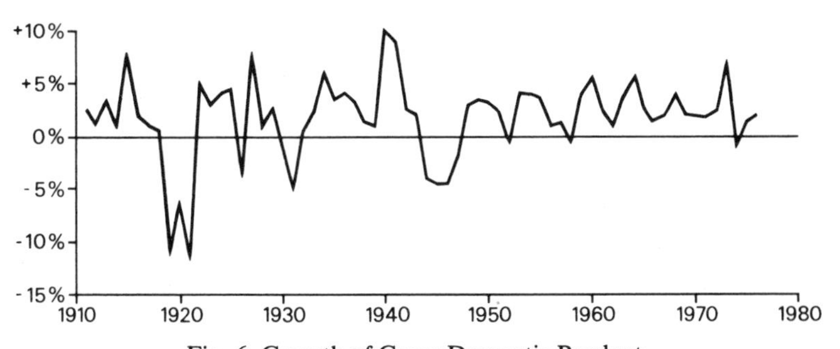

Fig. 6 Growth of Gross Domestic Product

living enabling more goods and services to be purchased. The result was an increase in the rate of economic growth in the mid-1930s which was sustained in the late 1930s by the rearmament programme.

World War II once again caused a growth of output with many of the old staple industries like coal-mining and shipbuilding being brought back into full production as far as possible. The government again took strong powers to intervene in the economy and in view of the new menace of air attack the dispersal of industry to remoter western areas became very important. As during World War I production fell away towards the end of the war, but quickly recovered with a strong post-war boom which was prolonged by the Korean war (Figure 6). This enabled Britain's industries, both old and new, to be buoyant for nearly a decade after the war.

The economy of the twenty years from the early 1950s was characterised by strong cyclical movements, sometimes referred to as 'stop/go' (Figure 6). The stop part of the cycle was necessitated by the weak balance of payments which made it necessary for Chancellors of the Exchequer to deflate the economy to restore the balance. After a brief recovery, and often as a general election approached, the economy was reflated but this proved short lived as the trade balance deteriorated. The result was that the average rate of growth was low compared to other advanced countries, which before 1973 had experienced sustained high rates of economic growth. One of the results of Britain's poor performance was unemployment, which increased at each downturn in the cycle, and rose highest in the assisted areas. After very low levels in the 1950s and early 1960s, unemployment rates increased from 1966 reaching their highest level for forty years in the recession of the mid-1970s. There is no doubt that the low rate of economic growth has made a solution of Britain's regional problems more difficult, not only because the low overall demand for labour hit the weakest areas most, but because the diversion of jobs to these areas is more difficult when there is little economic growth. The pro-

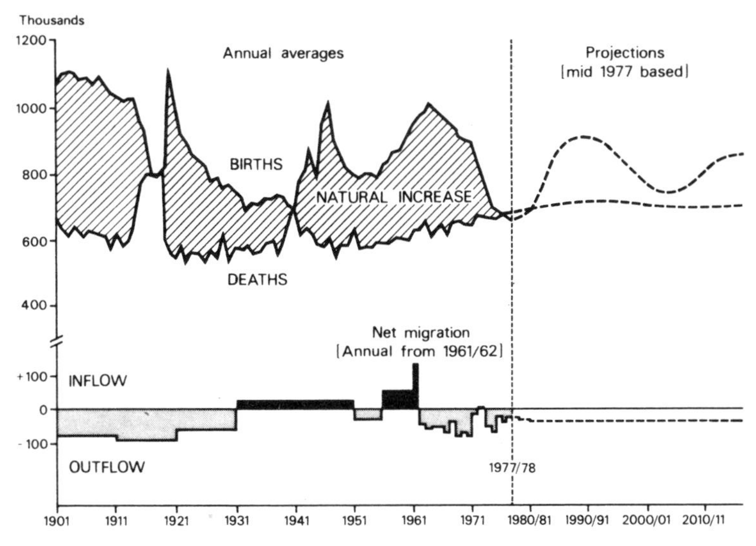

Fig. 7 United Kingdom Births, Deaths and Net Migrants

spect of an imminent downturn has also discouraged firms from long-term investment planning for growth.

Population Changes

In the period from the World War I to the early 1970s, Britain experienced steady if unspectacular growth in population. The 1921 Census recorded 44.6 million people and by 1971 this had risen to 55.5 million, an increase of 26 per cent (Table 2). The death rate in peace time has remained steady, if slightly declining, so that fluctuations in birth rate have been the main factor in changes in natural increase (Figure 7). After a post World War I bulge, the birth rate fell steadily to the 1930s causing concern that there might be population decrease. Following World War II there was another baby boom partly compensating for low war-time births, but by the early 1950s the birth rate appeared to be falling again. However from 1955 the birth rate began to increase reaching a peak in 1964, falling slowly in the late 1960s and more rapidly in the 1970s at least till 1977. Once again there is the prospect of a stationary population which

TABLE 2 UK Population Growth

	Total (000)	*Per Cent Annual Change*
1921	44,627	
1931	46,038	0.46
1939	47,762	0.47
1946	49,217	0.44
1951	50,225	0.41
1961	52,708	0.49
1971	55,515	0.53
1977	55,852	0.10

was achieved at least temporarily in 1976–7. The causes of the changing birth rate are not entirely clear but may be the result of several factors such as changes in the average age that women have children, changes in the number of children desired and the aspiration of many women for more career opportunities.

Throughout the period there have been outflows of people to the former dominions and colonies and to the USA, as well as regular inflows of Irish and irregular inflows of other nationalities (Figure 7). Before, during and after the war these immigrations were mainly from Europe, but in the late 1950s and early 1960s there was a considerable influx of coloured immigrants from the former colonies, both of these movements causing net immigration for short periods. These immigrants have often been willing to take jobs which British workers were unwilling to do.

Part of the population increase has arisen from the prolongation of life resulting from improved health and other social services. In 1921, people over sixty formed only 9 per cent of the population but by 1971 this had increased to 19 per cent, the numbers of the over 60s being about 10½ million. As the numbers of the elderly have increased, so has the development of private and national pension schemes so that retirement from full-time work has become an accepted part of life. Normally women now retire at sixty and men at sixty-five, but there is currently a suggestion that the latter should fall by at least a year or two. The growth of this retired population and its location are beginning to have an effect on regional development as will be mentioned in Chapter 3.

At the same time as this growth in the numbers of the retired population, the increased length of schooling, both by the raising of the leaving age to sixteen in 1973 and the increased numbers staying on after this age, has contributed to a slower growth of the population of working age and a tendency for the ratio of dependents to working population to increase.

The Changing Economic Structure

The growth of population has in general been matched by a growth of employment which, after a severe decline during the inter-war depression, grew steadily to a peak in 1966, since when it has fallen slightly and fluctuated according to economic conditions. There was a 24 per cent increase in employment between 1921 and 1971, 12 per cent for males but 52 per cent for females (including part-timers). The great increase in women working can be expressed another way in terms of the female activity rate, the proportion of women economically active to the population of working age, which increased from 32 per cent in 1921 to 43 per cent in 1971. Most of this increase has taken place in the post-war period (see Table 15) and is mainly the result of more married women working (Department of Employment Gazette, 1974). On the supply side, women are spending less time in child rearing, have more labour saving devices in the home, and increasingly wish to work. There has also been an increase in the demand for women workers as the expansion of jobs has been in those fields not requiring manual strength where women are under no handicap.

The changing employment structure is shown in Figures 8 and 9. The primary sector recorded a large decline between 1921 and 1971, both absolutely and relatively, mainly due to changes in coal-mining and agriculture. The manufacturing sector grew until the mid-1960s, since when it has

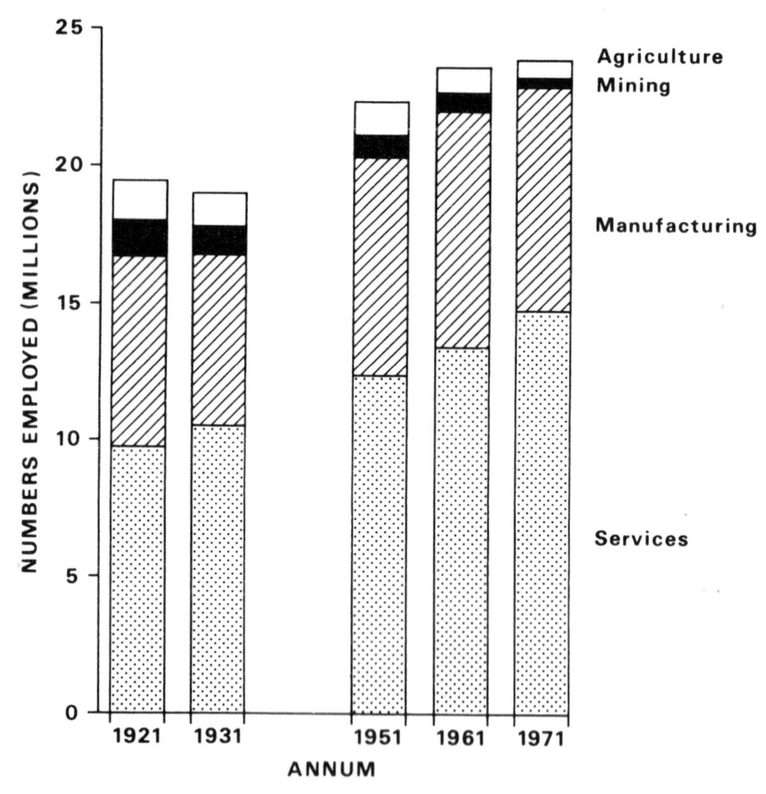

Fig. 8 United Kingdom Employment Structure 1921–71

experienced absolute and relative decline, but within this sector there have been significant variations in performance, with well-known declines in textiles, clothing and shipbuilding and increases in engineering, vehicles and metal goods. Within each of these 'Orders' of the Standard Industrial Classification (SIC) there are also variations. Thus within the Vehicles order, motor vehicle employment grew rapidly for most of the period, but railway engineering declined. The statistics for the Order and even lower divisions called Minimum List Heading level (MLH) conceal the fact that there was an ever widening product range, both for consumers and industry. Likewise the range of machinery used in manufacturing (and other sectors) has increasingly replaced labour-intensive operations. Until recently there has been less

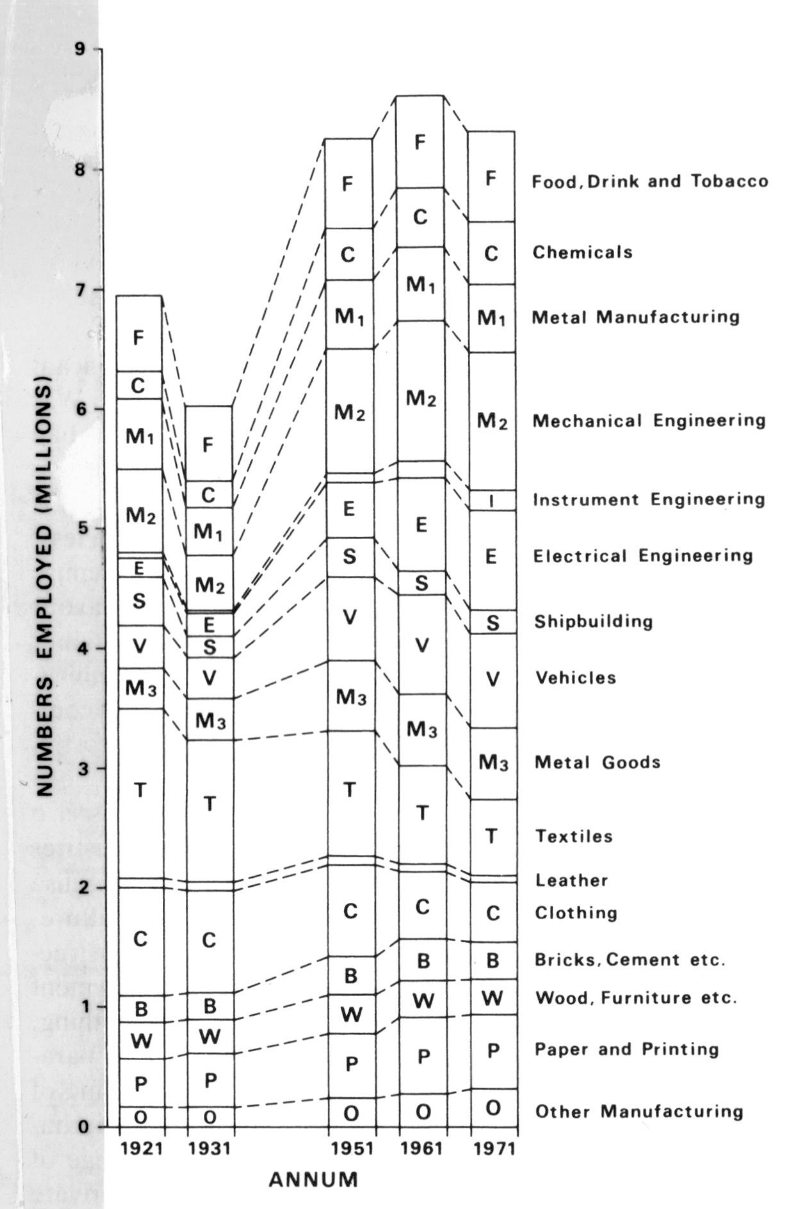

Fig. 9 United Kingdom Manufacturing Employment 1921–71

mechanisation in the service sector and this, plus shifts in expenditure patterns, accounts for the rise of employment in this sector. Not all services showed growth in employment, and notable decreases were recorded in railway and water transport and private domestic service. The public services, including education, health, and central and local government all showed large gains, but there were also increases in commercial services.

Changes in some of these services have had significant effects for regional development. At the time of World War I, public utilities (water, gas, electricity) were often urban based, with cost variations reflecting urban size and accessibility to coalfields. By the 1970s these utilities were universally available and regional cost differences were much less. Transport changes have also been significant with the demise of the slow train, horse and cart, and tramp steamer in favour of the flexible lorry, high speed passenger and container trains, and large bulk and container ships. Telecommunications have also greatly improved so that all forms of communication are quicker, easier and relatively less costly, hence helping to reduce restraints on location.

The employment structure for men and women has also changed significantly. In 1921 there were certain industries where male employment was overwhelming, usually because manual labour was involved. These included agriculture, coal-mining, metallurgical and heavy engineering, construction and transport. Opportunities for female employment were limited to a few industries like textiles and clothing, whilst within services private domestic service was of paramount importance followed by distribution. The decline of many of the male-employing activities coupled with mechanisation has enabled women to penetrate a wider range of industries, although service employment (but not private domestic service) is still most important.

Such changes in activities have produced a new employment structure: probably nearly 6 million of the 19.5 million jobs of 1921, or 30 per cent, had been lost by 1971, whilst some 10.5 million new jobs had been created representing 40

TABLE 3 The Share of the Largest One Hundred Manufacturing Companies in UK Manufacturing Net Output 1909–70

Year	*Per cent*	*Year*	*Per cent*
1909	15	1948	21
1919	17	1953	26
1924	21	1958	33
1930	26	1963	38
1935	23	1968	42
1939	23	1970	45

Source: L. Hannah 1976, 216

per cent of those existing at that time. With such change in the employment situation every region has been involved in creating new job opportunities.

Not the least of the economic changes during this period has been the changes in company structure, which has affected both the manufacturing and services sector. In both cases large firms have come to dominate industries and markets and even entire sectors. For manufacturing this dominance is expressed by showing the share of the one hundred largest companies in net manufacturing output (Table 3). Hannah's figures, which agree with those of Prais (1976, 4), suggest that industrial concentration increased from the late nineteenth century to about 1930, then remained steady for a few years and, since the late 1940s, have steadily increased until these largest one hundred companies probably now account for half the net output. Correspondingly all other firms have had their share reduced, and particularly those employing less than 200 persons (Bolton Report 1971, 58–60). The large firms which dominate the economy are multi-product, multi-plant and most likely multi-national. In 1972 the average firm among the top 100 employed 31,000 in 72 plants (compared with 27 in 1958), with an average plant employment of 430 (Prais, 1976, 61). There has also been a similar concentration in the retail sector, with chain stores dominating the high street and exerting an influence through their buying policies on manufacturing.

The causes of this concentration are not simple. Production and organisational economies of scale have been growing but account for only a small part of the increase. However, the advantages of size have been perceived to be important by industry itself, the government and the financial institutions and, with the absence of strong monopoly legislation, have enabled the large firm to grow faster.

The Increasing Role of Government

Since World War I, as has been previously mentioned, the government has become increasingly involved in the running of the economy. It spends an increasing share of the gross national product (GNP) and employs (including indirectly through local government) a growing proportion of the employed population (Hannah and Kay, 1977, 112). Where and how this money is spent, and where these people are employed has important effects for regional development. Over the period the government has from time to time been aware of this and used its influence according to predetermined policies, to be discussed below, whilst at other times, as will become apparent later, the regional implications have been ignored. The government's relationship with industry has evolved and changed over the years. Through nationalisation the government has become a major industrial employer itself. Through purchases from industry, particularly for defence, the government has for a long time had a potential way of influencing the location of industry. Since World War I the government has helped industry through research, setting up its own research establishments and assisting industrial associations to establish their own. More recently governments have become involved in restructuring industries to form larger and more competitive enterprises, and also in lending money for investment. The state has also become involved in the provision of industrial training facilities. In this and other ways discussed above (such as electricity and roads) the government is concerned with providing the infrastructure for industry.

More than ever before, and certainly as compared with the nineteenth century, the government is expected to solve problems and create living conditions acceptable to the electorate. Physical planning has grown steadily in power and effectiveness since World War I, becoming firmly established after the passing of the Town and Country Planning Act of 1947 (Ashworth, 1954, Cherry, 1974 and Cullingworth, 1964). One of its principal concerns has been the planning of growth around the major conurbations which has been achieved with the aid of green belts, new towns and town development schemes (Figure 10). The London region has benefited considerably from such plans, becoming much less congested than would otherwise have been the case, and thus perhaps more attractive to industry (Hall, 1969). The provision of growth points has enabled a considerable decentralisation of activity from London which has overflowed into the South West, East Anglia and East Midland regions (Figure 10). The government has also been concerned with the fate of regions. In the nineteenth century areas and regions declined, and unemployment and out-migration increased, without governments taking any counter-action. Since the 1930s such an attitude would have been unthinkable. The government is now expected to intervene, and in so doing has become a new force for regional development in Britain (McCrone, 1969, McCallum, 1979).

The Evolution of British Regional Policies

The growth of unemployment in the 1920s in some of the older industrial areas led the government to establish the Industrial Transference Board in 1928 to help workers migrate to districts where work was available. This was partly a recognition of the then accepted view that contemporary industrial trends were probably inevitable and, even if they were not, it was no function of government to interfere with the location of industry.

The great increase in unemployment after 1929 was felt most severely in the depressed areas of Central Scotland,

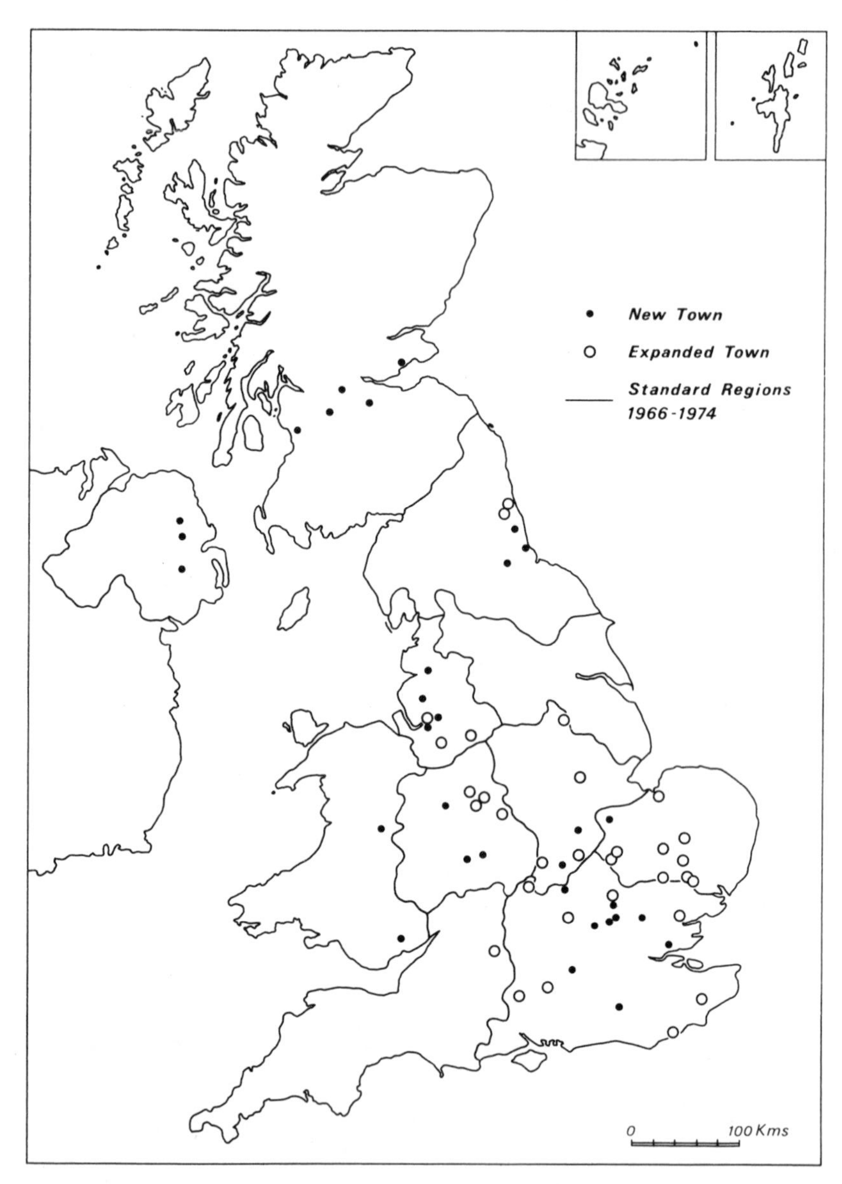

Fig. 10 New and Expanded Towns

West Cumberland, North-East England, South Wales, Lancashire and some smaller coalfield areas. By 1932 when 19 per cent of the insured population of the UK were unemployed, the figure was often twice this level in these areas. As a result of public pressure, in 1932 the government began surveys of these districts through the Board of Trade. In 1934 the Special Areas (Development and Improvement) Act was passed, scheduling the first four areas mentioned above, as recipients of a small amount of money, mainly used for infrastructure (Figure 11). More money was made available in 1936 and 1937, both from government and private sources. With this firms were encouraged to expand in the Special Areas (SAs) and were assisted through the establishment of trading estates notably at Team Valley (Gateshead), Hillington (Glasgow) and Treforest (South Wales). These new developments marked a significant turning point in the evolution of regional policy emphasising the idea of taking work to the workers rather than the previous policy of taking the workers to the work (Pitfield, 1978). These government efforts were being supplemented by similar initiatives from local authorities in the areas of high unemployment (see Chapter 10). The government also began to place orders in the SAs, many resulting from the rearmament programme of the late 1930s. Some of these areas benefited from the new aircraft factories which it was argued, should be built in the safer western areas, though some were built in Coventry and Birmingham. The government also made it possible for firms developing in the SAs to receive tax and rate rebates. All these measures were useful and important innovations but the time between their introduction and World War II was too short to judge their effectiveness. When the war came there was considerable government-enforced dispersal of industry, much to the SAs, but the paramount concerns were strategic and the need to obtain production quickly.

Meanwhile the Commissioners for SAs, dissatisfied with the uneven distribution of new industry in the country, fought for and obtained a Royal Commission on the Geographical Distribution of the Industrial Population. Its report

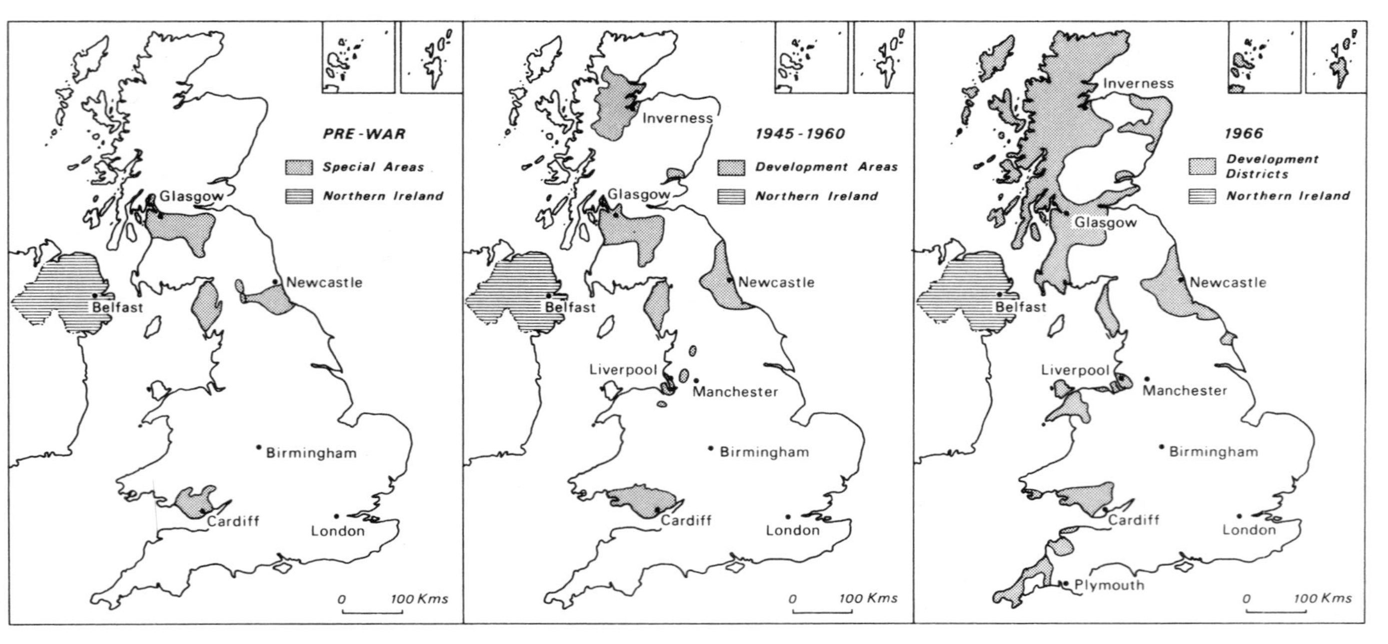

Fig. 11 Assisted Areas 1934 to 1966

in 1940, known as the Barlow Report, was to have a profound influence on post-war regional policy. The Commission were asked to consider the advantages and disadvantages of the concentration of industry and population in large cities and conurbations. In their report they acknowledged that there were many benefits from concentration, such as accessibility to markets, labour and external economies, but they emphasised that there could also be diseconomies such as traffic congestion, as well as the disadvantages of air pollution, greater unhealthiness, lower fertility and strategic vulnerability. Weighing up these factors, and no doubt influenced at the beginning of the war by the strategic factors, they came to the conclusion that on economic, social and strategic grounds the further growth of large cities was undesirable. In their proposals they called for a national distribution of industry policy and for industry to be decentralised from cities to satellite towns. They put forward the concept of the 'proper distribution of industry' which broadly meant distributing industry according to the existing pattern of population and thus rebuilding employment in the depressed areas. In a government White Paper in 1944 on 'Employment Policy' these proposals were accepted.

The 1945 Distribution of Industry Act legislated for these proposals, renaming the SAs as Development Areas (DAs). The former SAs often enlarged became DAs and there were some later additions most notably that of Merseyside in 1949 (Figure 11). The Board of Trade was also given power to build factories, make loans and grants and help with infrastructure. Most importantly all new factory building over a certain size had to obtain an Industrial Development Certificate (IDC) which could be refused if it was contrary to distribution of industry policy. After 1947 the lower limit below which an IDC was not required was placed at 5,000sq ft. Until 1950 the government also had the power to refuse a building licence. It was hoped that firms refused an IDC in, say, London or Birmingham, would be persuaded to move to a DA. Since 1945 Northern Ireland has had its own legislation which in general has made similar provisions to those of the DAs but with incentives at a slightly higher level. In addition to the DAs and Northern Ireland, the Board of Trade attempted to steer industry to some of the smaller localities badly affected by the rundown of war-time activities, such as the Royal Naval dockyard towns and Barrow in Furness. Post-war legislation also gave the government power to build New Towns, and at Cwmbran (South Wales), Aycliffe and Peterlee (North East), and Glenrothes (Fife) this was used to the benefit of the DAs.

In the post-war boom national and regional unemployment was low by pre-war standards and, in spite of the continuing dependence of the DAs on a narrow range of industries, some critics suggested that regional policy was no longer necessary. The Labour government had already begun to relax controls in 1948 where export industries were concerned, and the election of the Conservative government in 1951 saw a further relaxation over the granting of IDCs which became much easier to obtain in the South East and Midlands. Incentives were still available for firms moving to DAs, but much less pressure was put upon them to move there. The only exception to the decline of regional policy in the early 1950s was a Northern Ireland act of 1954 which made it possible for the Ulster government to assist industrial development.

The increase in unemployment in the late 1950s, particularly in the former depressed areas where the old industries were beginning a further decline, led to a reactivation of regional policies in 1958. The 1958 Distribution of Industry (Industry Finance) Act and the 1960 Local Employment Act which replaced it, made finance available to relatively small areas, after 1960 known as Development Districts (DDs), which were based on Employment Exchange areas where the rate of unemployment was about twice the national average. The reintroduction of these incentives, and the tightening up of IDC control, including the closing of various loopholes, caused a swing of investment in favour of the DDs. In 1963 the Conservative government increased the incentives in the DDs and extended some of them to cover what were deemed more appropriate areas (Figure 11). The new Labour government of 1964 sought to expand regional policy and did so by passing the 1966 Industrial Development Act. This not only increased the amount of aid but greatly extended the assisted areas which were once again called Development Areas. These now covered most of the poorer regions such as Scotland, Northern England and Wales. In 1967 these areas began to benefit from a new subsidy on labour called the Regional Employment Premium (REP) and also a rebate on Selective Employment Tax. The REP was introduced to meet the criticism that many of the incentives encouraged capital intensive industry where there were relatively few jobs, yet jobs were desperately needed in the DAs. In 1967 the government also created the Special Development Areas to cover small areas within the DAs which were adversely affected by the run down of coal-mining, and within which extra incentives were provided. Finally, following the publication of the Hunt Committee report in 1969 new 'Intermediate Areas' (IAs) were designated to cover districts adjacent to DAs which were suffering as a result of their proximity, and where lower level incentives would be offered (Figure 12). The 1960s were thus a period of great activity on the part of the government in seeking to attract industry to the areas of high unemployment.

These regional policy measures were supplemented by other actions to help the industries of the assisted areas. These included protection for the coal industry, re-equipment grants for the cotton industry and special funds for shipbuilding. In addition the maintenance and development of the steel industry in these areas has been encouraged. More indirectly, assisted areas have also benefited by greater funds for infrastructural developments such as trunk roads and motorways. Against this peripheral regional assistance must be set the subsidies which London Transport receives to support commuter services and the benefits of special programmes like Concorde to the South West.

Despite these various attempts to stimulate industry in the regions, employment in the London area was continuing to

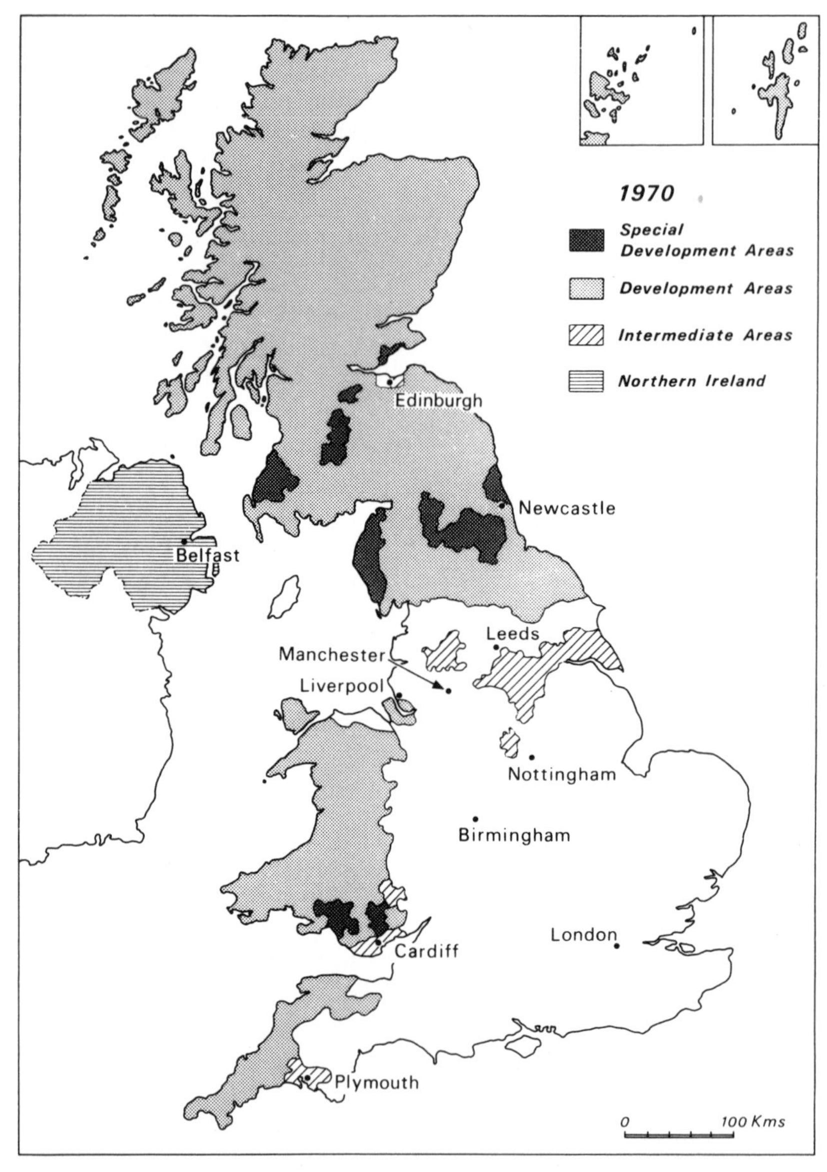

Fig. 12 Assisted Areas 1970

grow, not so much by additional factory jobs but from an increase in office workers employed by government, commercial companies and in the headquarters of large industrial undertakings. Hitherto it had been felt that control over industrial jobs would be sufficient since these were the 'basic' jobs in a regional economy, whilst service employment including offices was assumed to be related to the basic population. The realisation that at least some office jobs were footloose made some control essential both for inter- and intra-regional planning. In 1963 the Conservative government began to plan the dispersal of some of its own activities and in 1964 the new Labour government introduced the office equivalent of the IDC, the 'Office Development Permit' (ODP). Office developments in the South East and Midlands required an ODP, but since this was granted or withheld for general office developers, this instrument was less flexible than the IDC which was issued to particular users. Policies for this sector were extended in 1973 when it became possible for firms to receive grants for the movement of office jobs to the assisted areas.

The return of a Conservative government in 1970 at first suggested a relaxation of regional policies, including controls, similar to the 1951 situation, but this tendency did not last long. The 1972 Industry Act maintained government help to the assisted areas but on a different basis. A new Labour government returned in 1974 pledged itself to greater regional assistance and introduced at least two new policy measures. The 1975 Industry Act enabled government to enter into 'planning agreements' with industrial companies through which it was hoped to influence firms towards more investment in the assisted areas. Secondly in 1975 the Labour government established Development Agencies in Scotland and Wales charged with the task of stimulating industry in these regions. On perhaps a lesser scale, the regional offices of the National Enterprise Board were also charged with the task of stimulating industry in the assisted English regions. In all three cases the agencies were able to buy shares in companies, a new feature of regional policy. By 1975/6 the annual

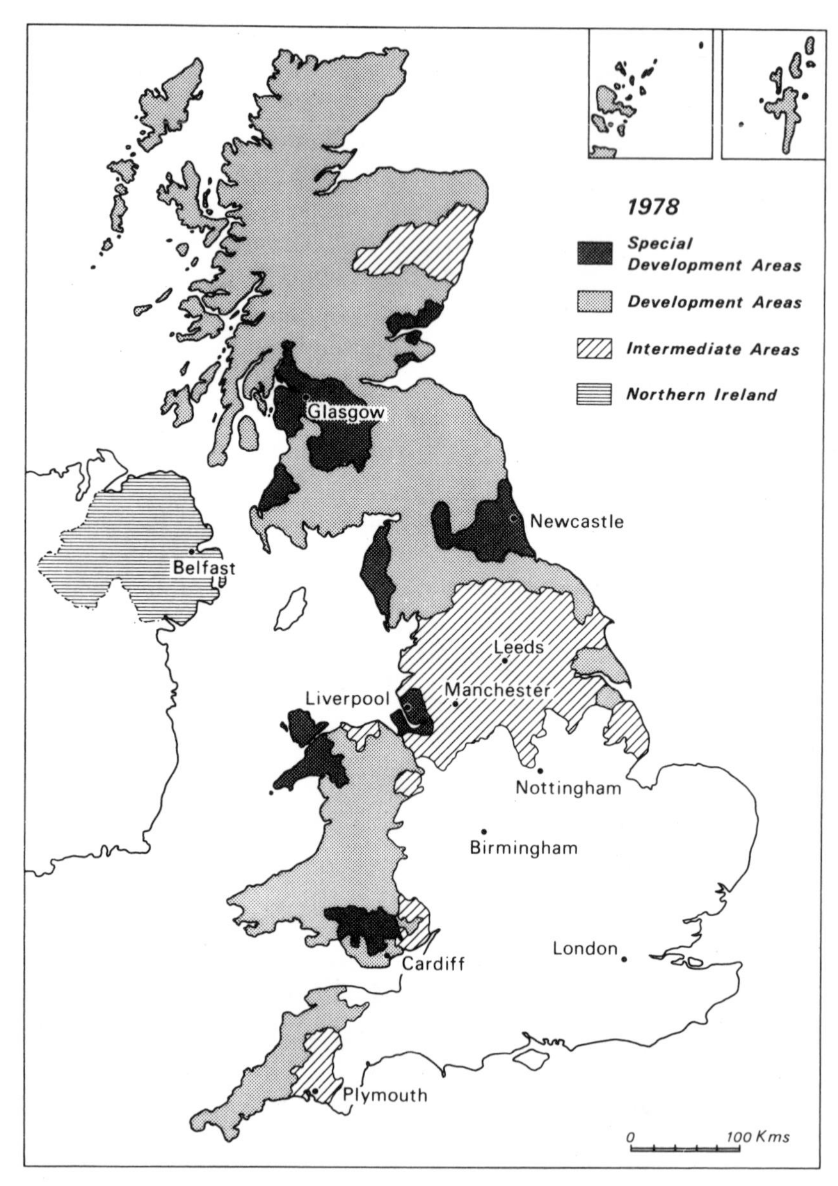

Fig. 13 Assisted Areas 1978

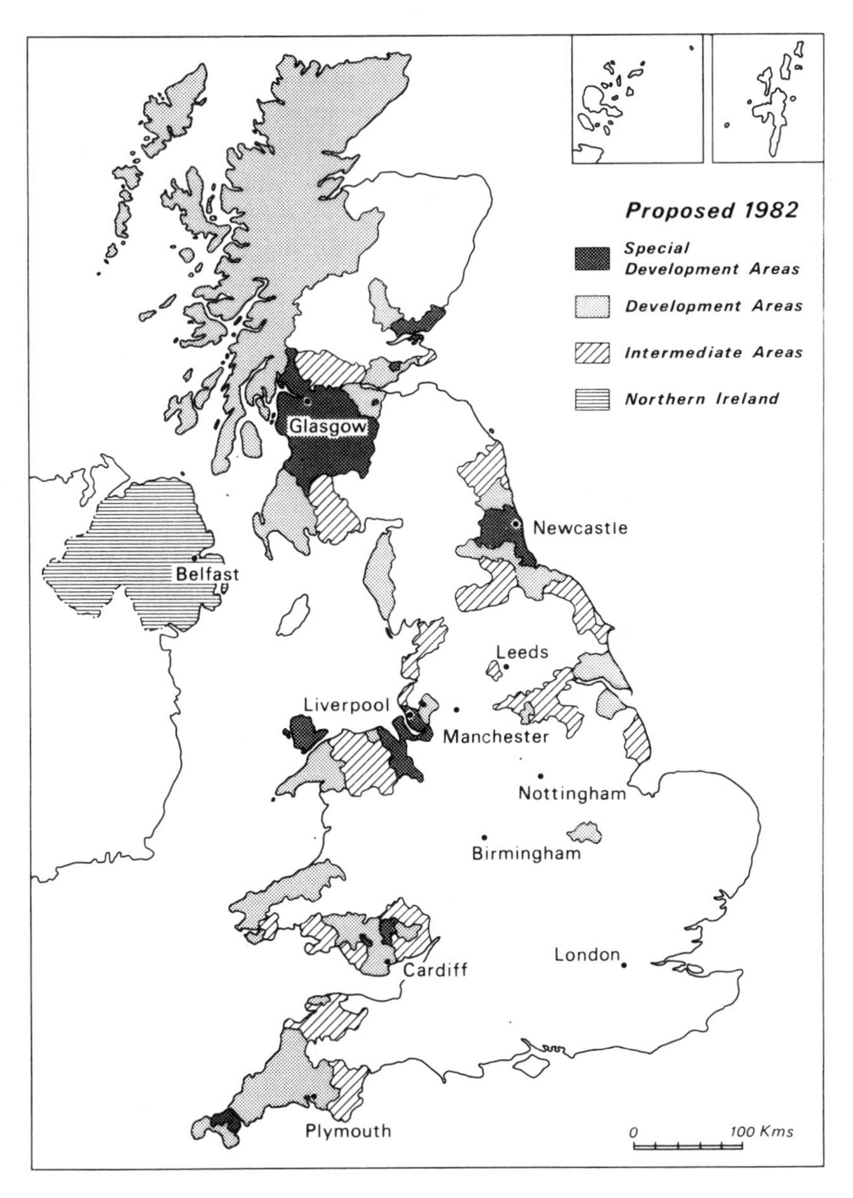

Fig. 14 Proposed Assisted Areas 1982

expenditure on regional policy had reached nearly £700 million, in real terms slightly higher than the levels of the late 1960s (Moore, Rhodes and Tyler, 1977).

At the end of 1976 the financial and economic problems of the country led to public expenditure cuts which embraced regional policies. The regional employment premium was abolished from the beginning of 1977 except for Northern Ireland where it has been maintained. Meanwhile the high levels of unemployment in most parts of the country has led to extensions and upgradings of the assisted areas (Figure 13) but at the same time made it difficult to refuse IDCs in the South East and Midlands and this, coupled with the fear of losing firms to EEC countries, has lessened the impact of IDC control. The Labour government's assistance to industry continued but it was increasingly on the basis of stimulating strategic sectors and less on a geographical basis. One positive gain since 1975 has been the new EEC regional policy which on a modest scale has given further help to the assisted regions (Armstrong, 1978).

The new Conservative government elected in May 1979 began an immediate review of all public spending including regional policies and in July 1979 announced a revised policy. In order to avoid sudden changes in policy the proposals are to be phased in over three years and it is suggested that an expected expenditure of £609 million in 1982/3 under the old policy will be cut by £233 million, a saving of 38 per cent. Aid is to be concentrated on the areas of highest employment and many assisted areas removed from the list (Figure 14). These include many lightly populated areas in Wales and Scotland as well as densely settled areas in the North West and Yorkshire. The new map of assisted areas will be similar to that of the early 1960s (Figure 11). Grants in the Development Areas and Intermediate areas will also be reduced. At the same time the IDC exemption limit will be raised to 50,000sq ft in the non-assisted areas (previously 15,000sq ft, except for the South East where it was 12,500sq ft) and abolished in the Intermediate Areas. Although the proposals will not come fully into effect until August 1982, a review will be carried out in 1981. The new Conservative government appears likely to maintain the newer regional development bodies such as the Scottish and Welsh Development Agencies, but with smaller funds and more prescribed interventionism. It has also made it clear that industries like steel and shipbuilding, mainly found in the north and west part of the country, are less likely to receive subsidies than under the previous Labour government.

It is clear that throughout the period of over forty years during which governments have been involved in regional economic policy the main motive has been the concern about the relatively high levels of unemployment experienced in certain regions of the country. The relaxation and subsequent reactivation of policy in the 1950s aptly illustrates this point. Whilst strategic factors were important in encouraging regional policy before, during and immediately after World War II, they have hardly appeared valid in the subsequent age of nuclear weapons. While lip service has often been paid to other arguments for regional policy such as the need to diversify industrial structures, the inflationary effects of labour shortages in the South East and Midlands and the economic waste of under-utilised labour resources in the assisted areas, in the last resort it has always been the unemployment argument that most mattered. Neither of the two main political parties could afford to ignore this issue and let the other gain votes in the regions. In particular the Labour party, drawing a large proportion of its votes and seats from the lagging regions, has been the leader in arguing for regional policies. As a result regional policy has become a permanent feature of government activity for political as much as social reasons.

In general policies since the mid-1930s have been simple and straightforward, designed to attract jobs of whatever sort, to the assisted areas. The government has never sought to distinguish between industries sending particular industries to particular regions, although the newer development agencies have naturally sought to attract the more promising growth industries. Whilst regional theorists in the

1960s emphasised the inter-related industrial complex and/or growth pole, the government refused to adopt such policies and the same applies to more recent ideas which have emphasised office complexes and the relationships between offices and manufacturing industry.

CHAPTER THREE

An Outline of Regional Development

The aim of this chapter is to provide an outline of certain key indicators of regional development during the period and thus introduce some of the topics to be dealt with more fully in later chapters. We shall begin with population which provides an overview of regional development.

Population Change

The regional pattern of population change in the post World War I period provides a strong contrast with the pattern of the previous fifty years. In the half century before 1921, the regions growing at above the national average included Wales, Northern England, North-West England, Yorkshire, the East Midlands and the South East, whilst predominantly rural regions like East Anglia, South-West England and Northern Ireland all grew more slowly. In the half century after 1921 it was the five southern and midland regions which increased at above average rates, whilst the northern and western regions, with the exception of Northern Ireland, grew more slowly. (Table 4.) With the exception of Northern Ireland these rates of population change reflect the general economic performance of the regions since World War I.

Within the whole period there were significant variations in the rate of change for the regions (Table 4). In the inter-war period only three regions grew at above average rates, with the South East clearly outshining the two midland regions. The coal-mining and industrial regions all grew either slowly or in the case of Wales and northern England actually lost population. The rural regions of East Anglia,

TABLE 4 Population Changes 1921–71

	Per Cent Change				
	1921–39	*1939–51*	*1951–61*	*1961–71*	*1921–71*
South East	18.6	3.0	7.5	5.8	39.5
East Anglia	3.1	12.0	5.9	13.5	42.0
South West	5.7	13.2	5.8	10.6	39.9
West Midlands	13.8	10.9	7.6	7.4	45.9
East Midlands	13.1	7.5	6.8	9.5	42.3
Yorkshire, E & W	6.2	3.6	2.2	2.9	16.0
North West	3.6	3.3	1.9	2.6	11.9
Northern	−0.1	4.5	3.6	1.4	9.1
Wales	−0.7	5.4	1.7	3.3	2.8
Scotland	2.7	1.6	1.6	1.0	7.1
N. Ireland	2.9	5.8	3.9	7.8	22.1
UK	8.5	5.2	4.9	5.3	26.1

Source: Census Reports, Modified Regions

TABLE 5 Recent Population Change in the United Kingdom

	Population (000)				*Per Cent Change*		
	1961	*1966*	*1971*	*1977*	*1961 –6*	*1966 –71*	*1971 –7*
South East	16,071	16,719	16,994	16,834	4.0	1.6	−0.9
East Anglia	1,489	1,575	1,683	1,827	5.8	6.9	8.6
South West	3,712	3,920	4,088	4,279	5.6	4.3	4.7
West Midlands	4,762	4,946	5,122	5,154	3.9	3.6	0.6
East Midlands	3,330	3,497	3,635	3,747	5.0	3.9	3.1
Yorkshire and Humberside	4,677	4,809	4,869	4,876	2.8	1.2	0.1
North West	6,407	6,539	6,603	6,519	2.1	1.0	−1.3
North	3,113	3,125	3,138	3,116	0.4	0.4	−0.7
Wales	2,635	2,694	2,724	2,768	2.2	1.1	1.6
Scotland	5,184	5,201	5,217	5,196	0.3	0.3	−0.4
N. Ireland	1,427	1,476	1,538	1,537	3.4	4.2	−0.1
UK	52,807	54,500	55,610	55,852	3.2	2.0	0.4

Source: Regional Statistics
Regions: Post-1974 Standard Regions

the South West and Northern Ireland also increased relatively slowly. During World War II and the late 1940s, East Anglia and the South West had the highest rates of increase, while both the midland regions continued to perform well. Renewed economic activity also benefited the older industrial areas whose rates of growth came closer to the national average than in the previous period. Surprisingly the South East grew more slowly than every other region except Scotland, presumably reflecting wartime migration from London and controls on development.

In the 1950s, when development controls were weak, the rates of change were typical of the whole 1921–71 period with the five southern and midland regions increasing faster than the national average and the rest below. This pattern was similar to the inter-war situation with the exception that East Anglia and the South West were now incorporated into the zone of faster growth. Since the early 1960s these two regions and the East Midlands have had the highest rates of increase, whilst the South East and West Midlands have seen their rate of growth fall, perhaps reflecting development controls and overspill movements to adjacent regions (Table 5). In the 1960s Northern Ireland had a high rate of growth but this has stopped in the 1970s, no doubt reflecting the troubles in the province. Meanwhile the relative performance of Wales has improved to become the fourth fastest growing region in the 1970s. The overall slowing down of population growth in this decade, and the stability of the mid-1970s, has meant that gains in one region can only be had by losses elsewhere. Thus for the first time since the 1930s regional population decline has re-appeared affecting Scotland, Northern Ireland, the North, North West and even the South East.

Explanations for these changes can be sought in terms of natural changes (births and deaths) and especially net migration. Variations in crude birth and death rates often reflect age structure, but when this is taken into account regional differences are small, the most marked exception being Northern Ireland where high birth rates have produced above average rates of natural increase which, in the absence of cor-

TABLE 6 Population Net Gains or Losses by Migration

	Migration in 000				
	1921–31	*1931–9*	*1939–51*	*1951–61*	*1961–71*
South East	615	748	−279	481	−37
East Anglia	−21	9	44	24	121
South West	27	47	262	78	224
West Midlands	−76	100	88	61	−13
East Midlands	−20	32	78	65	83
Yorkshire, E & W	−58	−41	−90	−98	−58
North West	−154	−59	−70	−124	−114
North	−231	−149	−60	−86	−108
Wales	−259	−182	7	−49	−4
Scotland	−392	−32	−247	−255	−325
N. Ireland	−62	−41	−58	−92	−67

Source: Census Reports and estimates, Modified Regions 1921–31

respondingly high net outward migration, accounts for the higher rate of population growth in the province.

Net migration is the major factor explaining differences in regional performance. Throughout the period 1921–71 the five southern and midland regions have gained people, whilst the northern and western regions have lost people, though once again there are differences within the period (Table 6). In the inter-war period regional differences were most marked with the South East attracting large numbers, the two midland regions, the South West and East Anglia just about holding their own, whilst the northern and western regions lost heavily (Willats and Newson, 1953). There was in particular a very strong migration out of Wales, mainly to England, and also from Scotland from where in the 1920s many went overseas. One study of the 1930s has shown that there was a high positive correlation between levels of unemployment and net out-migration and also that the rate of migration was affected by distance from the areas of growing employment, which may explain why Wales lost so heavily (Makower, Marchak and Robinson, 1939 and 1940). Another study relating to this period by Friedlander and Roshier (1966) and using census birthplace data, suggests that the main inter-regional movements within England and Wales were from South Wales and north-east England to the South East. Brinley Thomas (1934 and 1937) in a study based on the exchange of insurance cards suggests that in addition to these two regions the South East was also drawing significant numbers from the South West. In contrast the population growth of the West Midland's industrial areas was mainly furnished by intra-regional migrants. Similar trends in net migration reappeared in the 1950s and once again a correlation with unemployment was noted (Oliver, 1964), although by this time out-migration from Wales was less heavy. During the 1960s the South East and West Midlands have both experienced net out-migration perhaps reflecting the slowing down of development caused by tight planning controls (Champion, 1976). In the longer term regions have been losing people to regions more southerly and particularly to the South East (Figure 15). In recent years there has been a movement from here to East Anglia, the South West and East Midlands in both planned overspill schemes and voluntary moves. Older industrial regions like Scotland continue to lose large numbers, but in the case of Wales and the North the late 1960s revealed a reduced rate of out-migration perhaps once again reflecting regional policy successes (Champion, 1976). However, at the same time there was an increase in out-migration from the North West and Yorkshire which apart from Merseyside received little benefit from these policies.

At the macro scale net migration flows have shown movements away from regions of low employment growth, high unemployment and low earnings towards regions of growth and prosperity. In general therefore migration has been seen in its classic role as an adjustment mechanism, responsive to economic change and helping to bring greater equilibrium between the supply and demand for labour (Gober-Meyers, 1978). However, the rates of net out-migration do not simply reflect economic performance, and other factors such as past variations in birth rates and their lagged effect on the number of workforce entrants and also the willingness of people to

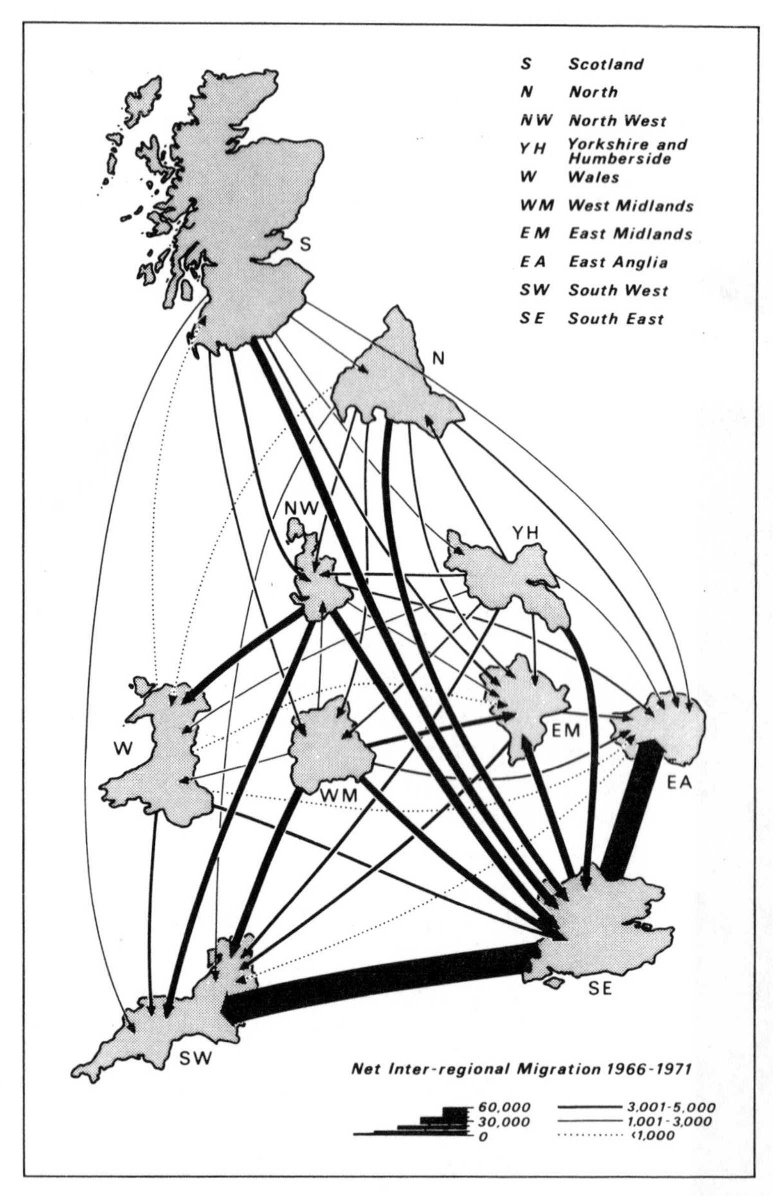

Fig. 15 Inter-regional Migration 1966–71

migrate to and from regions may also be important (Eversley, 1971).

Since migration is selective these aggregate flows may conceal significant sub-group characteristics. As elsewhere it has been found that young adults form a majority of migrants. In a study for the period 1921–31 and covering South Wales and Durham as typical depressed areas, it was found that about 53 per cent of the out-migrants were aged 15–29, and that these represented nearly 20 per cent of the age group (Singer, 1937). Another study of migrants from South Wales to Oxford in the 1930s showed that 79 per cent were aged 16–34 and that 33 per cent were 20–24 (Daniel, 1939). More recently disaggregation of the figures for 1966–71 (shown in Figure 15) reveals that the majority of the migrants to the South East are in this young adult age group and were drawn from every British region except the East Midlands, South West and East Anglia. These regions are also attracting young adults but in addition the last two are also attracting a significant number of migrants over 60. Studies of retirement migration reveal a movement of this age group away from the large urban centres and particularly the London area towards environmentally attractive areas predominantly along the coasts of southern and eastern England (Law and Warnes, 1976).

It is also known that migrants contain a greater than expected proportion of skilled and higher socio-economic groups (Musgrove, 1963). The fact that these groups are more migratory than other groups in the population does not necessarily mean that a net redistribution is taking place between British regions. However, since (as we shall discuss later) there has been a tendency for these more skilled jobs to develop in certain regions, it is reasonable to suggest that there is a net movement to these regions. In support of this conclusion studies of rural areas have shown that they are losing a high proportion of the better qualified school leavers (Jones, 1965 and Williams, 1959). During the inter-war period the Industrial Transference Scheme, begun in 1928 to assist movement from the depressed areas, reinforced this trend by only encouraging and assisting those most likely to find employment, who would generally be the more able (Owen, 1937). The evidence, therefore, although fragmentary, does suggest that the net out-migration from the northern and western regions of the country has involved a significant loss of the younger and more able elements of the population.

Inter-regional changes may in fact conceal or distort other important changes in the distribution of the population. In the nineteenth century there was a strong movement of people from rural areas into towns and cities where they lived at high densities. This trend continued into the twentieth century but has increasingly been complemented by a counter flow of people from the city; at first to low density suburban developments, which in the case of large towns and cities has been followed by growth in adjacent villages and towns (Hall, 1971 and 1973, D.O.E. 1976). Such dispersal, which has been partly encouraged by planning policies including green belts and new towns, is particularly noticeable in the growth zones of the London region and the Midlands (Lind, 1969). In the case of London this outward growth clearly envelopes parts of the adjacent East Anglia and South West, and involves the movement of jobs as well as people. One interpretation of this trend is that people are placing an increasingly high priority on good environments and are able to satisfy their aspirations because of easier and cheaper communications. The movement of retired people to the coastal areas of southern and eastern England, referred to above, is perhaps but one example of this trend made more feasible for this group because the ties to work have been released. It is significant that when people have been asked whether they would be prepared to work in particular regions, the South West has emerged as the most popular region (Harris and Clausen, 1966).

Social Structure

The concept of social class is one which is widely understood in society and yet one which is very difficult to define precisely. A person's class is a result of a combination of factors

TABLE 7 Social Class in UK Regions

Region	*Class* *I*	*II*	*III (NM)*	*III (M)*	*IV*	*V*
1.			*Per Cent of UK Total*			
UK	4.7	17.2	11.3	36.4	17.3	8.3
2.			*Location Quotient*			
South East	1.3	1.1	1.2	0.9	0.9	0.8
East Anglia	0.9	1.1	0.9	0.9	1.2	0.9
South West	1.0	1.2	1.0	0.9	1.0	0.8
West Midlands	0.9	0.9	0.9	1.3	1.2	0.9
East Midlands	0.8	0.9	0.9	1.2	1.0	0.9
Yorkshire & Humberside	0.7	0.9	0.9	1.1	1.0	1.1
North West	0.9	0.9	1.0	1.0	1.0	1.2
North	0.8	0.8	0.8	1.1	1.0	1.2
Wales	0.8	1.0	0.8	1.1	1.0	1.2
Scotland	0.9	0.9	0.8	1.0	1.1	1.2
N. Ireland	0.7	1.2	0.8	0.9	1.1	1.5
3.			*Per cent of class total*			
South East	41.7	35.8	39.0	27.3	28.5	25.5
East Anglia	2.7	3.3	2.6	2.8	3.7	2.7
South West	6.6	8.0	6.7	6.2	6.7	5.8
West Midlands	8.3	8.3	8.1	10.6	10.2	8.5
East Midlands	5.2	5.6	5.5	7.3	6.2	5.4
Yorkshire & Humberside	6.3	7.4	7.7	9.9	9.0	9.5
North West	10.8	10.8	11.8	12.3	12.4	14.5
North	4.5	4.9	4.9	6.8	5.8	7.3
Wales	3.8	4.8	3.9	5.2	4.9	5.9
Scotland	8.3	7.9	7.6	9.4	9.9	11.2
N. Ireland	1.7	3.1	2.1	2.2	2.7	3.8

Source: 1971 Census, Standard Regions 1966–74
Classes: I—Professional, II—Intermediate, III (NM)—Skilled non-manual
III (M)—Skilled manual, IV—Partly Skilled, V—Unskilled

such as income, education and occupation. Any attempt such as that by the Register General to classify people into classes must therefore be arbitary, but will hopefully reflect the situation in general. The census classification is based on employment status and since 1951 there has been a division into either social classes or socio-economic groups. Unfortunately in both cases changes in classification between censuses make comparison over time difficult and the degree of disaggregation of the statistics makes recalculation impossible. For convenience we shall use the simpler division of social classes, for which the 1971 regional figures are given in Table 7.

The most striking feature of these tables is the concentration of higher class groups in the South East, South West and East Anglia with the peripheral regions having more than their share of the lower class groups. Characteristically the midland regions occupy an intermediate position being well represented in the skilled manual classes (Hall and Smith, 1968). It would seem probable that the South East has always had a larger share of the higher classes than its population would suggest, but it would be useful to know whether this proportion has been increasing. A limited study of Waugh (1969) of the professional and managerial groups for the period 1961–66 suggests their numbers in the southern regions are increasing more rapidly than elsewhere, and that this is partly a result of inter-regional migration and partly through the higher generation rate of such jobs in these regions. This form of regional imbalance is a topic which will be returned to in later sections.

Employment Changes

The pattern of regional employment changes for the whole period is very similar to that for population, with the notable exception of Northern Ireland, where for 1921–71 there was virtually nil employment growth compared to average population change (Tables 8 and 9). The only census figures for the inter-war period relate to 1921–31, where it needs to be remembered that the 1931 census was taken at a time of severe depression, so that total employment fell. In spite of this national picture, employment in the South East rose by nearly 10 per cent and there were also increases in the South West and West Midlands. Elsewhere jobs declined, particularly severely in Wales, Scotland, the North and North West.

TABLE 8 Regional Employment Changes 1921–71

	Employment (000)			*Per Cent of Total*		
	1921	*1951*	*1971*	*1921*	*1951*	*1971*
South East	5,436	7,005	7,860	27.9	30.9	32.6
East Anglia	483	559	668	2.5	2.5	2.8
South West	1,133	1,399	1,587	5.8	6.2	6.6
West Midlands	1,584	2,125	2,334	8.1	9.4	9.7
East Midlands	1,272	1,558	1,747	6.5	6.9	7.2
Yorkshire & Humberside	1,730	1,889	1,881	8.9	8.3	7.8
North West	2,897	3,027	2,940	14.9	13.3	12.2
North	1,203	1,320	1,347	6.2	5.8	5.6
Wales	1,057	1,040	1,072	5.4	4.6	4.4
Scotland	2,149	2,193	2,155	11.0	9.7	8.9
Northern Ireland	566	564	560	2.9	2.5	2.3
Total	19,510	22,679	24,151	100.0	100.0	100.0

Source: Census Reports, Modified Regions

TABLE 9 Inter-censal Employment Changes

	Per Cent Change				
	1921–31	*1931–51*	*1951–61*	*1961–71*	*1921–71*
South East	9.6	17.5	8.9	3.0	44.6
East Anglia	−2.5	18.7	4.6	14.2	38.0
South West	2.4	20.6	5.1	7.9	40.1
West Midlands	0.1	34.1	7.9	1.7	47.3
East Midlands	−1.0	23.7	8.1	3.8	37.3
Yorks, E & W	−4.7	14.5	2.8	−3.1	8.6
North West	−10.0	16.1	−0.4	−2.5	1.5
North	−14.5	28.3	2.2	0.4	12.0
Wales	−15.1	15.8	2.5	0.5	1.4
Scotland	−13.8	18.4	0.4	−2.2	0.3
GB	−2.3	19.8			
N. Ireland			−3.3	2.9	−0.9
UK			4.8	1.4	23.6

Source: Census Reports, Modified Regions

TABLE 10 *Recent Changes in Regional Employment*

	Employees in Employment (000)			*Per Cent of Total*		
	1966	*1971*	*1976*	*1966*	*1971*	*1976*
South East	7,522	7,247	7,247	32.3	32.8	32.2
East Anglia	599	607	670	2.6	2.7	3.0
South West	1,465	1,429	1,514	6.3	6.5	6.7
West Midlands	2,363	2,207	2,186	10.2	10.0	9.7
East Midlands	1,465	1,411	2,497	6.3	6.4	6.6
Yorkshire and Humberside	2,086	1,918	1,968	9.0	8.7	8.7
North West	2,862	2,657	2,638	12.3	12.0	11.7
North	1,277	1,207	1,255	5.5	5.5	5.6
Wales	1,028	962	995	4.4	4.3	4.4
Scotland	2,120	2,003	2,071	9.1	9.1	9.2
Northern Ireland	466	473	491	2.0	2.1	2.2
Total	23,253	22,122	22,539	100.0	100.0	100.0

Source: Department of Employment, Post-1974 Standard Regions
Figures may not add up due to rounding

During the long inter-censal period from 1931–51 some of these jobs were regained so that all regions had high rates of increase. Once again the 1950s reflects the long-term position of the regions with the five southern and midland regions having above average rates of increase and the others below, including losses in the North West and Northern Ireland. This pattern was repeated in the 1960s with the exception of Northern Ireland where the number of jobs was at last increasing for the first time. Also for the first time East Anglia and the South West had the largest percentage increases, perhaps reflecting an overspill from the South East. In spite of considerable aid, the number of jobs in Wales and the North only just increased, whilst in Scotland, the North West and Yorkshire there were declines.

Focusing on the more recent period beginning in 1966, a new pattern of change emerges (Table 10). The most successful regions in terms of employment growth are East Anglia, the South West and the East Midlands, but the assisted areas of the North, Wales, Scotland and Northern Ireland no longer occupy the lowest position. The slowest growing or most declining regions are the North West, West Midlands and, perhaps surprisingly in view of the previous fifty years, the South East.

Economic Structure

A characteristic feature of nineteenth-century Britain was the high degree of local and regional specialisation (Rawstron, 1964) accompanied by marked localisation of activities. These features were still present in 1921 and Figure 16 shows how each region began the period with a distinctive economy as revealed by a simple division into four sectors. Agriculture employed 7.8 per cent of the labour force but its share was two to four times greater in East Anglia, Northern Ireland and the South West. Mining and quarrying, employing 7.2 per cent of the labour force, was very important in Wales and the North and also high in Yorkshire and the East Midlands. Just over one-third of all jobs were in manufacturing, but its share was nearly one-half in the North West, West Midlands and Yorkshire. Finally about one-half of all jobs were in services, but this figure was only reached in three regions, East Anglia, the South West and massively so in the South East where over two-thirds were in this category. By the mid-1970s these differences had been diminished but not eliminated (Figure 17). Agriculture and mining had declined in employment, manufacturing had become more widespread and services had grown everywhere, occupying a dominant position in the employment structure of every region. But still the services were over-represented in the South East and under-represented in the two midland regions, where manufacturing remained at above average importance. However, in the North and Wales the diminution of primary activities had brought the regional economic structure much closer to the national one.

One technique used to measure the degree of specialisation, the coefficient of specialisation, compares the percentage distribution of employment in a region with the national pattern, the positive differences being summed and divided

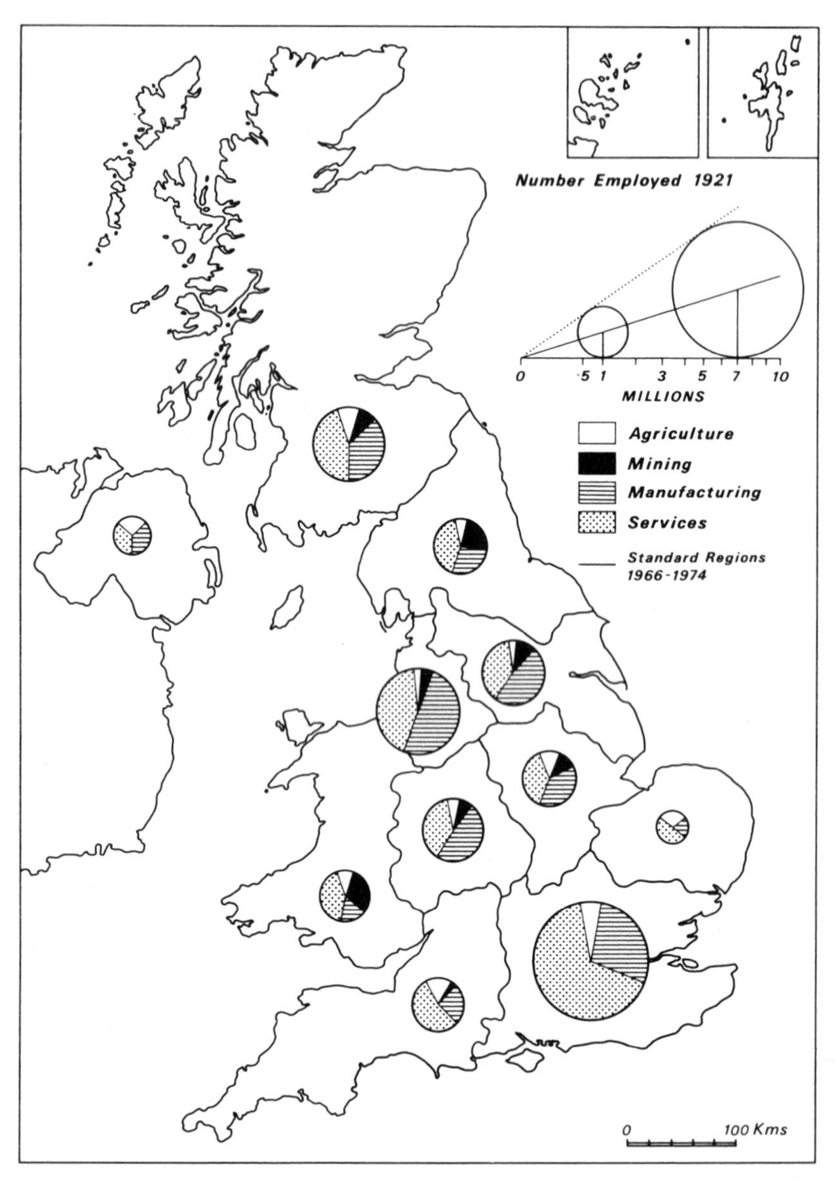

Fig. 16 United Kingdom Regional Employment Structure 1921

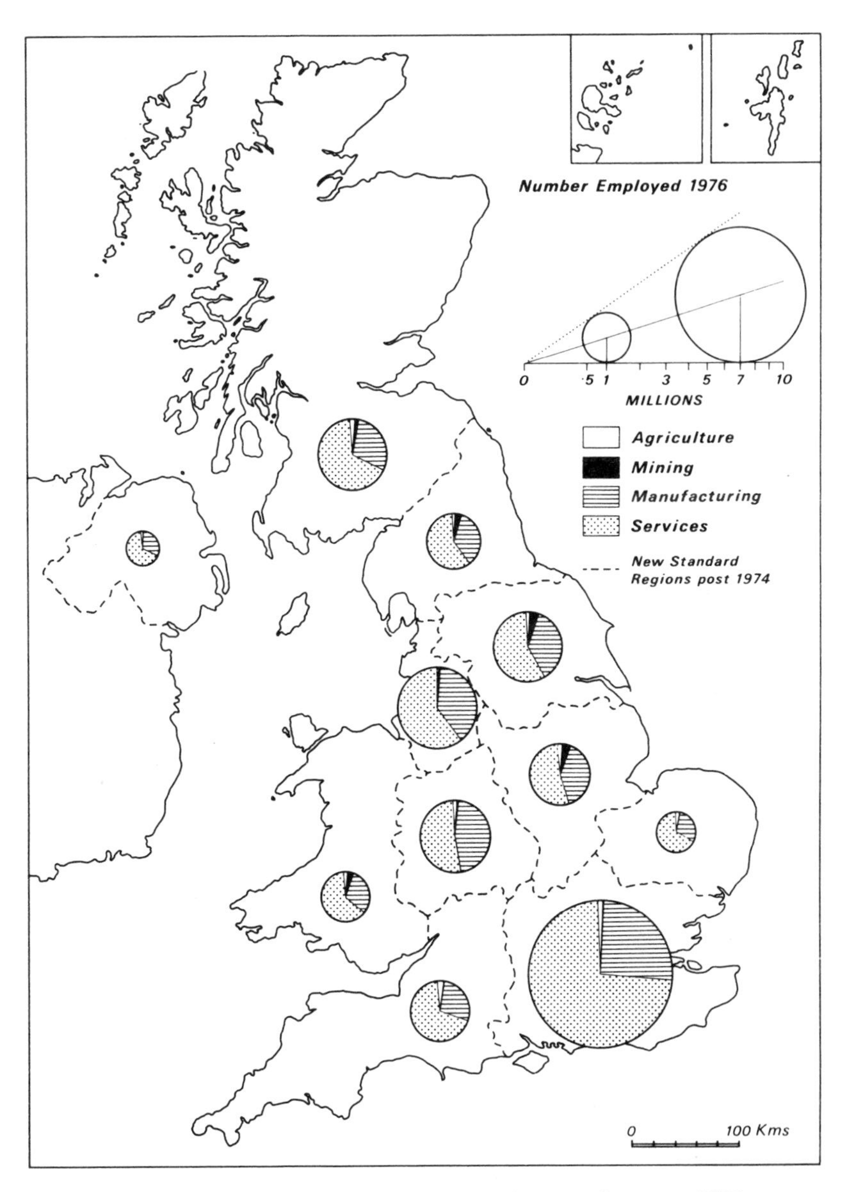

Fig. 17 United Kingdom Regional Employment Structure 1976

TABLE 11 Specialisation and Redistribution in Regional Employment Structure

	Coefficient of Speeialisation		*Redistribution*
	1921	*1971*	*1971/1921*
South East	0.22	0.11	0.19
East Anglia	0.27	0.14	0.28
South West	0.17	0.10	0.27
West Midlands	0.25	0.20	0.23
East Midlands	0.18	0.14	0.26
Yorkshire, E & W	0.19	0.13	0.23
North West	0.19	0.10	0.26
North	0.26	0.11	0.32
Wales	0.29	0.12	0.37
Scotland	0.11	0.07	0.26
N. Ireland	0.32	0.21	0.32
UK			0.24

Based on 25 orders, Modified Regions

by one hundred: a high degree of specialisation would give a coefficient near 1, a high degree of diversification would result in a figure near 0. The same technique may be used to compare the distribution at two different dates, when it is known as the coefficient of redistribution. Two problems arise in the use of the technique: firstly the degree of disaggregation of the employment structure may produce different results according to the number of sectors used; secondly linked activities may be found in different orders so that the true degree of specialisation may be underestimated. Thus a Lancashire town may have been dominated by the cotton industry but other industries dependent on textiles such as textile machinery and chemicals, as well as services, would all be in other orders. When a large number of sectors are used for planning regions, the degree of specialisation appears quite low (Table 11). In 1921 Northern Ireland, Wales, East Anglia and the North were the four most specialised regions, whilst the North West, East Midlands, South West and Scotland were the most diversified. By 1971 every region had become more diversified. Northern Ireland remained the most specialised, but the West Midlands now appears the second most specialised followed by the East Midlands and East Anglia. At the other extreme Scotland, the North West and South West remain the most diversified. The progress at diversification of regions like Wales and the North can be seen from these two coefficients as well as in the coefficient of redistribution. Most regions changed rapidly but least progress was made by the South East, West Midlands and Yorkshire. These results, showing increased diversification, confirm the work of previous studies. Leser (1948 and 1949) found that there had been an increase in diversification during the World War II period from 1939 to 1947, most noticeably in Wales, the most specialised region in Great Britain in 1939, and also in the North. Conkling (1964) in his study of South Wales also found that this period was important for diversification.

Whilst the specialisation of regions like Wales and the North is confirmed by these tests, the low figures for regions like the North West and Scotland may at first sight seem puzzling, although their size and the degree of disaggregation may explain some of their diversification. However, even allowing for this, it is clear that the economies of the peripheral regions in 1921 were far from identical. The problems of the peripheral regions lay not so much in specialisation but in specialisation in declining activities. One test of this is the share of employment in declining industries which has been calculated for the periods 1921–31 and 1921–71 (Table 12). The figures for 1921–71 are under-estimates since classification changes prevent all declining industries being included. This test is very crude since all declining activities are included, whether their employment declined by 5 per cent or 55 per cent, and also the rates of decline varied between the regions. For both periods the South East has by far the lowest share of declining activities, while for the whole period the West Midlands also scores well, followed by the South West. At the other extreme Wales, the North and Northern Ireland score poorly, having a high share of declining activities. The remaining regions all have figures clearly above the national figures showing potential weaknesses.

TABLE 12 Regional Shares of Employment in Declining Activities

	1921–31		*1921–71*	
	%	*Rank*	%	*Rank*
South East	34.8	11	32.2	11
East Anglia	50.3	8	54.7	5
South West	44.3	10	50.0	9
West Midlands	47.0	9	38.1	10
East Midlands	56.3	4	57.0	4
Yorkshire, E & W	56.1	5	54.6	6
North West	55.7	6	50.5	8
North	61.1	2	60.7	2
Wales	61.5	1	65.4	1
Scotland	54.8	7	51.3	7
N. Ireland	57.6	3	59.5	3
UK	45.3		40.1	

Modified Regions

Another indication of the weakness of economic structures can be gained by considering the loss of jobs over the period 1921–71. A crude indication of job loss can be obtained by comparing employment in industries in 1921 and 1971 and adding up the losses. Unfortunately classification changes prevent some declining activities from being counted and the figures do not cover losses in firms which closed but were replaced by new firms somewhere in the same region. The results are shown in Table 13, where it is seen that the five worst regions were all in the north and west. East Anglia and the East Midlands also lost a high percentage of jobs, but the South East and the West Midlands had the lowest percentage loss of jobs. An indication of job gains can be obtained by subtracting job losses from the 1921 total and adding the net gain in employment from 1921 to 1971. The results are shown in the third and fourth columns where a clear contrast is seen between the southern and midland regions and the rest of the country which this time includes Yorkshire. These job gains in the assisted regions would have been much smaller had there been no regional policy. A more detailed consideration of regional employment performance will be made in Chapter 4.

TABLE 13 Regional Job Losses and Gains 1921–71

	Jobs Lost (000)	*% of 1921*	*Jobs Gain (000)*	*% of 1921*
South East	1,061	19.5	3,486	64.1
East Anglia	150	31.0	334	69.2
South West	324	28.6	779	68.7
West Midlands	319	20.1	1,086	68.6
East Midlands	371	29.1	845	66.6
Yorkshire, E & W	475	27.4	636	36.7
North West	1,027	35.5	1,053	36.4
North	446	37.1	597	44.1
Wales	468	44.3	491	45.5
Scotland	744	34.6	759	35.1
N. Ireland	237	41.8	227	39.8
UK	5,466	28	10,078	51.7

Modified Regions. Figures for Northern Ireland relate to 1926–71

Finally mention should be made of the high degree of geographical concentration which existed in some industries at the end of World War I. This can be measured using the coefficient of localisation in which the percentage distribution of an industry by regions is compared to the share of the population and the positive differences summed and divided by 100. A figure near 1.0 will show a high degree of localisation whilst one near 0 will show a distribution close to that of the populations. The main concentrations in 1921 existed in textiles with figures of 0.71 for cotton (620,000 jobs) mainly found in the North West; 0.81 for linen, flax and hemp (86,000) mainly in Northern Ireland; 0.69 for wool (261,000) mainly in Yorkshire; 0.87 for jute (34,000) found in Dundee; 0.65 for hosiery (96,000) mainly found in the East Midlands and likewise for lace (26,000) with a figure of 0.73. There were also high degrees of concentration in some of the metal trades although unfortunately the high degree of aggregation of the figures does not permit many examples. Textile machinery manufacture was also localised with a figure of 0.63, as was scales manufacture, with 0.52; brass goods 0.74; cutlery and small tools 0.68; and bolts and nuts 0.61. Several of the latter were concentrated in the West Midlands. The newer and growth industries of the twentieth century generally showed less localisation at the beginning of the period, and owing to dispersal policies have become less geographically concentrated.

Unemployment

The combination of decline in traditional activities, slow growth of new ones and insufficient net outward migration caused such high relative rates of unemployment in the peripheral regions that regional policies were initiated to help solve the problem. As we have seen, upward trends and marked spatial variations in unemployment rates have been important in the determination of regional policy. Unemployment rates, which measure the proportion of the working population out of work, need to be looked at in relation to the absolute numbers involved: for example, London may have a low unemployment rate but still a large number out of work, whilst an area in mid-Wales with a high unemployment rate but only a small number unemployed would find it difficult to supply labour to attract a factory to the district.

Unemployment figures may be obtained from the censuses after 1921, whilst monthly and annual figures are available from the Department of Employment. The regularity of the latter should not allow their deficiencies to be ignored which particularly relate to female unemployment which is under-registered since married women have no incentive such as unemployment benefit to encourage them to enrol at labour exchanges.

In spite of these statistical problems the pattern of unemployment rates, from whatever source, is remarkably clear-cut (Table 14). Between 1931 and 1977 the five southern and midland regions, with the possible exception of the South West, had rates below the national level, whilst the five northern and western regions had rates above this, with Yorkshire around the national figure. A more detailed spatial picture would reveal an even starker centre-periphery pattern (Keeble, 1976, 81), with a basin of low unemployment

TABLE 14 Regional Rates of Unemployment in the U.K.

	Per Cent Unemployed (Males and Females)					
		Census Figures			*Dept. of Employment*	
	1931	*1951*	*1961*	*1971*	*1971*	*1977*
South East	7.8	1.1	2.2	4.1	2.0	4.5
East Anglia	9.4	1.9	2.5	4.4	3.2	5.4
South West	8.1	1.8	2.4	4.4	3.3	6.9
West Midlands	12.0	1.3	2.1	4.7	2.9	5.8
East Midlands	9.6	1.2	2.0	4.3	2.9	5.1
Yorks, E & W	12.2	1.6	2.6	5.2	3.8	5.8
North West	16.2	2.2	3.5	6.1	3.9	7.5
North	19.2	3.0	3.8	6.9	5.7	8.4
Wales	16.5	3.5	4.2	6.9	4.4	8.1
Scotland	16.1	3.5	4.5	7.4	5.8	8.3
GB	12.0	1.8	2.8	5.2	3.4	6.0
N. Ireland	*	6.6	9.4	8.3	7.9	11.2
UK		1.9	3.0	5.2	3.5	6.2

Census figures relate to modified regions. Department of Employment figures relate to Post-1974 Standard Regions
* No figures available for Northern Ireland.

centred on the London and Birmingham regions and levels increasing away from this. Some of the highest levels are found in the west, Northern Ireland, west Scotland, Wales and the south-west peninsula, although there are also high rates in the north-east coalfield. Over the period the rankings of the regions has remained remarkably similar, with times of expansion or recession being faithfully recorded in all regions. If anything peripheral regions have suffered slightly more in recessions, perhaps because of their industrial composition and perhaps because companies in peripheral regions have been less inclined to hoard labour.

Activity Rates

Unemployment rates only reflect declared unemployment and omit those who might work if there were more opportunities. This hidden unemployment can be revealed by the use of activity rates which show variations in the proportion working. Activity rates can be calculated using census data or

TABLE 15 United Kingdom Regional Activity Rates 1921–71

	Male Activity Rates				
	1921	*1931*	*1951*	*1961*	*1971*
South East	85.2	89.7	87.1	87.0	82.2
East Anglia	85.8	88.1	85.9	84.7	80.5
South West	84.2	87.5	84.9	83.2	78.1
West Midlands	88.3	92.3	90.3	88.8	84.1
East Midlands	88.8	89.3	88.6	87.4	82.4
Yorkshire E & W	89.8	92.1	88.1	86.7	81.1
North West	89.2	91.7	88.0	86.6	81.4
North	87.5	90.7	87.4	86.1	80.2
Wales	87.7	90.1	86.0	84.3	78.6
Scotland	87.1	91.0	88.3	87.1	81.4
GB	87.1	90.6	87.6	86.3	81.5
N. Ireland	*	*	86.7	86.0	79.9
UK			87.6	86.3	81.4

	Female Activity Rates				
	1921	*1931*	*1951*	*1961*	*1971*
South East	34.1	36.1	36.5	39.6	44.5
East Anglia	27.5	27.5	27.4	30.0	38.5
South West	29.0	28.8	28.1	31.0	37.4
West Midlands	33.7	36.8	38.7	41.5	45.3
East Midlands	30.9	32.7	33.7	36.6	42.2
Yorkshire E & W	32.7	34.6	35.5	38.6	42.2
North West	39.3	41.9	40.5	42.0	44.3
North	22.4	24.1	28.4	31.3	39.7
Wales	21.2	21.0	25.0	28.0	35.6
Scotland	32.3	34.9	33.6	35.8	42.4
GB	32.3	34.2	34.7	37.5	42.6
N. Ireland	*	*	34.5	35.3	36.0
UK			34.7	37.4	42.5

Source: Census Reports. Modified Standard Regions. Proportion of active population over population of minimum working age
* No figures available for Northern Ireland and thus for the UK

Department of Employment statistics. The latter are not suitable for long time periods and also exclude the self-employed, armed forces and family workers, so we shall refer to the census data.

Male activity rates are high since men usually work for most of their non-childhood years. In the post-war period there has been a slight fall in male activity rates caused by longer periods of education and earlier retirement, made possible by greater provision of pensions. Regional variations (Table 15) are small and reflect the factors just mentioned and the opportunities for the elderly to work. Hence the South West with its large retired population has the lowest male activity rate and the West Midlands, with more job opportunities and fewer retired, the highest rate.

Female activity rates show greater regional variation and largely reflect the industrial structure and the opportunities which it provides for women to work (Bowers, 1970, 27). In 1921 there were considerable regional variations in these rates, with regions like Wales, the North and East Anglia where coal-mining and agriculture were dominant having low rates. In contrast the highest rate was found in the North West where the textile industry was dominant. The South East and West Midlands had above average rates (Table 14).

By 1971 female activity rates had increased by a third, and there had been a considerable convergence in the rates, reflecting increased opportunities for women to work in all regions, but particularly in the former coal-mining and agriculture dominated regions. Even in the North West female activity rates increased, although the South East, with its jobs in services, and the West Midlands had the highest rates. Wales still remained at the bottom of the league, and East Anglia, the South West and Northern Ireland also had rates below the average. Moving from the standard regional level to the subdivision level reveals a zone of high female activity rates covering the main urban belt from the London region through the core areas of the East and West Midlands to Lancashire and the West Riding (Moseley and Darby, 1978). In addition to industrial structure, these variations in female activity rates may reflect problems of access to work (Andrews, 1978), particularly difficult for women in rural areas, the age structure and retired population, and the demand for labour. If these problems could be overcome and the national female activity rate raised to the highest regional level, then in 1971 there would have been 626,000 more women at work.

TABLE 16 United Kingdom: Relative Income by Regions

Year	*1949–50*	*1954–5*	*1959–60*	*1964–5*	*1970–71*	*1976–7*
UK Mean	*£400*	*£546*	*£732*	*£1004*	*£1545*	*£3477*
UK Index	*100*	*100*	*100*	*100*	*100*	*100*
South East	107.5	107.5	108.1	108.1	107.7	106.5
East Anglia	93.2	90.8	91.4	94.8	96.4	101.3
South West	93.5	94.4	94.3	96.5	96.9	95.1
West Midlands	98.8	104.1	102.9	102.2	99.8	100.0
E (North) Midlands	(97.8)	(99.9)	(98.2)	(97.6)	96.1	101.2
Yorkshire E & W	98.3	98.4	97.3	95.8		
Yorkshire and Humberside				95.8	96.4	97.8
North West	94.8	97.6	97.0	95.6	95.2	96.4
North	92.2	95.6	93.8	92.4	94.1	95.7
Wales	88.8	91.8	92.6	92.9	92.4	92.8
Scotland	95.0	94.6	92.1	93.1	95.8	93.2
N. Ireland	83.6	85.4	82.0	81.9	86.0	87.1

Source: Reports of the Commissioners of Her Majesty's Inland Revenue and Regional Statistics

Regions: 1949/50 to 1964/5 Modified Standard Regions
1970/1 Standard Regions 1966–74
1976/7 Post-1974 Standard Regions

Income Variations

In many countries income variations are considered prime indicators of regional inequality and great emphasis is given to reducing such differences. In the United Kingdom however, less importance has been attached to these figures as an index of regional inequality though there is a distinct pattern of regional differences. Figures for regional incomes have only become available in the post-war period and may be obtained from either the General Household Survey or the Inland Revenue. The latter is probably more comprehensive and accordingly has been used for Table 16.

The South East region has the highest incomes, followed by the West Midlands whose position has slipped in recent years. At the bottom Northern Ireland has average incomes of about 15 per cent below the UK mean. All the other regions have average incomes between 0 and 10 per cent below the UK mean. The average income of a region reflects several aspects of its economic structure. High unemployment as in Northern Ireland will obviously reduce incomes. The type of economic activities available also has an important bearing on incomes. In rural areas, such as East Anglia, the South West, central Wales and the Highlands of Scotland where agriculture is important, the low incomes of this industry will depress the average. By contrast the high wages of the motor vehicle industry raise averages where it is present as in the West Midlands. Finally investment incomes, which are heavily concentrated in the South East, are another factor (Coates and Rawstron 1971, 25). The range of income variations is not great when compared to other European countries such as Italy, but it is not absolute or relative difference which matters in this case, but how these differences are perceived by those in the poorer regions. The growth of television and other media has made many people more aware than ever before of such differences and has created dissatisfaction in the regions. Although the changes over the period have been slight, in addition to the decline of the West Midlands the outward spread of the prosperity of the South East into East Anglia and the South West may be noted.

Conclusion

According to the spatial equilibrium theory of regional development inequalities between the regions should be reduced and possibly eliminated. Has there been such a convergence with respect to employment opportunities and incomes? Certainly compared to great differences in the early 1930s there has been a reduction in the inequalities but the basic pattern of differences remains. There are clearly many factors involved in explaining these continuing disparities, which will be discussed later, but one which is relevant to this chapter is the role of migration. Has migration been insufficient to reduce these differences and if so why? Suggested causes of immobility include good unemployment benefits reducing the necessity for movement; insufficient regional differentials in wages to encourage movement caused by trade union influence; the British system of local authority housing which inhibits movement since transfers are difficult, to which may be added the declining number of properties for renting; and finally the strong social and family links which exist in many communities and inhibit movement. If migration is seen as the sole or main equilibrating mechanism for regional differences, then clearly there has been insufficient migration and the factors listed above may be an explanation. However, insofar as other factors are involved we must delay any conclusions until later in this work.

CHAPTER FOUR

The Performance of Regional Economies

In the last chapter some important indicators of regional development were described. Of the indicators discussed the most important is employment since most of the population rely directly or indirectly on the income from a job. Therefore changes in the number and type of jobs in a region to a large extent provide an explanation of the other indicators of regional development. Before looking at the factors involved in regional employment change it will be useful to make a further analysis of the way employment was changing during the period. How did regions vary in the ability to create new jobs and how did inherited industrial structure influence the course of employment change? To answer these questions we shall use two tests.

The first of these tests attempts to measure the rate of job loss and gain. Each region is simultaneously both losing and gaining jobs and must seek a positive balance to remain a viable economy. The decline of employment may reflect such factors as greater automation, the inevitable decline of certain industries, business inefficiency and locational disadvantage. Loss of jobs causes no problems if at the same time a region has the ability to generate new employment at a sufficient rate to replace those jobs lost. The vitality of a region may be measured by its rate of job creation. Ideally, there should be statistics available showing the total number of jobs both lost and gained during a given period but unfortunately the published employment figures do not give this information. However, a crude index of loss and gain can be obtained by comparing inter-censal figures for each industry and then summing the figures to give some indication of gross changes. The rates of change per 1,000 employed have been calculated for minimum list headings (MLH), the most detailed level at which information is available. Many MLHs are fairly small and cover distinct industries; in other cases the MLHs are aggregates of quite varied industries (e.g. Other Mechanical Engineering), the large size and miscellaneous character of which produce less satisfactory results. Changes within such groups cannot be measured so that overall results are underestimates of the true rates of job losses and gains. Nevertheless in the absence of better figures they do give some indication of the underlying processes.

A second method of measuring regional employment performance is by comparing actual change with expected change. This is most commonly achieved by a technique called 'shift and share analysis' which standardises rates of change across regions. It is postulated that during any given period each regional economy will grow at the same rate as the national economy. This is called the regional share (R). However, each regional economy is composed of a different bundle of industries which are growing at different rates. An economy with a high proportion of fast growing industries could be expected to grow faster than the national rate and conversely an economy with a high proportion of slow growing industries would grow more slowly. This difference in expected performance because of structure is called the proportionality shift (P) or sometimes the composition component. Since not every industry in every region will grow at the same national rate for the industry, there will be a difference between R + P and the actual change, referred to as the differential shift (D). Consequently employment change in a regional economy will be equal to R + P + D and equations can be derived for each of these shifts or components (Stilwell, 1969). The value of this technique lies in the fact that it seeks to isolate and quantify the structural element in regional growth. Using this technique it is possible, for example, to estimate the extent to which the problems of the assisted areas are the result of having a high proportion of declining industries and the extent to which the prosperity of the West Midlands was due to having a growing motor vehicle industry. Notwithstanding these advantages a number of criticisms have been made of this technique.

First, Stilwell (1969) has drawn attention to the fact that the longer the period of comparison the less reliable is the structural input since with time the structure will be changing. To overcome this problem he has suggested a modification which incorporates the structure at the end of the period as well. This is called the 'reversed proportionality shift'.

Secondly, it can also be argued that the formula is unduly complicated and that the expected performance is simply the sum of the industries growing at the national rates of change (i.e. R + P). Such a formula has been used by Moore and Rhodes (1973) and will be used in this chapter.

Thirdly, another criticism centres around the weakness of the data used. Employment statistics are classified on an industrial base and in the Standard Industrial Classification are divided into Orders and Minimum List Headings (MLH). Many researchers have been content to use the order level, though these cover very broad groups of industries within which there are quite different rates of change and different regional distributions: for example the Vehicles order contains both the motor vehicle industry and the railway engineering industry. It is now generally agreed that the use of the order level statistics will distort the structural component (P), and that more satisfactory results are obtained using the MLH level (Buck, 1970).

Fourthly, it has been suggested, that although the concept underlying the technique is good the quality of the data is not good enough to justify its use (Buck, 1970). The classification of firms to a MLH contains a certain arbitariness, particularly when a firm's several activities span the MLH boundaries. Usually such a firm is classified according to its major activity, but this could change over time without the classification being adjusted. Moreover, changes from one MLH to another of major firms could wreck the interpretation of the results, a much greater problem at the local as opposed to the regional level.

Paradoxically, a fifth criticism of the technique is that some industries are too narrowly defined and that linkages between activities are consequently ignored (Mackay, D.I., 1968). For example, within the textiles order the textile finishing trades are classified as a separate industry but in fact they are very closely linked to particular textile industries (cotton, wool, hosiery, etc) to which they are also close geographically. When national rates of change are applied to the textile finishing MLH across the regions, it appears to have performed well in the East Midlands and badly in the North West reflecting the trades which it serves. Whilst this is accurate, the expected rate of change for textile finishing in the North West might have been more realistically predicted by applying the rates of change for the cotton industry. Instead the normal method produces a negative differential for the North West and a positive one for the East Midlands when in fact their industries may have performed very much as could be expected when the linkages are known. In this and other cases linked activities are divided by the classification and the interpretation of the results made more difficult. Perhaps the most important linkage, which an over-simplistic use of this technique may obscure, is between basic and non-basic activities. As employment in the basic industries of an area increases so does the population producing an increase in the demand for services and service jobs and in service type industries such as bakeries and printing. Similarly, when the basic activities are in decline or stagnation there will also be a decline in these service activities. Therefore when national rates of change are applied across the regions to the service trades the differential will to a certain extent reflect changes in the basic sector of the economy and also of population (Brown, 1972, 130).

It will be apparent from the above comments that the interpretation of the differential shift is not easy. When the technique was first used some commentators were over-quick to suggest that a region with a positive differential shift had locational advantage and vice versa. It could, however, reflect several factors including government regional policy and business efficiency as well as the problems mentioned earlier—adequacy of data, classification and linkages. Only a detailed analysis of the results involving full knowledge of industrial change will permit an adequate interpretation of the meaning of the differential shift. The technique of shift and share analysis is not an end in itself—it does not provide an explanation of regional performance—but is merely a tool which describes and illuminates certain aspects of regional employment performance.

In the rest of this chapter, the census industrial statistics from 1921 to 1971 will be analysed at the lowest level of classification using job loss and gain rates, and a modification of the shift and share technique in which the expected performance is compared to the actual. The results are shown in Tables 17, 18, 19 and 20. The reasons for using census statistics are discussed in the Appendices. One problem in using census data is that census dates are arbitary and inter-censal periods do not coincide with economic changes and so are not necessarily homogeneous. It is desirable therefore to briefly mention the salient economic features of each period. In the first inter-censal period from 1921–31 the economy was declining into a depression, but the main interest of the decade is in showing regional performance in the absence of location of industry policy. In the undesirably long inter-censal period from 1931–51, the economy picked up and showed substantial increases in employment while for over half the period, particularly in the 1940s, the location of activities was tightly controlled. The next period from 1951–61 was one of growth and low unemployment in which there was only a weak regional policy, though the effects of the earlier decade continued to influence performance. Finally the decade from 1961–71 was one of growth and strong regional policy.

TABLE 17 Regional Employment Performance 1921–31
Rates per 1000 Employed in 1921

	Job	*Job Gains*			*Actual*	*Expected*		*Primary*		*Secondary*		*Tertiary*	
	Losses	*Total*	*Mnft*	*Tert*	*Change*	*Change*	*Diff*	*Expect*	*Diff*	*Expect*	*Diff*	*Expect*	*Diff*
South East	54.5	152.6	36.4	114.8	+98.1	+47.5	+50.6	−6.7	−1.2	−7.9	+24.4	+62.1	+27.4
East Anglia	99.2	73.6	14.8	58.0	−25.7	+1.6	−27.3	−37.5	−19.2	−14.8	−2.0	+54.0	−6.0
South West	89.9	114.7	17.8	94.0	+24.8	+7.4	+17.4	−24.7	−12.4	−23.5	−2.2	+55.7	+31.9
West Midlands	104.0	105.1	37.5	67.1	+1.1	−12.5	+13.6	−26.3	+0.2	−30.2	+4.7	+44.1	+8.8
East Midlands	97.6	101.9	37.8	62.1	+4.2	−37.5	+41.8	−46.6	+15.0	−30.2	+15.8	+39.4	+11.0
Yorkshire E & W	115.4	70.1	17.7	49.7	−45.2	−61.5	+16.3	−32.7	+28.3	−72.9	−0.5	+44.1	−11.4
North West	161.7	63.7	21.3	41.5	−98.0	−58.6	+39.4	−16.4	−1.3	−84.2	−8.8	+42.0	−29.3
Northern	214.3	68.8	17.5	50.8	−144.9	−119.1	−25.9	−72.8	+0.2	−87.3	−18.8	+41.1	−7.3
Wales	193.7	42.8	9.0	32.4	−150.9	−78.8	−72.1	−89.2	−28.9	−25.8	−15.7	+36.2	−27.5
Scotland	194.3	57.7	13.9	43.2	−136.6	−61.6	−75.0	−35.7	−1.9	−71.9	−42.3	+46.0	−30.8
Great Britain	120.5	97.6	25.6	68.6	−22.9	−22.9		−28.0		−44.9		+50.5	

Source: Calculated from the Census Reports, Modified Regions. No figures for Northern Ireland available

TABLE 18 Regional Employment Performance 1931–51
Rates per 1000 employed in 1931

Region	*Job Losses*	*Job Gains Total*	*Mnft*	*Tert*	*Actual Change*	*Expected Change*	*Diff*	*Primary Expect*	*Diff*	*Secondary Expect*	*Diff*	*Tertiary Expect*	*Diff*
South East	103.7	278.2	138.1	139.2	+174.4	+255.3	−80.8	−2.9	+1.8	+126.9	−9.8	+131.3	−72.8
East Anglia	105.7	296.9	95.7	198.5	+191.9	+114.8	+76.9	−20.0	+19.3	+97.5	−24.8	+37.3	+82.7
South West	123.7	330.1	132.4	195.6	+206.1	+166.2	+40.0	−13.5	+ 7.1	+84.8	+16.6	+94.9	+16.3
West Midlands	78.5	419.4	253.8	164.3	+340.9	+378.6	−37.6	−14.1					
East Midlands	85.5	300.9	154.8	144.5	+215.7	+118.0	+97.9	−29.7	+17.8	+108.9			
Yorkshire E & W	101.4	246.2	142.1	103.8	+144.7	+135.2	+9.5	−25.3	+2.8	+113.8	−8.5	+46.7	+15.2
North West	179.3	279.4	162.3	116.9	+100.1	+85.8	+14.3	−9.4	−5.1	+35.3	+9.3	+59.9	+10.1
Northern	93.2	379.8	209.2	165.2	+283.1	+138.0	+145.3	−43.1	+21.0	+128.4	+72.7	+52.5	+51.4
Wales	171.1	329.1	172.6	152.8	+157.6	+44.5	+113.0	−53.8	−36.3	+60.2	+103.1	+38.1	+46.2
Scotland	106.2	289.6	152.6	134.0	+183.4	+152.6	+30.8	−22.1	−1.0	+114.0	+21.4	+60.6	+10.5
Northern Ireland	221.0	217.7	88.4	127.8	−3.4	+49.2	−52.6	−24.2	−63.2	+22.3	−18.6	+49.9	+29.1
United Kingdom	118.1	299.5	156.5	141.7	+189.5	+189.5		−16.6	+113.7			+92.4	

Source: Calculated from the Census Tables, Modified Regions

TABLE 19 Regional Employment Performance 1951–61
Rates per 1000 Employed in 1951

Region	*Job Losses*	*Job Gains*			*Actual Change*	*Expected Change*	*Diff*	*Primary*		*Secondary*		*Tertiary*	
		Total	*Mnft*	*Tert*				*Expect*	*Diff*	*Expect*	*Diff*	*Expect*	*Diff*
South East	73.4	162.9	59.2	103.4	+89.5	+87.0	+2.5	−7.6	−0.3	+37.9	+4.0	+56.7	−1.2
East Anglia	108.6	151.7	51.7	99.0	+43.2	+24.4	+18.8	−47.1	+3.8	+15.6	+16.6	+55.9	−1.9
South West	99.2	151.9	48.2	103.1	+52.7	+22.8	+29.9	−26.6	+0.4	+20.2	+8.8	+29.3	+20.7
West Midlands	74.4	153.9	60.7	93.0	+79.4	+95.3	−15.9	−14.4	−1.8	+73.7	−35.1	+35.9	+21.7
East Midlands	80.8	160.8	64.0	96.3	+80.1	+16.1	+63.9	−30.3	+10.1	+11.2	+25.6	+35.3	+28.3
Yorkshire E & W	91.9	119.3	42.9	76.4	+27.3	+24.9	+2.4	−18.7	+1.3	—	+1.6	+43.7	+0.4
North West	123.3	118.0	55.1	64.5	−3.7	+20.8	−24.4	−8.2	−2.3	−18.6	+3.9	+47.5	−26.1
Northern	96.6	113.6	42.8	70.6	+17.0	+15.0	+2.0	−32.7	−0.9	+14.0	+9.1	+33.7	−6.2
Wales	101.3	126.4	39.7	86.5	+25.0	+26.3	−1.2	−39.6	−9.4	+22.9	+3.5	+43.0	+4.7
Scotland	91.9	96.2	32.2	63.7	+4.3	+38.2	−33.9	−24.9	+3.3	+10.0	−25.7	+53.0	−11.6
Northern Ireland	152.4	119.8	48.6	68.8	−32.6	−42.3	+9.6	−44.0	−8.3	−42.7	+18.7	+44.4	−0.9
United Kingdom	91.1	139.5	52.2	87.0	+48.4			−18.5		+14.5		+52.3	

Source: Calculated from the Census Tables, Modified Regions

TABLE 20 Regional Employment Performance 1961–71
Rates per 1000 employed in 1961

Region	Job Losses	Job Gains Total	Job Gains Mnft	Job Gains Tert	Actual Change	Expected Change	Diff	Primary Expect	Primary Diff	Secondary Expect	Secondary Diff	Tertiary Expect	Tertiary Diff
South East	77.0	106.5	19.3	87.1	+29.5	+72.9	−43.4	−6.3	+0.8	+10.6	−30.6	+68.6	−13.7
East Anglia	85.0	227.7	100.8	125.8	+142.7	+21.7	+121.0	−39.2	−0.3	+0.1	+83.1	+60.7	+38.3
South West	83.2	162.2	66.0	95.0	+79.0	+13.2	+65.9	−23.6	+3.5	−8.9	+50.6	+45.6	+11.8
West Midlands	98.7	116.0	37.6	73.5	+17.2	+26.8	−9.6	−18.6	+1.1	+4.9	−22.3	+40.5	+11.6
East Midlands	100.4	139.9	48.2	91.4	+39.6	−29.7	+69.2	−46.8	+8.3	−16.4	+31.1	+33.5	+29.7
Yorkshire E & W	130.5	98.2	25.1	73.0	−32.4	−40.5	+8.1	−37.2	+9.2	−39.1	−3.9	+35.8	+2.7
North West	140.3	103.1	35.5	67.5	−37.1	−12.3	−24.8	−11,3	−2.8	−40.8	−6.7	+39.8	−15.3
Northern	146.2	150.2	57.7	90.7	+4.0	−42.3	+46.3	−63.3	−10.0	−14.8	+30.8	+35.8	+25.5
Wales	135.2	140.5	63.7	76.4	+5.3	−29.9	+35.2	−61.1	−2.1	−8.7	+43.6	+39.9	−6.3
Scotland	142.2	121.0	44.2	76.3	−21.1	−14.3	−7.3	−33.1	−7.5	−22.6	+13.4	+41.3	−13.2
Northern Ireland	180.1	208.7	77.5	128.1	+28.6	−46.6	+75.0	−35.6	−9.8	−47.9	+35.1	+36.9	+49.7
United Kingdom	108.6	122.8	38.3	84.1	+14.2			−24.2		−11.3		+49.8	

Source: Calculated from the Census Tables, Modified Regions

Job Losses and Gains

Confirmation for the idea that the northern and western regions have been suffering from a relatively severe run down of employment is obtained from the column of the tables showing job loss rates, where it is seen that the five southern and midland regions have in most cases had the lowest losses. In three of the four inter-censal periods the South East had the lowest rate, and this was particularly noticeable in the 1920s. East Anglia and the South West had the highest rates of this group, a fact which may reflect the importance of agriculture in their economies. In the northern and western group of regions the rates were nearly always above the national average and in some cases nearly twice as great.

However, the problems of these northern and western regions has not merely been the high rate of job loss, but also the inability to generate new jobs. This can be seen most clearly in the 1920s and 1950s when regional policies were either non-existent or not important. In the column showing total job gain rates this group of regions had below average figures whereas the five southern and midland regions which were suffering least from job losses and therefore least in need, had the highest rates. In the other two inter-censal periods, 1931–51 and 1961–71, significantly when regional policies were important, the picture is not clear cut in this way and indeed some of the highest rates were obtained in the assisted areas. At the same time both East Anglia and the South West had high rates. The next two columns show how these gains were divided between the manufacturing (secondary) and tertiary (services) sectors. In the 1920s the South East, West Midlands and East Midlands were outstanding in their manufacturing job gain rates and also did well in the tertiary sector where they were joined by the South West. This good performance is repeated in the other uncontrolled decade, the 1950s, where the group is joined by East Anglia. The effect of regional policy may be seen in the other two decades where the gain rates in manufacturing were much more even, and where in the 1960s the rates for the South East and West Midlands have been considerably reduced. Although this apparent effect of regional policy is interesting, we still need to inquire further into the effect of industrial structure on regional employment change and for this we turn to shift and share analysis.

Shift and Share Analysis

The effect of structure can be seen in the columns showing expected rates of change. In the 1920s, a period of net employment decline, only four regions, the South East, East Anglia, South West and West Midlands were expected to increase above the national rate (Table 17). In the case of the first three this was expected on the basis of services and for the West Midlands on the basis of manufacturing. All the other regions were expected to decline faster than the national rate, generally because of their poor structure in all three sectors. In the event this league table was only slightly changed with the deletion of East Anglia from the top rung and the addition of the East Midlands to the upper group. The South East performed much better than expected in both manufacturing and services and this was also true to a lesser extent of both midland regions. Meanwhile the South West benefited from a better than expected performance in the tertiary sector and both the East Midlands and Yorkshire in primary activities. The last four regions, the North West, North, Wales and Scotland all did worse than expected.

In the next inter-censal period, 1931–51, there were significant differences between the expected and actual performance (Table 18). Only the South East and West Midlands were expected, on the basis of their good structure, to grow faster than the national rate, but in the event neither did as well as expected and only the West Midlands was above the national average with the South East having a large negative differential. All the other regions, except Northern Ireland, performed better than expected, most noticeably in the case of the East Midlands, the North and Wales.

In the 1950s the South East and West Midlands were once again expected to grow more rapidly than the rest of the country and both achieved this despite a negative differential from the West Midlands (Table 19). In addition East Anglia, the South West and the East Midlands all grew much faster than expected, to raise themselves up to or above the national level. All the other regions were expected to and did grow below the national rate, with the North West and Scotland performing poorly. However, Northern Ireland, although having a net loss of jobs, declined less than expected due to a good performance in manufacturing.

In the 1960s, the final period for which census figures are available, we once again find that the South East and West Midlands were expected to grow faster than the rest of the country, and had in this decade been joined by East Anglia and the South West (Table 20). In the event these last two regions performed much better than expected in both the secondary and tertiary sectors, while the South East and West Midlands did less well. As before, the East Midlands performed much better than expected in all three sectors. The remaining regions were, as previously, expected to grow less rapidly than the rest of the country, in this case actually to lose jobs overall. However, in the cases of the North, Wales and Northern Ireland there was a remarkable turn around with a large positive differential producing overall employment growth. However, the North West and to a lesser extent Scotland performed poorly whilst Yorkshire's performance was only slightly modified by a slower decline of its primary sector.

It has only been possible to mention the salient features from these analyses of regional employment and the tables will repay further study. It will be noted that the aggregate results are by no means mirrored in the figures for the different sectors each of which has its own distinctive pattern. These variations will be discussed in the three chapters which follow. Here it will be sufficient to highlight a few conclusions and questions. In the periods of non-existent or weak regional policy the vitality of the South East and also the West Midlands has been noted. The high rate of increase in jobs is more than could be expected from a favourable structure. What are the causes of this? East Anglia and the South West which began the period with either a poor or middling performance have now become the most successful regions. Is this merely an overflow from the South East or are there other factors involved? Throughout the period the region which has performed well most consistently is the East Midlands. In spite of an apparently adverse structure it has managed to buck the trend and grow rapidly in each intercensal period. What are the causes of this vitality and to what extent is this conclusion a result of the technique used? The regions of the north and west are the reverse of the South East and West Midlands for in periods of weak regional policy they have performed poorly, particularly in the inter-war period. Cursed with an unfavourable structure they have performed still worse. Is this a factor of location, of economic environment or something else? Located on the boundary between the prosperous and less prosperous regions is Yorkshire whose performance has also mirrored this position. Neither failing badly nor succeeding well, it has appeared to be slipping over to the wrong side. Once again we can look for the factors involved. Finally we have noted the contrast in regional employment performance between the periods of weak and strong regional policy. This is a topic which has received much attention and will be discussed in the next section.

Comparisons and Applications

Shift and share analysis has been used to study British regional employment changes by a number of writers including A.P. Thirlwall (1967), F.J.B. Stilwell (1969) and A.J. Brown (1972); and also in a modified form by Moore and Rhodes (1973), Buck and Atkins (1976) and D. Keeble (1976). Comparison of these studies is difficult as they are not consistent with respect to period or area of study: some use figures for the United Kingdom, others only for Great Britain; some use the regional boundaries of the early 1960s, others those of the late 1960s; some use statistics at the order level, others at the MLH level; and finally some have covered all three sectors whilst others have been concerned only with manufacturing. Most studies are also based on Department of Employment statistics which, unlike the census statistics used here, are available on an annual basis (see Appendix A). There is agreement with the work reported above on the weakness of the Scottish economy (Moore and Rhodes, 1974b), and on the comparatively good performance of the Welsh economy (Moore and Rhodes, 1975), whilst the early improvement in the 1950s of the Northern Ireland economy is noted by Thirlwall (1967). More important, perhaps, is the improved performance of the assisted regions from the 1950s to the 1960s which has been noted by Moore and Rhodes (1973) in their attempt to evaluate the effects of regional economic policy.

In a comparison of expected and actual changes in the manufacturing employment of the four main assisted regions, Moore and Rhodes (1973) found that during the 1950s and up to 1963 these two figures were similar, suggesting that expected performance based on applying national rates of growth to industrial orders was a good predictor of actual performance during this period of weak regional policy, although as noted above there were significant variations between the assisted regions. In the period after 1963 there were, however, significant differences between actual and expected performance, with the assisted areas doing much better than predicted. This difference was assumed to be caused by regional policies, which it was suggested during the period 1963–1970 resulted in 150,000 extra jobs in the manufacturing sector, excluding shipbuilding and metal manufacturing which were the beneficiaries of special government policies. When allowance is made for these industries and for the multiplier effects in the service sector, plus the results of a similar exercise for the Merseyside and South West Development Areas which only covered parts of regions, an additional 70,000 jobs were suggested giving a total regional policy effect for the period 1963–70 of 220,000.

In a later study Moore and Rhodes (1976b) estimated the policy effect for the whole period 1960–71 at 300,000 jobs while in separate papers on Scotland (Moore and Rhodes, 1974b) and Wales (1974) they estimated the policy effect on the former region at 70/80,000 jobs and for the latter at 62/72,000.

In his study of employment changes in 1953–9 and 1961–66, A.J. Brown (1972, 318) argued that the policy effect was not only any positive differential in employment performance derived from a shift and share analysis but should include any negative differential which existed in the earlier period of weak policy and which could be assumed to have been wiped out. For the period 1961–66 he found the policy effect in the four assisted regions to be 70,000 jobs a year or for the five year period 350,000 jobs, considerably higher than the Moore and Rhodes estimate.

The analysis used in this chapter differs from that of Moore and Rhodes and A.J. Brown in being based on census data disaggregated to the MLH level, but the same methods employed to measure the effect of regional policy may be used. In the period 1951–61 the negative differential for all manufacturing industry in the four main assisted regions was 36,100 whilst for the decade 1961–71 this had changed to a positive differential of 136,400 giving a total policy shift for the 1960s of 161,500 jobs using the A.J. Brown method. If the figures are made comparable to those of Moore and Rhodes by excluding the metal manufacturing and shipbuilding orders, the respective figures are −35,000 and +161,000 giving a total shift of 196,000 jobs. Whilst the negative differential for the period 1951–61 differs from the Moore and Rhodes figures, the total policy effect for manufacturing in the four main assisted regions very nearly agrees with their estimate of 200,000 (Moore and Rhodes, 1976b). Using the Moore and Rhodes figure of 50,000 to cover additional employment created in the Merseyside and South West Development Areas, and in the metals and shipbuilding industries, would suggest that regional policy employment effects in the manufacturing sector were between 211,000 and 246,000 in the decade 1961–71. The major part of this policy effect was due to industrial movement. During the period 1960–71 at least 177,000 manufacturing jobs were moved to the five main assisted regions (see Chapter 9). The remainder of the policy effect will have been due to indigenous growth.

Conclusion

In this chapter we have examined the idea that regional employment changes reflect industrial structure and have seen that while this is important it has never been the only or even principal factor explaining change. In the inter-war period and the 1950s, the South East performed much better than structure would suggest, while the northern and western areas much worse. In periods of government control and influence through regional policies such as the 1940s and 1960s the pattern was reversed. Given the crudeness of the shift and share technique it would be spurious to lay too much emphasis on the precise division between the structural and differential components of the analysis. However, since the 'differential' component is important it is of great interest to examine the other causes of variations in regional employment growth. This might be due to differences either in the movement of activities between regions or in the rates of indigenous growth of activities, topics which will be examined in Chapters 8 and 9. Meanwhile our consideration of structure will be taken further as the three sectors are examined in the following chapters.

CHAPTER FIVE

Regional Employment Changes in the Primary Sector

In the first chapter a number of themes were indicated for the study of regional economic change in Britain. These included the role of structure and the fact that each region begins the period with a different combination of industries, using that term in its widest sense, which grow or decline at different rates. In the next three chapters an attempt will be made to explore the role of structure, examining how far and why employment changes in the major activities have moved according to previous spatial patterns, and how far other factors from locational advantage to government regional policy have intervened to alter the pattern. It will not be possible to consider all the factors in regional economic change, some of which are reserved for later chapters. The division of the three chapters is based on the three sectors, primary, secondary and tertiary, each of which is to a certain extent influenced by a different set of location factors. In the primary sector there is a close link with physical resources which are fixed in location. The manufacturing activity of the secondary sector is potentially far more flexible in location being attracted by several factors such as materials, markets and labour, whilst in the tertiary sector the supply of services to consumers means that market orientation is of very great, although by no means exclusive, importance. The following commentary will be based on employment statistics derived from the censuses from 1921 to 1971 and discussed more fully in Appendices A and B.

The primary sector, covering agriculture, forestry, fishing, mining and quarrying, has experienced the greatest absolute and relative decline in employment since World War I of the three sectors. In 1921 nearly three million people were employed in this group of activities representing 15 per cent of the labour force. When allowance is made for the service sector, much of whose employment may be considered non-basic as it is widely found, probably about 30 per cent of the basic labour force was in this category. The relative importance of this sector in 1921 in regional economies varied, partly depending on the development of other activities: where these were weakly represented as in East Anglia, Northern England, Wales and Northern Ireland, over a quarter the labour force was found in these activities; in contrast there was less than 8 per cent in the South East and North West. Between 1921 and 1971 the numbers employed in the primary sector fell by nearly two thirds or 1,859,000 jobs affecting every region. The lowest relative loss was in the South East where it was 52 per cent (147,000 jobs) and the highest in Wales where it was 76 per cent, a loss of 324,000 jobs. In 1971 no region had more than 10 per cent of its workforce in this sector; it was just below this level in East Anglia and Wales, and lowest in the North West and South East where fewer than 2 per cent were engaged in primary activities.

Agriculture, Forestry and Fishing

Agriculture is the most important primary activity. The numbers employed in agriculture in each region reflect the size of the region, the opportunities afforded by land and climate, and the type of agriculture practised. Since the 1860s the agricultural labour force has been in almost continuous decline. In the period 1921–71 about 800,000 jobs were lost, or over half the labour force. The main reason for this decline has been the replacement of men by machines. Although tractors were introduced before World War I, there were still less than 5,000 in 1925. This had increased to 55,000 in 1939 and reached a peak of over 480,000 in the mid-1950s (Coppock, 1971). At the same time many other types of machines were introduced such as combine harvesters and milking machines. Every region has been affected by these changes and the rate of decline has been fairly even across the country (Figure 18). Small variations in this rate of decline have been determined by factors such as the extent of arable farming, encroachment of urban land and diffusion of new techniques. Mechanisation has had greatest impact in the arable eastern areas rather than the pastoral west. The loss of jobs has also been greater in semi-urban regions like the North West and South East where land has been lost to building and where there is more competition for labour. Finally the new techniques have generally been introduced in the southern part of the country and spread to other areas. The higher rate of labour loss in Northern Ireland and Scotland may thus reflect some catching up with other regions in the level of mechanisation.

Forestry and fishing both employ much smaller numbers. After World War I it was decided for strategic reasons to encourage afforestation and under the leadership of the Forestry Commission large areas of upland Britain have been planted (Mather, 1978). About 20,000 are now employed and although its impact on regional economies is negligible, the industry does make a significant local contribution in these upland areas. Employment in fishing declined from 66,000 in 1921 to about 20,000 in 1971, and has fallen still further in the late 1970s with the ban on Icelandic fishing. Once again the overall impact is small but many fishing ports along the east coast have been significantly affected.

Mining and Quarrying

Most of the activity in this industry must inevitably take place at the location of the mineral deposits which are determined by geological factors, but the scale of activity will be determined not only by the general demand for the material but by the quality of the deposit, the cost of production and the cost of access to markets.

Coal mining has always been the most important extractive industry in Britain. Production increased rapidly during the

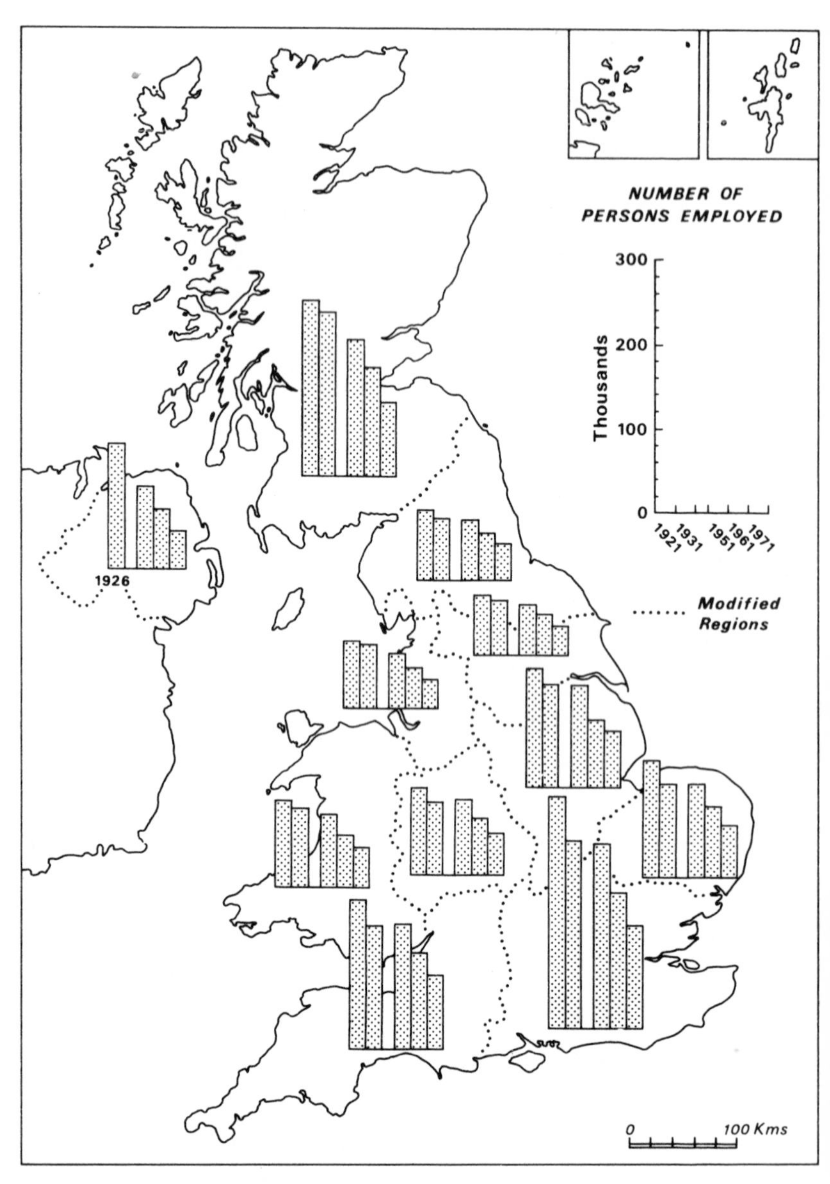

Fig. 18 The Regional Distribution of Employment in Agriculture, Forestry and Fishing

nineteenth century to reach a peak of 287 million tons in 1913 of which over one-third was exported. In 1921 over 1¼ million were employed in this activity and, since most employment in mining and quarrying is in this group, Figure 19 accurately reflects the regional pattern of the industry. The industry was most important in Wales and Northern England where over ¼ million were employed and where the coastal locations of the coalfields facilitated the development of a large export trade. Over 100,000 people were also employed in other regions such as Scotland, the North West and the two midland regions. Only in Northern Ireland, East Anglia, the South West and the South East was the industry either absent or on a small scale.

Since World War I coal output has fallen reflecting the almost total loss of export markets as well as a decline in home demand. In both cases other fuels—oil, natural gas and nuclear power—have eaten into markets traditionally held by coal whilst the more efficient use of coal has reduced demand in still held markets. Only in its use for electricity generation has the market for coal increased. In 1957 the electricity industry accounted for 21 per cent of UK coal consumption; by 1972–3 its share had risen to over 53 per cent (North and Spooner, 1978).

Production fell during the inter-war depression but rose in the late 1930s, and after the war, under the new National Coal Board's plans for expansion, it increased again in the early 1950s (Simpson, 1966). By the mid-1950s output was between 220 and 230 million tons, but after 1957 demand and output declined once again. Over the next two decades a further 100 million tons of production was lost accompanied by a massive programme of pit closures and redundancies. The labour force which had been around 750,000 in the mid-1950s was savagely cut, falling below 300,000 in 1976, representing a loss of one million jobs since 1921. This 77 per cent reduction in jobs compared to a 56 per cent decline in output reflected significant increases in productivity which had taken place mainly in the post-war period.

The regional patterns of decline reflect changes in access to

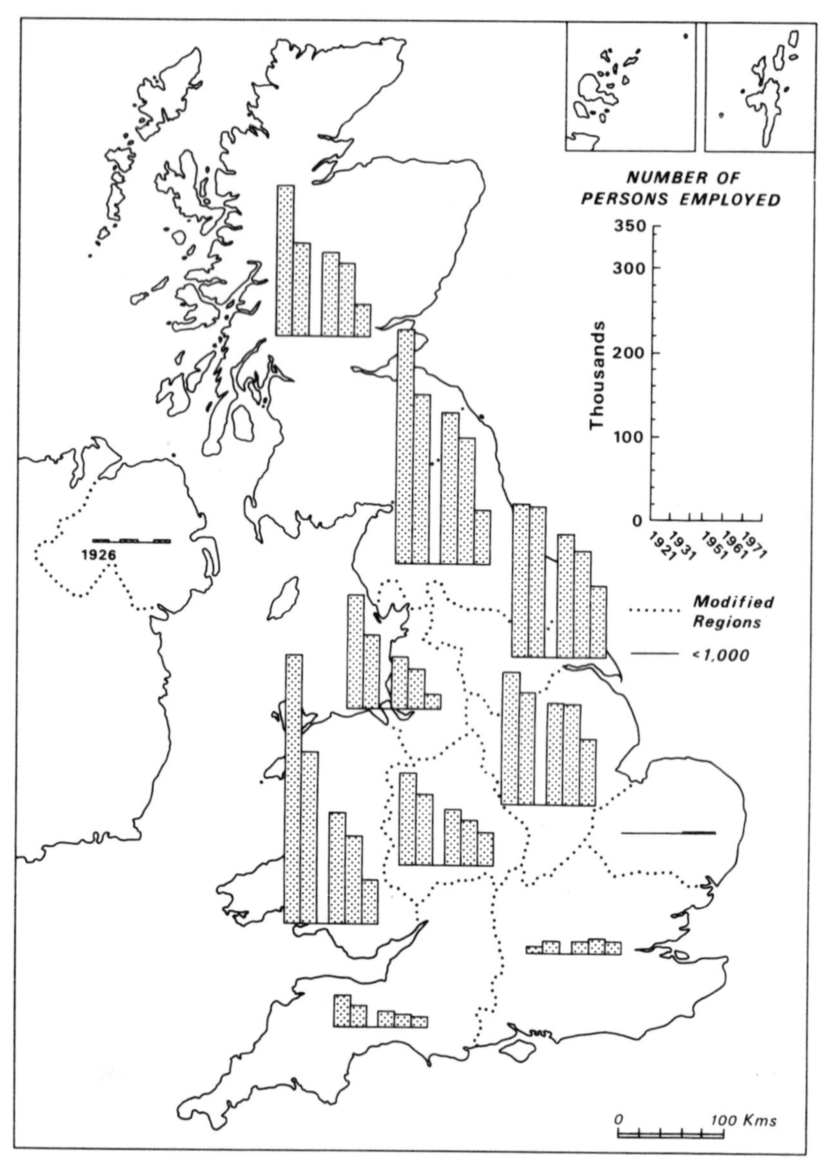

Fig. 19 The Regional Distribution of Employment in Mining and Quarrying

markets, costs of production and easy access to reserves (Blunden, 1975). In Yorkshire and the East Midlands mining conditions are good with thick gently dipping seams and relatively few faults. It has thus been easy and economical to introduce mechanisation and accordingly these areas have become the most efficient and lowest cost producers in the country (Table 21). At the same time these areas have a central location near to the principal centres of population from London to Lancashire–Yorkshire so that the Central Electricity Generating Board has been anxious to build large modern coal-fired power stations in the areas (Rawstron 1964b), thus providing ready markets for local coal. Although the older western areas of these coalfields have been closed in recent years development and expansion in the eastern concealed coalfields continues and the 1980s will see the commencement of production from the Selby coalfield (Yorkshire) and possibly from the Vale of Belvoir (East Midlands). (North and Spooner, 1977.) Whilst production and employment has fallen slightly in both these areas the decline has been much less than elsewhere and over a long period there has been a relative shift towards these regions. In 1913 they produced 27 per cent of UK coal output and in 1977 56 per cent (Table 21).

In contrast the coalfields of Wales, the North West, North and Scotland have suffered very great decline. The pace of decline has varied over time between these regions with the South Wales coalfield badly affected in the inter-war period and the North East hit in the 1960s. In general the physical conditions in these regions are poorer making mechanisation more difficult and less economical with resulting high production costs. At the same time home and overseas markets have been lost with the latter particularly affecting South Wales and the North East. Higher costs and in some cases more remote locations have not helped these areas to obtain new markets such as electricity generation. One small compensation has been the good anthracite and coking coals found in parts of South Wales and the North East which has helped to preserve some markets. The inevitable decline of

TABLE 21 UK Coal Production and Productivity

	1913 tons	*1929 tons*	*1950 tons*	*1977–8 tonnes*
A Production (millions)				
South East	0.1	1.1	1.7	0.6
South West	3.0	2.4	1.3	—
West Midlands	20.8	18.2	17.0	9.8
East Midlands	33.7	32.7	40.1	37.1
Yorkshire	43.7	46.4	42.6	31.0
North West	24.6	15.7	12.5	4.0
North	58.7	55.6	39.7	16.2
Wales	60.3	51.6	25.2	10.5
Scotland	42.5	34.2	23.2	8.7
UK	287.4	257.9	216.3	120.2
B Per Cent of Total Production				
South East	0.0	0.4	0.8	0.5
South West	1.0	0.9	0.6	—
West Midlands	7.3	7.1	7.9	8.1
East Midlands	11.7	12.7	18.5	30.9
Yorkshire	15.2	18.0	19.7	25.8
North West	8.6	6.1	5.8	3.3
North	20.4	21.5	18.4	13.6
Wales	21.0	20.0	11.7	8.8
Scotland	14.8	13.3	10.7	7.2
C Output per Man (Indexed UK = 100)				
South East	20	98	93	46
South West	73	83	66	—
West Midlands	96	87	97	116
East Midlands	117	100	135	131
Yorkshire	105	100	100	105
North West	88	73	82	85
North	95	104	82	82
Wales	93	99	74	60
Scotland	117	127	92	87

Source: Annual Abstract of Statistics and Regional Statistics (1979)

coal production in these regions has been slowed down by the benefits of cross-subsidisation from the more profitable areas and the overall protection given to the industry by the government (Manners, 1971). In spite of this, the loss of coal-mining jobs in these regions between 1921 and 1971 is considerable as is shown by the following figures: Wales—252,000; Northern England—195,000; Scotland—129,000; and North West England—112,000. The size of these job losses is clearly one of the major causes of high unemployment in these regions and thus of the regional problem itself. Notwithstanding the large-scale pit closure programmes which have already occurred, there are still many unprofitable collieries remaining and further closures and redundancies seem inevitable.

The other extractive industries comprise a disparate group of mineral workings ranging from the widely found sand and gravel workings to the more valuable and localised extraction of iron ore and tin. Collectively employment has fallen from 115,000 in 1912 to 53,000 in 1971 but the regional impact has been uneven. The greatest decline has been in the exploitation of minerals from the older and harder rocks of the north and west for which there has been a fall in demand. In contrast there has a slight increase in employment for the softer materials found in the south and east which, like sand and gravel, are used in the building industry and where a growing population has provided a local market.

Britain's energy position was transformed in the mid-1960s by discoveries of natural gas (in 1965) and oil (in 1969) in the North Sea (Chapman, 1976). The development of these resources and their early regional impact has been delayed till the 1970s and there is considerable speculation about possible future effects, which will be discussed more fully in Chapter 12.

Conclusion

Since World War I about two million jobs have been lost in the primary sector. These activities, particularly coal-mining, were more concentrated in the northern and western parts of the country, and additionally the rate of decline has been proportionally greater there as well. The significance of this loss is much greater than the figures suggest since 98 per cent of the workers were male and so these jobs provided the economic basis in many areas of the country in both lightly peopled rural areas and densely settled mining districts. Given modern productive methods these industries will never again play such a vital role in the economic and social life of the regions, but their disappearance has created many problems.

CHAPTER SIX

Regional Employment Changes in the Manufacturing Sector

The manufacturing sector has always been regarded as the most important in the economy because it provides basic jobs on which the wealth of the community depends. In 1921 nearly 7 million were employed in this sector in the UK and, after a fall in the depression, the numbers increased steadily till the mid-1960s when there were over 8½ million jobs. Since 1966 employment has fallen by over a million and the decline has been particularly rapid since 1971. In the period 1921–71 the five southern and midland regions all increased their absolute and relative share of manufacturing jobs as did the North and Wales, but in the North West, Yorkshire, Scotland and Northern Ireland there was both absolute and relative decline (Table 22). Since 1966 there has been widespread absolute decline in manufacturing employment which by the 1970s affected every region except East Anglia (Table 23). In contrast with earlier periods, the South East and West Midlands experienced a relative decline with significant absolute losses of jobs. East Anglia, the South West, East Midlands, the North and Wales have continued to increase their share of manufacturing employment. Within the total number employed by manufacturing industry the trend for those engaged in non-production activities—such as management, clerical workers, scientists and salesmen—has been one of increase whilst the number of production workers has been declining since the 1950s (Crum and Gudgin, 1978). These non-production activities show a greater concentration in the South East region, where head offices and research laboratories are commonly found, a topic which will be discussed in Chapter 8.

TABLE 22 Changes in Regional Manufacturing Employment, 1921–71

	Employment (000)			*Per Cent of Total*		
	1921	*1951*	*1971*	*1921*	*1951*	*1971*
South East	1509	2186	2281	21.6	26.5	27.4
East Anglia	107	121	185	1.5	1.5	2.2
South West	291	349	440	4.2	4.2	5.3
West Midlands	778	1081	1116	11.2	13.1	13.4
East Midlands	488	622	694	7.0	7.5	8.3
Yorkshire E & W	812	832	740	11.6	10.1	8.9
North West	1440	1404	1196	20.6	17.0	14.4
North	353	416	461	5.1	5.0	5.5
Wales	189	279	338	2.7	3.4	4.1
Scotland	806	775	695	11.6	9.4	8.4
N. Ireland	198	194	171	2.8	2.3	2.1
UK Total	6972	8259	8317	100.0	100.0	100.0

Source: Census Reports, Modified Regions

TABLE 23 Recent Changes in Regional Manufacturing Employment

	Employment (000)			*Per Cent of Total*		
	1966	*1971*	*1976*	*1966*	*1971*	*1976*
South East	2363	2171	1851	27.5	26.4	25.5
East Anglia	173	190	196	2.0	2.4	2.7
South West	429	439	420	5.0	5.4	5.8
West Midlands	1197	1104	979	13.4	13.7	13.5
East Midlands	631	618	587	7.4	7.7	8.1
Yorkshire & Humberside	860	777	711	10.0	9.6	9.8
North West	1251	1131	1006	14.6	14.0	13.9
North	462	463	439	5.9	6.4	6.1
Wales	317	324	302	3.7	4.0	4.2
Scotland	726	669	608	8.5	8.3	8.4
N. Ireland	175	170	147	2.0	2.1	2.0
UK Total	8584	8056	7246	100.0	100.0	100.0

Source: Department of Employment, Employees in Employment. New Standard Regions (Post-1974 regions)

In Chapter 1 some of the factors affecting the location of industry were discussed. The traditional approach has been to examine cost variations in respect of factors such as the procurement of materials, labour and the distribution of final products to explain observed locational patterns. However, where the spatial margins of profitability are wide it is necessary to use a more behavioural approach and examine variations in the formation of new firms, the location of foreign firms and the spatial behaviour of the large corporation including patterns of movement. These factors will be examined in Chapters 8, 9 and 10. In this chapter employment change amongst the various manufacturing industries will be examined since differences in industrial structure and the growth or decline of industries have been the most important forces affecting regional and local prosperity. Although differences in industrial structure at the broad level have been widely discussed in studies of regional development, frequently differences within major groups have been ignored and one of the themes of this chapter is how subgroup performance has affected regional employment growth. We shall adopt a simple two-fold division into those industries which have experienced employment growth and those with employment decline over the period.

Industries with Declining Employment

Since World War I over 2 million jobs have been lost in manufacturing, and the location of these losses has been very significant for regional development. The main declining industries are shown in Table 24 where it is seen that some of the most significant decreases have been in industries which are geographically concentrated inevitably causing local hardship. In studying declining industries it is of interest to examine whether job losses have been evenly spread within the districts containing the industry or whether the decline has been accompanied by migration of the industry to areas where it was previously not found.

The textile industries, which show the largest declines,

TABLE 24 Principal Industries with Declining Employment, 1921–71

	Employment Decline	
	1921–71	*1971–76*
Spinning/Weaving of Cotton, Flax, Hemp, etc.	609,000	37,000
Clothing (excluding footwear)	285,000	55,000
Shipbuilding and Marine Engineering	239,000	8,000
Woollen and Worsted	143,000	32,000
Railway Engineering	128,000	5,000
Textile Finishing	62,000	6,000
Textile Engineering	38,000	13,000
Grain Milling	28,000	3,000
Jute	24,000	2,000
Lace	19,000	—
Motor Vehicles		56,000
Other Machinery		50,000
Iron and Steel		36,000
Bread and Confectionery		31,000
Other Mechanical Engineering		30,000
Iron Castings		23,000

Source: 1921–71 Census Reports
1971–76 Department of Employment

were amongst the pioneering manufactures of the Industrial Revolution (Stamp and Beaver, 1971, Chapters 19, 20 and 21). Although usually treated as a group there are in fact several branches, in some of which—man-made fibres, hosiery and carpets—there has been recent growth. The major branch was the cotton textile industry: the past tense is used deliberately, for much of the remnant of the industry is now concerned with the processing of man-made fibres. Hence to follow the cotton industry over the past fifty years it is necessary to enlarge the definition to include the spinning and weaving of flax, hemp and man-made fibres. So defined this includes three industries: first the traditional cotton industry (excluding finishing) which in 1921 employed 620,000, 85 per cent of whom were found in the North West with the remainder being found in the East Midlands, Yorkshire and Scotland; secondly the linen industry with 86,000 employed in 1921, four-fifths in Northern Ireland and the rest mainly in Scotland; finally the silk industry, including rayon weaving, with 30,000 workers in 1921 found particularly in parts of the Midlands, North West and Yorkshire. In all nearly ¾ million workers were employed of whom over half were women (Figure 20). The decline of these industries through the loss of exports, and even in recent years to imports to the home market, is well known (Smith, 1969). Together with increased mechanisation, this accounts for the loss of over 600,000 jobs from 1921 to 1971, four-fifths of the earlier total. The decline has affected all the traditional areas, but in absolute terms the North West with the largest industry has suffered most, losing 460,000 jobs. At the same time there have been small increases in jobs in Wales and Northern England where a few new plants have been attracted by development area grants.

The second major textile industry is the woollen and worsted industry, which by the late nineteenth century had become concentrated in west Yorkshire with a smaller industry in Scotland. In 1921 four-fifths of those employed in wool manufacture were in Yorkshire compared to only one-twelfth in Scotland, the next most important region (Figure 21). The decline of the woollen industry has been slower and generally more recent than that of the cotton industry for it was never so dependent on exports. However, increased efficiency has reduced jobs bringing a drop in employment of 140,000 between 1921–71, 130,000 of which was in Yorkshire. The decrease was less in Scotland, whose share of the national woollen industry increased, while the Northern region also showed a small real gain in jobs as a result of firms being attracted there by the assisted area incentives and labour supplies.

There has also been employment decline in some of the smaller textile industries like jute manufacture, largely concentrated at Dundee, and lace, mainly found in the Nottingham area. The decline of all these textile industries has naturally had an adverse effect on the many ancillary industries, most notably those of textile finishing and textile engineering, which are usually found located close to the industries they grew to serve.

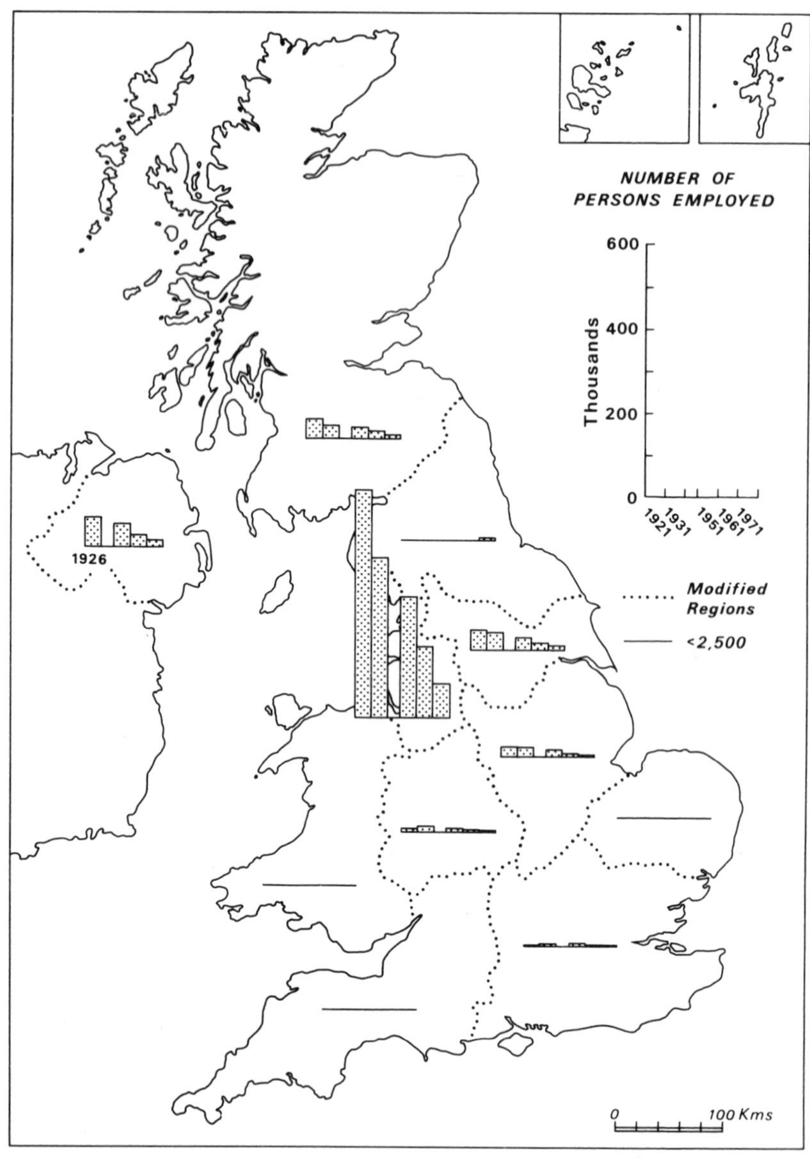

Fig. 20 The Regional Distribution of Employment in Cotton, Linen and Silk

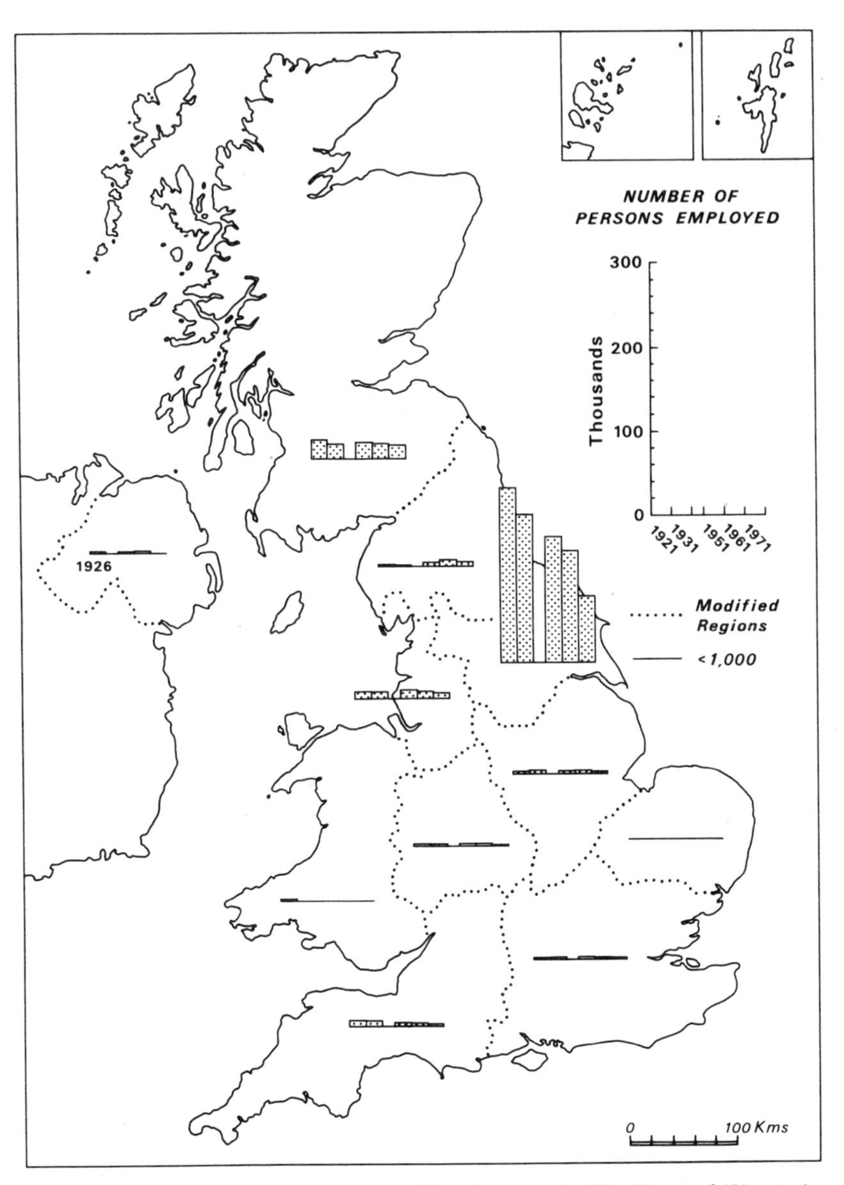

Fig. 21 The Regional Distribution of Employment in Woollen and Worsted

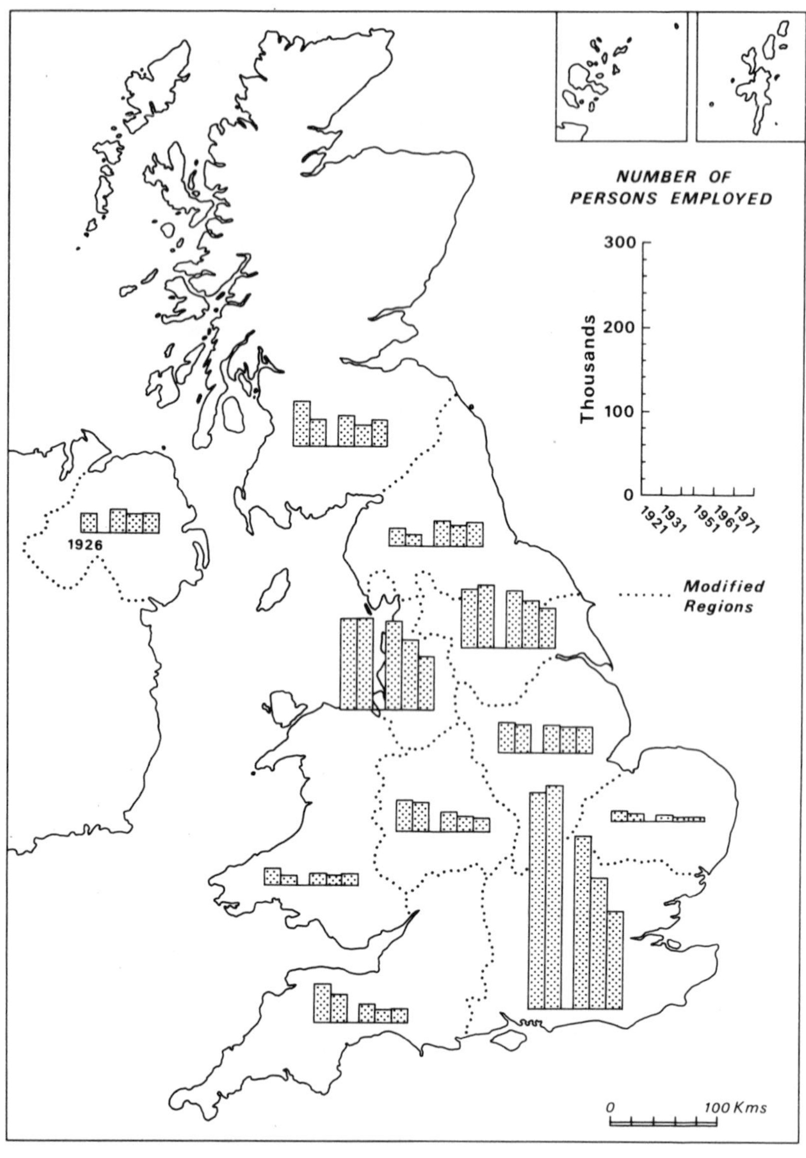

Fig. 22 The Regional Distribution of Employment in the Clothing Industries

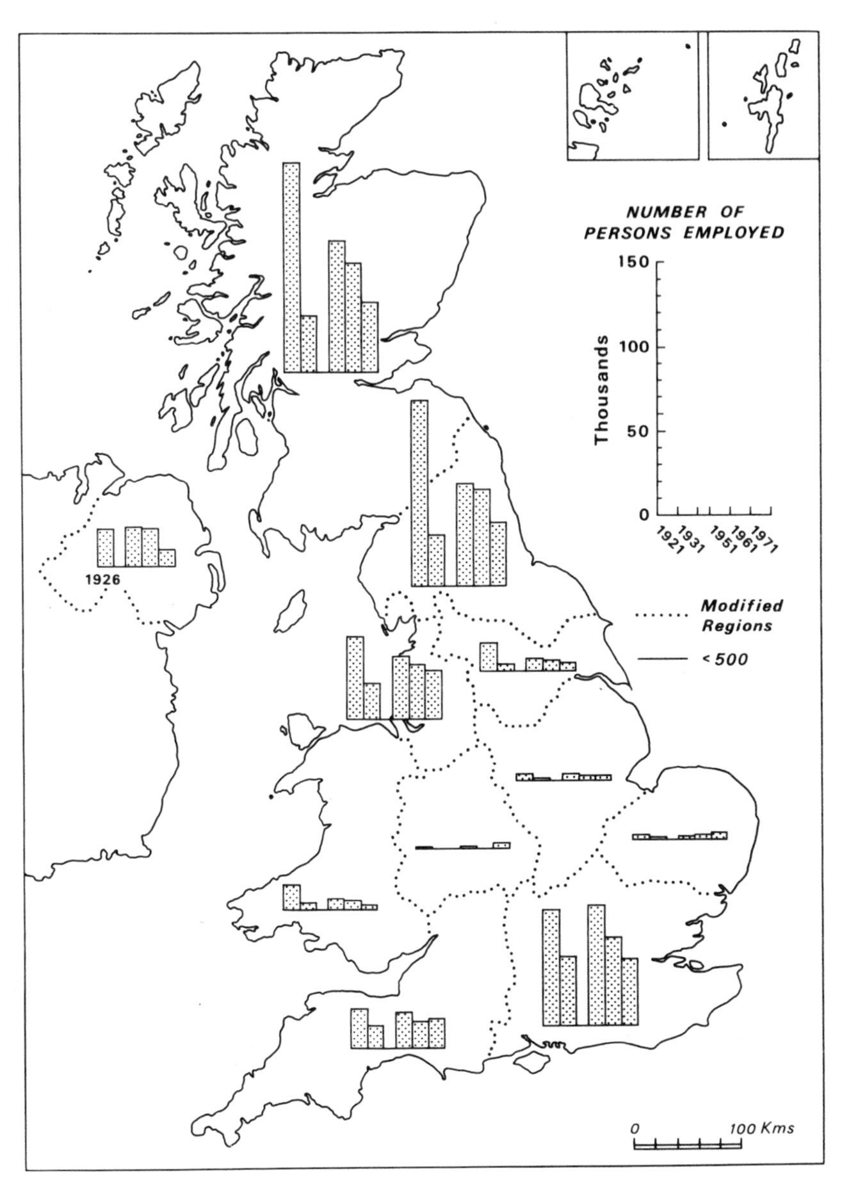

Fig. 23 The Regional Distribution of Employment in Shipbuilding and Marine Engineering

The clothing industries (excluding footwear) have also witnessed a major loss of jobs, from 683,000 in 1921 to 397,000 in 1971, a decline of 285,000. These varied industries have always been fairly widespread, partly reflecting bespoke manufacture where access to customers is important, but there have also been centres of specialisation such as London for fashion products, Leeds for men's suits, Manchester for rainwear, Londonderry for shirts, Luton for hats and so on. The decline in employment since World War I is a reflection of greater productivity, fashion changes and increased imports. The relative job loss has been greatest in southern England and the West Midlands, whilst there has been a gain of jobs in Northern England (Figure 22). Elsewhere the decline of jobs has been about average. The relative shift of the industry away from the traditional centres probably represents a search for cheap supplies of female labour encouraged by Development Area policies (Keeble, 1976, Chapter 7).

Another major declining activity has been the shipbuilding industry which by World War I was the largest in the world, reflecting the position of the country both as a marine power and trading state. Once again any discussion of employment changes in this industry needs to take into account the different types of activity included under this heading. The shipbuilding classification covers not only the building of merchant ships but also of fishing boats, pleasure craft, ship repair, marine engineering, the building of warships and the work of the Royal Naval dockyards. Using this definition there were approximately 430,000 workers in the industry in 1921 with Scotland (Clydeside) and Northern England (the North East) leading with over 25 per cent each. The South East with 16 per cent came next, this figure including the Royal Naval dockyards at Chatham and Portsmouth (Figure 23). By 1971 about 240,000 jobs had been lost with the two leading areas each losing about one-third of the total. These areas were badly affected because of the decline of merchant shipbuilding as were the North West (Birkenhead and Barrow) and Northern Ireland (Belfast). Elsewhere the loss was relatively less reflecting the dependence of these regions on other activities of the industry, although this still involved a large loss of jobs in the South East.

The metal manufacturing trades have only shown a slight loss of jobs over the whole period, but their decline in employment is likely to continue with important effects for regional employment. The metal manufacturing order, which in 1971 employed 551,000, includes not only the basic manufacture of iron, steel and non-ferrous metals, but also their further processing into castings and other components. The first aspect has traditionally been attracted to the source of raw materials, originally coalfields or orefields and more recently ports, and remains through inertia and government policy important in Wales, Yorkshire, the North and Scotland (Heal, 1974) (Figure 24). Processing is more attracted to market locations and it is here that the West Midlands has always been important, not least since World War I with the growth of the motor vehicle industry. The growth of markets in the South East has encouraged a small metal processing industry there, while since 1921 the industry has grown in the East Midlands with the development of Corby and Scunthorpe and the growth of foundries in that area. The major losses have been in Scotland where both sections of the industry have been in decline. In the 1970s the new technologies associated with the basic oxygen converter and surplus capacity in the industry have caused major rationalisation programmes resulting in the closure of many works in the northern and western regions of the country.

The decline of these activities has more significance than the mere employment figures might suggest. Many of these industries conform to the propulsive industries of 'growth pole' theory and developed in the nineteenth century with many local linkages. The cotton industry in the North West is a good example of this with linkages to engineering, chemicals and transport in the region. The decline of such growth poles has multiplier effects via these linkages causing greater problems to these regions in which the industries were situated.

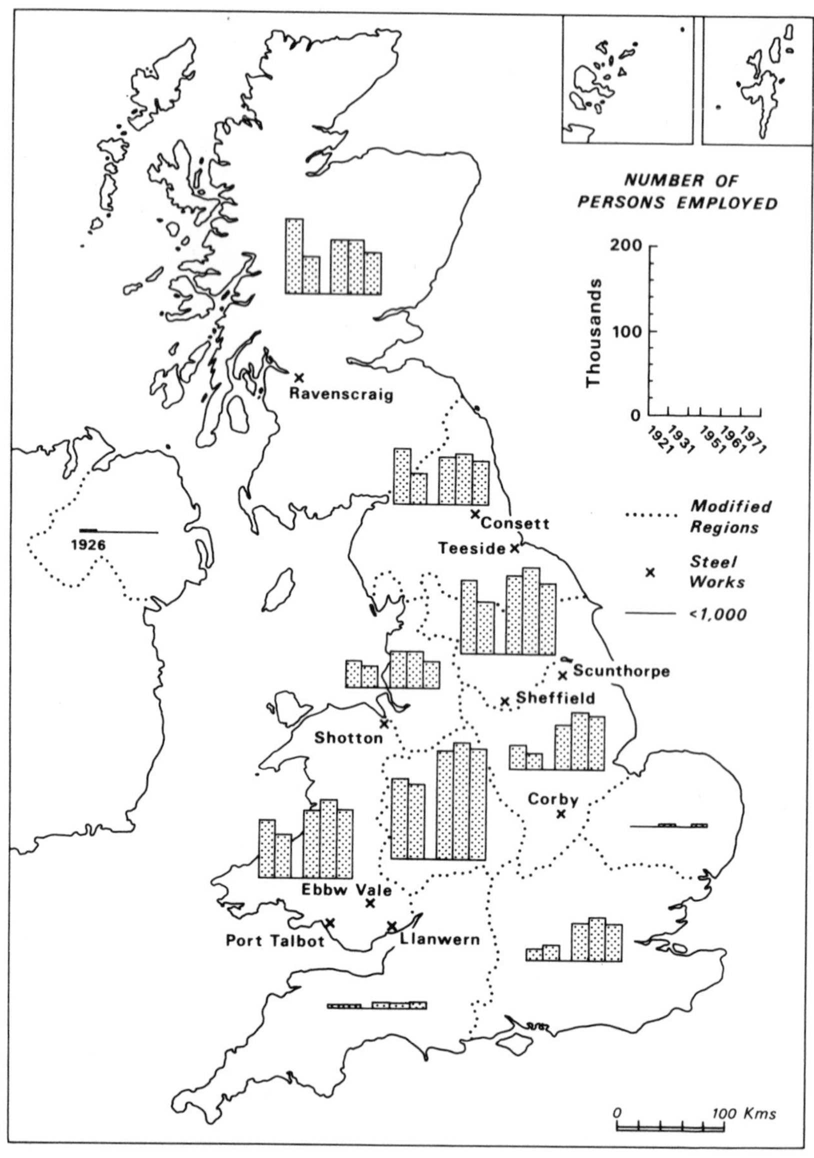

Fig. 24 The Regional Distribution of Employment in Metal Manufacturing

Industries with Growing Employment

We have already seen in Chapter 2 that employment growth has occurred particularly in the engineering and metal goods industries and to a lesser extent in chemicals, food, printing and other industries. There is a wide range of modern growth industries, not all of which are quickly recognisable to the public. Owing to their recent evolution and the changes in industrial classification it is not possible to tabulate the precise employment changes during the period. Further some of these activities have already peaked in jobs and are now shedding labour as a result of new production technologies. In this section we shall have space to examine only a few of the more important growth industries, some of which have their roots in the period before World War I.

The motor vehicle industry is one of the most important twentieth-century industries. In 1971 there were about 500,000 workers in this industry but this did not include many of those making vehicle components such as tyres, brakes, electrical instruments and glass windscreens, the addition of whom would probably increase the total employment in the vehicle industry by 50 per cent. In 1971 in spite of government location policy two-thirds of the employment was still found in the South and Midlands, reflecting the pattern of the early evolution of the industry (Bloomfield, 1978, 204). The first motor vehicles were pioneered on the continent in the 1880s and soon attracted attention in Britain, although the development of the industry was hampered till the abolition of the Red Flag Act in 1896. Many enthusiasts made cars and attempted to set up firms, but some of the more successful companies arose out of the cycle trades, coach-building firms and agricultural engineering firms. Coventry and Birmingham were important for cycle manufacture from which many car firms evolved. This transition was stimulated by the chance factor that the first Daimler company was established in Coventry, providing a source from whence the new technology could be diffused. Many firms arose in London where the principal market for what was then a luxury product was found. However, there were some other areas where pioneer firms were found including Scotland and the North West. In 1911 Henry Ford established a factory in Manchester at the terminus of the ship canal where imported Model T cars were assembled and quickly captured a large market. The period before World War I was a pioneering one in terms of product and production processes with manufacturers still making most of the components used. Thereafter the product became more sophisticated and sold in larger quantities, and with this evolution many other firms were drawn into component manufacture, whilst mass production methods were introduced into the main manufacturing firms or at least into those which remained successful.

The inter-war period saw a marked shift of the industry towards the South East caused by three developments: first, the growth of the Morris company at Oxford which, although a chance location, had the advantage of being between London and the West Midlands; second the takeover in 1926 of Vauxhall Motors at Luton by the giant American company General Motors which proceeded to expand the company; and thirdly, the American Ford company, in view of new British tariffs, decided to make an all-British car in a fully integrated plant at a new site on the Thames estuary at Dagenham. Opened in 1932 the new plant was expected not only to serve Britain but also Europe though because of tariffs this never developed. The growth of car component firms in this period was made possible by the increased sophistication of many of the components then being incorporated into vehicles and the economies of scale which specialist firms could gain. Not unnaturally many of these component firms were found in London and the West Midlands and were often old established firms which saw a new local market for their existing or modified products. In London Smith's, a clock making firm, took up the manufacture of car instruments, whilst in Birmingham Lucas turned from making oil lamps to electrical components (Nockold, 1978). A few firms in the North West and Yorkshire also became involved in component manufacture by modifying products for textile engineers such as gears and chains. The increasing economies of scale in the industry led to a rapid reduction in the number of firms and some firms which could not compete in the manufacture of cars turned successfully to the manufacture of commercial vehicles; for example in the North West there were several lorry firms, including the Leyland company in the town of that name.

In the post-war period the motor vehicle industry continued to grow until the early 1970s, at first mainly in existing or nearby locations. However, about 1960 government regional policy caused a marked shift of expansion towards the Development Areas with three large plants being built on Merseyside, two in central Scotland and smaller ones in South Wales (Keeble, 1976, Chapter 7). Some of the larger component suppliers, like the rubber companies, were also persuaded to move, though most firms in this category continued to supply assemblers from existing locations. The 1960s thus saw a shift away from the South East and West Midlands, but did not fundamentally reduce their dominance in the pattern. The new vehicle factories of the 1960s were built in anticipation of long-term growth in demand for the products of British companies. This growth has not materialised, in part due to the sluggishness of the British economy and in part due to the import penetration by foreign motor vehicle firms which has been a significant feature of the 1970s. The uncompetitiveness of British firms resulting from poor management and industrial relations has caused surplus capacity in the industry and a cut back in the labour force, and even the closure of one of the new works on Merseyside. The three non-British owned firms have become more integrated with their continental counterparts which should assist their long-term survival providing their productivity can be raised. The remaining British firm continues to fight for survival and the outcome of this could be very important for the thousands of jobs in the component factories of the West Midlands. However, as in so many British industries, even if output is maintained or even increased, there will be fewer jobs in the future, with repercussions for regions like the South East and West Midlands.

The aircraft industry is another vehicle industry which over the whole period has shown substantial growth, although since the 1960s employment has been falling. Since one of the main markets is defence its growth has very much reflected the changing demand for military aircraft. The early industry developed in a small way in the few years before World War I. Most of the pioneer aircraft builders were enthusiasts who were attracted to aerodromes like Hendon and Brooklands near London. The government played a crucial role at this stage through its balloon factory at Farnborough, later the Royal Aircraft Establishment, from where the design of military aircraft was controlled. Apart from enthusiasts, the armament manufacturers of Vickers and Armstrongs were also drawn into the industry, particularly during World War I when the industry expanded. There were only a few firms outside the London area such as the Bristol Aeroplane Company, A.V.Roe at Manchester and the Blackburn Company at Leeds and later Brough. During the war the industry expanded rapidly and motor vehicle firms noted for their engines such as Rolls Royce at Derby, Siddeley Deasy at Coventry and Napier in London were drawn into the aero-engine side of the industry. After the war the industry contracted and for over a decade survival was difficult. However, the movement of the Armstrong Whitworth Aircraft Company from Newcastle to Coventry in the early 1920s was perhaps significant. The survival and growth of all these firms was possible only because of the rearmament programme of the late 1930s and then World War II itself. However, much of the expansion of the industry was deliberately shifted to the western (or 'safe') areas while at the same time some non-aircraft firms like English Electric at Preston were recruited into the industry. The result was both a temporary and permanent shift westwards and northwards with new factories in Gloucestershire, Somerset, Flintshire, Lancashire and the Rolls Royce aero-engine works at Glasgow. The reduction of the industry after the war was much less than after World War I, and a large-scale industry continued until the 1960s when following the rationalisation of firms there were several plant closures. In 1971 there were still 212,000 workers in the industry, a figure which does not include all component manufacture.

The electrical engineering group of industries has been one of the fastest growing manufactures, increasing employment from 140,000 in 1921 to 857,000 in 1971 although showing decreases in the 1970s. In 1921 the South East, West Midlands and North West were already well represented in the industry (Figure 25) and subsequent growth has maintained the dominance of the South East, although the other two areas have grown less rapidly. In the post-World War II period, location policy has steered many new plants to the assisted areas boosting their share of the industry although this share is still often less than their share of the population. Apart from regional policy one of the main factors explaining regional variations in growth is the structure of the industry. The electrical engineering industry is very heterogeneous, manufacturing a variety of goods from giant turbines to light bulbs and from radar warning systems to hairdryers, each with its own spatial pattern and history.

The early electrical industry which developed in the thirty years before World War I was mainly concerned with heavy goods such as generators, dynamos, switchgear, large electric motors and cables. It supplied industrial firms and the many local authorities which were then establishing electricity supply: not surprisingly therefore it came to be located primarily in the main industrial areas—London, West Midlands, south Lancashire and, to a lesser extent, on Tyneside. At the beginning of the century several of the new firms had deliberately chosen to locate in midland and northern centres: British Westinghouse and Ferranti went to Greater Manchester, Siemens to Stafford, British Thompson Houston to Rugby and Reyrolle to Tyneside. The cable industry developed mainly on Thameside and south Lancashire. These industries continued to grow mainly in these locations, with only a little migration, reaching a peak employment

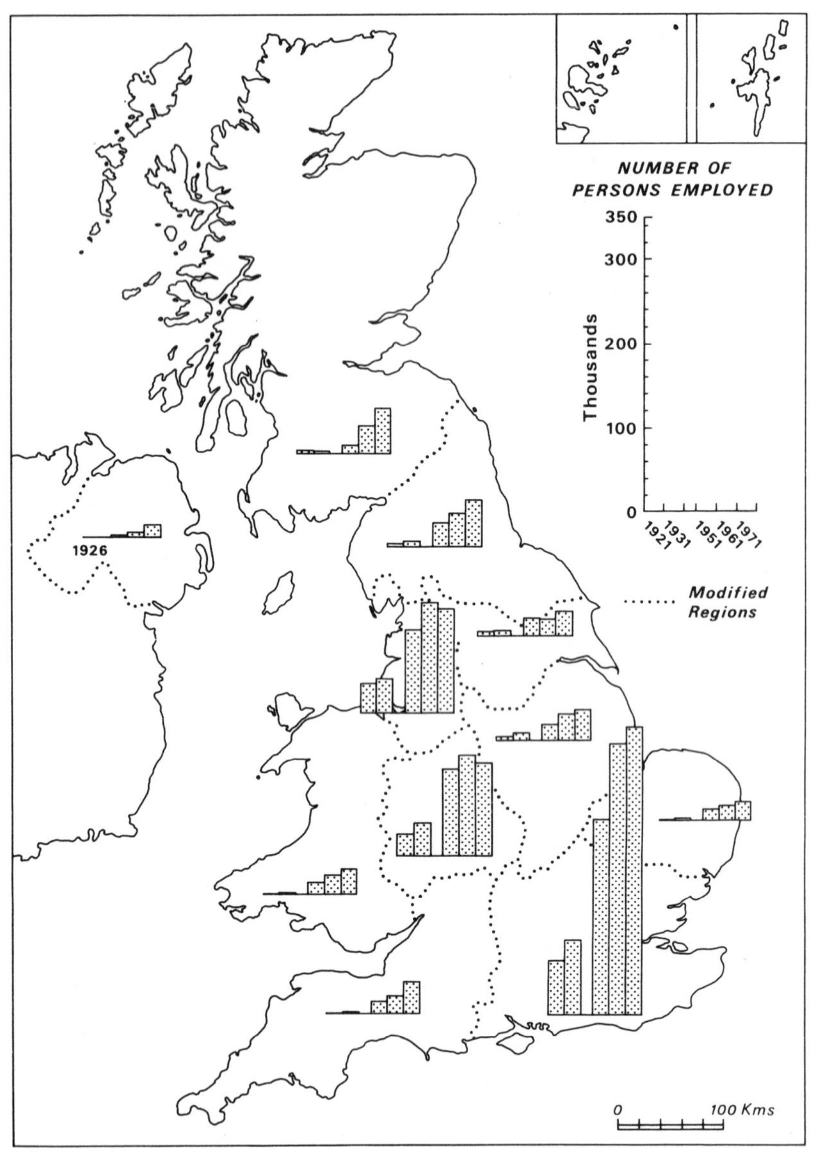

Fig. 25 The Regional Distribution of Employment in Electrical Engineering

around 1960 with over 250,000 workers. Since then, however, there has been a reduction in jobs and it is unlikely that these activities will ever employ as many again.

The first light electrical industry, the manufacture of electric light bulbs, developed mainly in London and there it evolved further into the manufacture of radio valves. Since the early radio industry was very much concerned with government and naval communications it was natural, as with aircraft, that it should be established close to government activities whose headquarters then as now were strongly concentrated in and around London. Only in the 1920s did the consumer radio industry develop and being based on the skills developed in the existing radio industry it not surprisingly was also mainly concentrated in the London region. The expanding television and electronics industry which later evolved out of the radio industry remained, despite location policy, strongly concentrated in the South East, though attempts have been made to steer the industry to the assisted areas, with some success in the case of Scotland. By 1971 nearly 350,000 were employed in the electronics industry of whom 58 per cent were in the South East (Keeble, 1976, Chapter 7). The micro-processor revolution of the late 1970s promises to increase the importance of the electronics industry as well as having implications for many other industries and above all for the number of jobs in the economy. Because of these wider and future effects it is considered more fully in Chapter 12.

The mechanical engineering order comprises an important group of industries which in 1971 employed over 1,100,000 compared to only 600,000 in 1921. Not all parts of this order have grown; for example textile engineering declined. Moreover this group of industries is much less easy to characterise than most other groups, since there is both a multitude of products and a situation where many firms make several products. In general, however, we may say that most firms provide machinery for other industries varying from typewriters in offices and printing machinery for printing firms, to excavators for the construction industry. Most of the firms in this group began as general engineers producing tailor-made goods for customers and many in this industry remain of this type. Proximity to customers is often important because of the contact needed as the machine is made. Sometimes firms have developed a special relationship with a particular branch of industry usually when that branch is localised near the firm. In the nineteenth century, general engineers in Lancashire and Yorkshire developed into textile engineers. To a certain extent the fate of such engineering firms has depended on the industries they served, although having developed a specialism these products could often be sold world wide. As new industries have developed so new branches of engineering have evolved to serve these industries and, not surprisingly, these firms are found in the regions where the industries they serve are found. Accordingly the South East and Midlands have seen considerable growth in employment in the mechanical engineering industries. Changes in the growth and decline of served industries coupled with government industrial location policies have contributed to a more dispersed mechanical engineering industry, well represented in most regions, particularly in the West Midlands, and under-represented only in Wales and Northern Ireland (Figure 26). Like the electrical engineering industry, employment levels in mechanical engineering are threatened by the micro-processor revolution which replaces mechanical parts by electronics and blurs the distinction between the mechanical and electrical engineering groups.

The twentieth century has not been characterised, as perhaps the nineteenth century was, by a few large, dominant and rapidly growing industries, which suggested a theory of regional development like that of 'growth poles' (see Chapter 1). In the twentieth century the growth process would appear to be much more diffuse across the industrial spectrum. It would be wrong, however, to conclude that the great multiplicity of manufactures, each to a certain extent unique, makes generalisation impossible. Already several factors have appeared significant in explaining the spatial pattern of growing industries. These include access to markets favour-

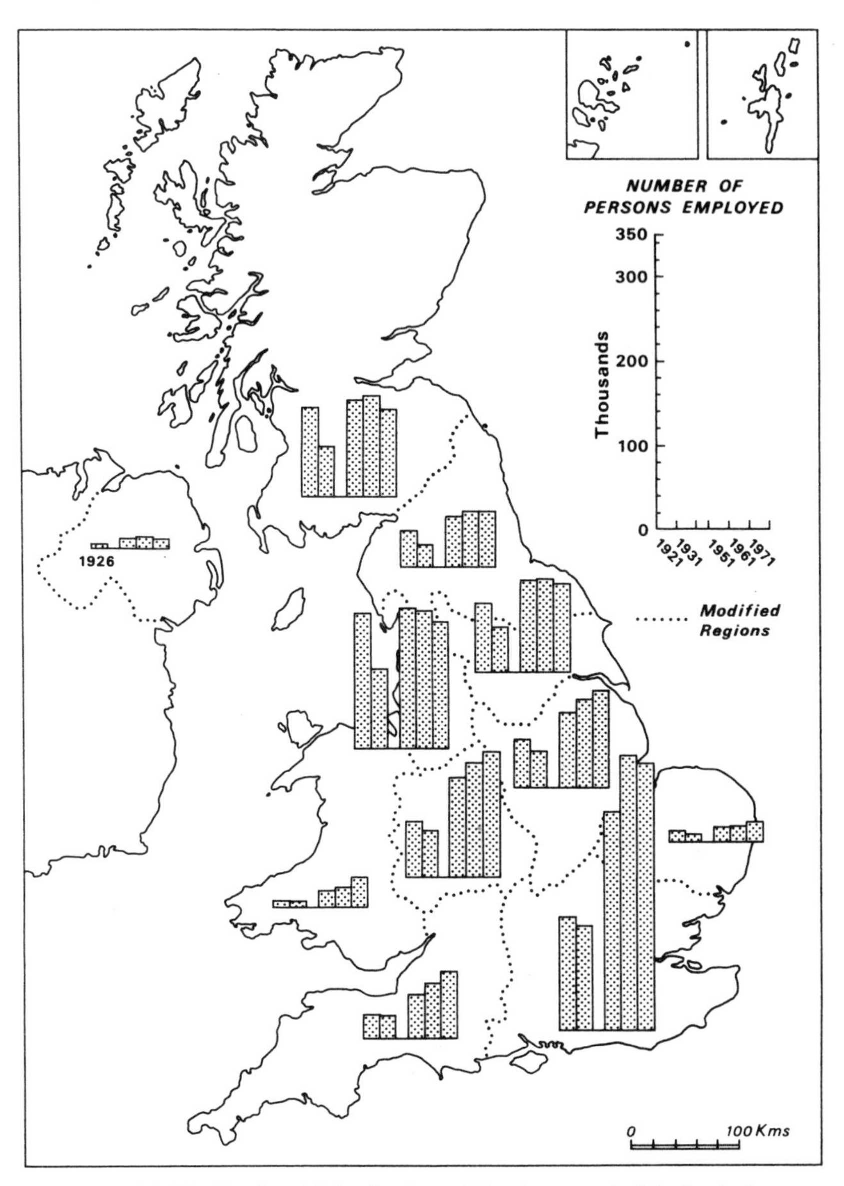

Fig. 26 The Regional Distribution of Employment in Mechanical Engineering

ing the South East, Midlands and to a lesser extent the North West; access to the particular market of the government has also been important; access to skills has been significant notably in the case of the West Midlands. In the past the external economies afforded by agglomeration may also have been important, whilst more recently the effect of government regional policies in diverting industry to the assisted areas has been noted. These and other factors will be further examined in later chapters.

CHAPTER SEVEN

Regional Employment Changes in the Service Sector

Since World War I employment in the service sector has risen from 9.6 million in 1921 to over 14.5 million in the 1970s, reflecting not only an increase in population but increased wealth with greater investment and consumption in this sector. The relative importance of the sector has increased not merely because of the additional employment, but also compared with the other two sectors, services are labour intensive and until recently have been less affected by mechanisation and automation. The distribution of regional employment in the service sector is shown in Tables 25 and 26, where it is seen that the South East has always been more important than its share of the population would suggest, but that surprisingly its proportion has slightly declined whereas for the whole period its proportion of the population has been increasing. In the other regions the share of employment has generally followed the other changes in population and total employment (Brown, 1972, 126), but significantly for some of the peripheral regions in recent years, the share of service employment has been increasing more than might have been expected. Compared with primary and secondary activities the geographical distribution of services have been little studied, perhaps because it has been thought that they were essentially related to and dependent upon the distribution of population which itself, it was argued, is determined by the first two sectors. However, this is a gross generalisation concealing significant geographical patterns in service employment. In this chapter we shall examine the factors affecting the distribution of service employment, and the changes that have taken place in the employment of the various services since World War I.

TABLE 25 Regional Employment in Services 1921–71

	Employment (000)			*Per Cent of Total*		
	1921	*1951*	*1971*	*1921*	*1951*	*1971*
South East	3,645	4,588	5,445	37.9	37.0	37.0
East Anglia	239	328	420	2.5	2.7	2.9
South West	626	884	1,047	6.5	7.2	7.1
West Midlands	593	890	1,137	6.2	7.2	7.7
East Midlands	486	695	907	5.1	5.6	6.2
Yorkshire, E & W	668	851	1,022	7.0	6.9	6.9
North West	1,242	1,497	1,657	12.9	12.1	11.3
North	489	653	779	5.1	5.3	5.3
Wales	443	542	634	4.6	4.4	4.3
Scotland	956	1,156	1,335	10.0	9.4	9.1
N. Ireland	217	269	341	2.3	2.2	2.3
UK Total	9,606	12,352	14,723	100.0	100.0	100.0

Source: Census Tables, Modified Regions

TABLE 26 Recent Changes in Service Regional Employment

	Employment (000)			*Per Cent of Total*		
	1966	*1971*	*1976*	*1966*	*1971*	*1976*
South East	5,027	4,972	5,305	37.2	37.6	36.5
East Anglia	357	365	428	2.6	2.8	2.9
South West	947	925	1,034	7.0	7.0	7.1
West Midlands	1,081	1,041	1,149	8.0	7.9	7.9
East Midlands	680	676	804	5.0	5.1	5.5
Yorkshire & Humberside	1,059	1,016	1,143	7.8	7.7	7.9
North West	1,554	1,491	1,599	11.5	11.3	11.0
North	686	663	751	5.1	5.0	5.2
Wales	588	560	626	4.3	4.2	4.3
Scotland	1,265	1,240	1,379	9.4	9.4	9.5
N. Ireland	271	287	329	2.0	2.2	2.3
UK Total	13,518	13,236	14,550	100.0	100.0	100.0

Source: Department of Employment: Employees in Employment Post-1974 Standard Regions. Differences in the figures (for 1971) between Tables 25 and 26 reflect the different sources and a likely underestimation in the Department of Employment figures

Location Factors

Many services show a hierarchical structure with activities at local, regional and national level. At the local level these branches are in direct contact with the public and therefore closely related to the distribution of population. The regional and national tiers perform managerial and specialist functions serving part or the whole of an organisation. As an example, the large clearing banks, like Barclays, Midland, Lloyds or National Westminster, may be cited as having local branches, regional headquarters and national headquarters, plus specialised functions mainly found in London. If we examine employment in these banks by regions we find that it is broadly proportional to population except in the South East where the head office and specialist services give increased employment. In most service activities the national headquarters and central functions have gravitated to London and the South East, though this is not inevitable, as is shown by our largest building society with its headquarters at Halifax and a large insurance group being found in Norwich.

Many service activities started as local firms serving a restricted locality, and some remain for ever like this. However, some grow, expanding into adjacant regions or acquiring branches elsewhere through takeover of similar firms, ending up with a national organisation. This can be seen in the history of our largest retail chain stores, such as Boots which originated in Nottingham, as well as banks and insurance companies. Although initially most activity and employment would take place in the local branches, there has been a tendency for the regional and national tiers to become relatively more important because they can gain economies of scale in the performance of certain activities which enable the organisation to remain viable, efficient and competitive. Initially such activities would include central buying and policy making, but in recent years the computer has accelerated this process. Whereas in the past the local branches of banks and insurance companies would carry out many clerical activities these have often been computerised at a central office resulting in many new jobs being located at this point. These shifts have altered the balance between the national and regional/local shares of employment, often to the advantage of the South East.

Not all service activities begin in this way. Some start as a national organisation, or national serving organisation, and may or may not develop regional or local tiers. Such activities are essentially national or need a national market to get started. The offices of foreign governments and foreign banks are mainly found at the national level, although occasionally they have a regional office as well. Many organisations, whether economic, social or political in purpose are set up with a single national office usually in London. In the past national (as opposed to local) government mainly operated at this level but through the extension of its activities it now has many regional and local activities concerned with the implementation of national policies. Not surprisingly we find that the balance of employment in these organisations is tilted towards the centre.

In addition to this hierarchical pattern two other factors operate in the distribution of service employment. Firstly, there is the ability of the consumer to pay for the services, which may vary from one part of the country to another. Thus there may be more hairdressers per head of population in the South East than elsewhere because people in this region can afford to go to the hairdresser more often: alternatively, this could be explained on the basis of taste, with southern people merely giving greater value to neater hairstyles.

Secondly, there may be a spatial diffusion process at work. Some services may commence in the most affluent region, normally the South East, before spreading to other regions and they will also become more developed in the region of initial growth. In some cases there may be a saturation level for the service so that eventually, after a period of diffusion, employment will be distributed amongst the regions relative to their population.

It should be obvious from the above discussion that whilst

some services are found throughout the population, others show a distinct concentration in one region or regions. Humphrys (1972) has called the former ubiquitous and the latter flexible, whilst Keeble (1978) referred to the latter as basic, in that they generate income for the region, and the former as non-basic. Such a distinction may be theoretically interesting but in practice it is difficult to apply. A bank, say in Warrington, may be locally serving and thus non-basic, whilst a bank in the City of London may be nationally serving and thus basic, but in practice their employment is found in the same classification of banks. Accordingly the classification of services adopted here will be slightly more pragmatic: those which are closely related to the distribution of population, at least at the regional level; and those which show some degree of concentration in one or several regions. Of necessity such a distinction is somewhat arbitrary, since in practice there is a continuum. A localisation coefficient of 0.1 has been used as an arbitrary cut-off point. A third category here will be for these services which have declined in employment over the period. A statistical synopsis showing employment changes is given in Table 27.

Services Distributed According to the Population

The significance of this group can be shown by the fact that in 1921 they accounted for 5½ million jobs or 27 per cent of the work-force, and by 1971 for 10¼ million or 42 per cent of the work-force. By definition, as discussed in the last section, the regional distribution of all these activities in 1971 was very similar to the distribution of population for that year. Since they are closely related to population their growth has been greatest in those regions with the highest rates of population growth and least in regions like Scotland with small population increases, though even slow-growing regions have benefited.

The largest increase of all has been in education, which between 1921 and 1971 added over one million jobs and between 1971 and 1976 provided nearly another 400,000, to

TABLE 27 Employment Changes in the Service Sector 1921–1971 by Minimum List Heading

Services distributed according to the population

Education	+1,001,000	Road Passenger	+ 156,000
Construction	+ 875,000	Hairdressing	+ 106,000
Distribution	+ 800,000	Catering, Hotels	+ 103,000
Medical	+ 777,000	Road Haulage	+ 63,000
Local Government	+ 295,000	Water Supply	+ 20,000
Motor Repair—at least	+ 234,000*	Gas	+ 3,000
Electricity	+ 165,000	Sport	no figures

Services showing some regional concentration

Other Misc. Services	+ 506,000	Other Transport	+ 110,000
Central Government	+ 239,000	Defence	+ 90,000
Postal Services	+ 202,000	Air Transport	+ 73,000
Banking	+ 193,000	Other Business Services	+ 73,000
Other Professions	+ 190,000	Accountancy	+ 65,000
Insurance	+ 147,000	Legal Services	+ 48,000
		Entertainment	no figures

Services with declining employment

Private Domestic Service	−1,151,600	Laundries	− 34,000
Railways	− 397,400	Shoe Repair not less than	− 32,000*
Sea Transport	− 125,000	Religion	− 16,000
Port and Inland Water Transport	− 89,000		

* Employment change 1951–71. No separate figures available before 1951

bring the total employed to almost 1.9 million or over 8 per cent of all employment. This increase has been due to a growth of population, longer compulsory and voluntary education, and higher standards of service requiring amongst other things more ancillary staff. The fall in the birth rate from 1964 to 1977 and public expenditure cuts in the mid- and late 1970s may have halted the growth of the sector, although it remains to be seen whether this is only temporary. Primary and secondary education are very closely related to the population; moreover, although parts of the tertiary system (such as universities) are potentially national in their catchment area and not necessarily regional in location, in practice there has been an attempt to give each region its share of such institutions. Variations from the expected share of employment are therefore small and may be related to regional variations in the tendency to stay on at school, in age structure of the population and in special education institutions. Since 1931 regional disparities in the numbers employed in education relative to the population have been considerably reduced.

The health service, like education, has also been greatly improved and extended since World War I. By 1976 over one million jobs had been added to the 1921 total. In the inter-war period there was a pronounced inequality of employment between the regions with the South East, through its greater ability to pay for a private health service, having more than its expected share. The aim of the National Health Service has been to equalise treatment throughout the country (National Health Service, 1962), and much progress has been made to this end, although significant regional disparities remain.

In the period 1921–71 the construction industry showed the second largest increase in jobs at over 875,000, reflecting higher standards of provision in housing, factories, offices and roads as well as general population increase. Regional activity may vary according to local growth rates, as it did to some extent in the inter-war period when the South East was noticeably more prosperous than other regions, but in the post-war period public contracts for roads, factories in Development Areas and urban renewal in the large cities have been important to the industry and also equalised activity between the regions.

With about three million jobs the Distributive Trades order (shops, warehouses, etc) is one of the most important of the services. The growth of 800,000 jobs is not particularly great when the population increase is taken into account and also the fact that 100,000 jobs were transferred into this order in 1958 when the SIC was changed. Since the mid-1960s employment has fallen slightly as small shops have gone out of business in competition with the large shops which have attempted to introduce more mechanisation. Most of the employment, such as that in shops, is strictly related to population (at the regional level), but some warehousing functions are more concentrated, particularly in the South East, where London is both the country's major market and port.

The expansion of local government service (here excluding education) is another example of the demand for higher standards of public service whether in social services, housing or planning. The increase in jobs, by 300,000 from 1921 to 1971, continued into the mid-1970s when it was halted, probably temporarily, by public expenditure cuts. Large government rate support grants to local authorities have evened out differences in the ability to pay for services to give a largely uniform high average standard.

Allied with local government is the provision of public utilities, gas, water and electricity. Originally local companies were set up to supply these, often controlled by local authorities. In the post-war period these have been taken over by state-owned regional and national organisations and national grids have been developed for the transfer of gas, water and electricity between regions. The East Midlands has become a power house for coal-fired power stations (Rawstron, 1964b) and now (since the late 1960s) most gas for the grid is obtained from the North Sea. These changes and increased efficiency have enabled the workforce to be reduced: from the 1950s in the gas industry and from the 1960s in the electricity industry. In spite of these grid transfers between regions, most of the employment in these industries is locally based dealing directly with the consumers. In the inter-war period the South East had more jobs than its share of the population would have suggested, probably reflecting, as with the services discussed above, greater purchasing power. However, in the post-war period once again such differences have been reduced.

Services Showing Some Concentration

While this second group is much smaller than the first its employment increased two and a half times from about 1.4 million or 7 per cent of the workforce in 1921 to 3.4 million or 14 per cent of the workforce in 1971. (Table 27). Whilst all its categories have employment in every region, they also show some concentration in at least one region and that region is always the South East. Basically these activities are attracted, at least for their higher order functions, to the London area, and may be related to the capital's role in the business, government and cultural life of the country.

The importance of the City of London as a financial centre dates back to at least the eighteenth century when institutions developed to assist overseas trade and to provide money for the government. These activities grew significantly as London became the capital of an empire and during this period it assumed the role of a world financial centre. In spite of the loss of empire and the declining role of Britain in world trade, London has been able to maintain its world leadership in many commercial spheres. In financial affairs London acts as a national capital, as an entry point for foreign companies, and in a world role. It has the headquarters of the leading British Banks, as well as of several British-owned banks which operate overseas. In addition there are over 200 foreign banks in London which employed over 10,000 in the early 1970s. In contrast Manchester and Edinburgh, the next most important banking centres in Britain, only have about a dozen overseas banks and these are subsidiary branches of London-based banks. Such foreign banks not only serve customers in Britain but operate at a world level from London because of the city's favourable facilities. In insurance the situation is similar, with leading insurance companies having their headquarters in London, and there are also the specialised facilities of Lloyds, where world shipping and aircraft are insured and where there is much cover insurance on behalf of other countries.

London has become the location for the headquarters of

the major British companies (see Chapter 8) and this has aided the growth of a whole range of ancilliary activities which appear under the headings of Other Transport, Other Business, Other Professions and Other Services. These naturally include accountancy services, legal services, advertising and market research, specialised services from consulting engineers, architects to typing, copying and translation agencies. The sheer scale of London as a financial and business centre enables many specialised services to exist, and the wealth of these attracts yet more activities to London.

Secondly, London is the seat of government whose non-local and regional activities for long naturally developed in the capital. As government has extended its control further over the economy and provided more services, so the number of civil servants has risen. Excluding defence departments and the forces the number rose from 178,000 in 1921 to 417,000 in 1971, rising continuously except for a peak during and after World War II. In 1972 approximately 64 per cent were described as local staff, 5 per cent as regional staff and 31 per cent as headquarters staff (Hardman Report, 1973). It is these headquarters staff which have mainly been concentrated in and around London. Even after some dispersal during the 1960s, 70 per cent were still found in the South East in 1972. Many government activities began years ago in a small way, naturally seeking to be close to their sponsoring departments, but only when they had grown in size was it seen that they were upsetting regional balance (Table 28).

Most of these jobs can be described as office jobs and it is the post-war office boom in London which has attracted most attention of the critics of regional policy. In 1961 over half the office jobs in the country were in the South East (Wright, 1967) and the continued expansion of office building in the early 1960s prompted the beginnings of office control policy. However, the result of much of this policy has merely been to decentralise offices from central London to the outer suburbs or parts of south-east England (see Chapter 9), so that the overall ascendancy of the region has remained, even if more diffused within it (Daniels, 1969).

TABLE 28 Regional Distribution of Civil Servants, 1978

	Financial Public Order and General	*Defence*	*Health Welfare Social Security*	*Economic Housing Community*	*Total*	*Per Cent*
South East	91.7	102.9	26.9	76.3	298.0	41.0
East Anglia	4.9	2.9	1.7	4.8	14.3	2.0
South West	13.5	53.3	5.2	12.7	84.7	11.6
West Midlands	10.3	11.3	6.5	8.4	36.5	5.0
East Midlands	8.4	9.8	5.1	6.0	29.3	4.0
Yorkshire & Humberside	12.4	10.3	6.5	8.7	37.9	5.2
North West	27.2	13.1	14.9	12.3	67.5	9.3
North	10.1	6.5	17.8	6.8	41.2	5.7
Wales	11.8	9.7	4.5	14.6	40.7	5.6
Scotland	28.2	22.2	7.7	12.3	70.5	9.7
Northern Ireland*	2.4	3.9	—	0.7	7.0	1.0
UK Total	221.2	245.9	96.9	163.6	727.6	100.0

* Excludes Northern Ireland Civil Service
Source: Regional Statistics 1979

Not only does the South East have a high share of office jobs but these contain a higher proportion of the more skilled posts, while in reverse the peripheral regions like the north have a higher proportion of the lower skilled clerical jobs (James, 1978).

In the armed forces and defence there is also regional imbalance in employment but in this case both the South East and South West have larger shares. Whilst there have always been army barracks in different parts of the country, there has also always been a concentration in and around London. In the mid-nineteenth century the Aldershot area was developed and in the twentieth century the Salisbury Plain district (in the South West region) has been extensively developed for defence establishments. Likewise the navy was concentrated in the south to protect England from the continent with three large naval bases at Chatham, Portsmouth and Devonport (Plymouth). The growth of the Royal Air Force since World War I has not led to the same degree of concentration but, in addition to southern areas, eastern districts have also been favoured for air bases. The numbers in the forces have varied a great deal depending on the strategic need. By the close of World War I there were over 4¼ million in the forces but this rapidly fell after the war and for much of the inter-war period the numbers were about 300,000. During World War II the numbers in the forces peaked at 4.6 million, but after mass demobilisation the numbers were allowed to fall more slowly in the post-war period to reach about 400,000 in the early 1970s. Not all of these are in the UK but they are counter-balanced by additional employment of civilians. In 1931 76 per cent of defence employment was in the South East and South West, whilst in 1971 this share had fallen to 58 per cent with East Anglia having another 5 per cent.

The South East also has a large share of Postal Services and Telecommunications, an activity which nearly doubled its employment from 223,000 in 1921 to 426,000 in 1971. Whilst post offices and telephone exchanges are found in every part of the country, many central functions are performed in the London area, including international exchanges, inter-regional exchanges and general administration and research, so that in 1971 the South East had 46 per cent of the jobs of which 30 per cent were in Greater London.

The growth of air transport has been another feature of the period under review. By 1976 there were 80,000 jobs, compared to 526 in 1921, but over 80 per cent of these were in the South East. Owing to the small size of Britain, most of the trade is provided by international journeys, and once again London shows its gateway role. Naturally most air journeys to Britain are to the capital and the South East so that London has been able to develop good services to most parts of the world. Provincial airports have often provided feeder services to London, and are only slowly developing international routes, which inevitably are less frequent and varied than London.

Finally mention may be made of London's role as the cultural centre of the country. The numbers employed in Entertainment (cinemas, theatres, broadcasting, music) has increased from 87,000 in 1921 to 118,000 in 1971, and the share of the South East has increased from 45 per cent in 1931 to 59 per cent in 1971. The growth of broadcasting, largely concentrated in London, has hit cinemas and theatres which previously were widespread so that outside the South East employment in this group has fallen since 1951. London's role as the capital is also seen in the way national organisations have their headquarters here. One indication of this is given by the statistic for employment in Professional and Scientific Organisations in 1971 where 9,000 out of the 11,000 jobs were in the South East.

Services with Declining Employment

The services discussed above have all shown an increase in employment over the period 1921–71, although some have since peaked and now have falling employment. In this section we shall discuss the few services which have shown a net fall in employment over the period.

The largest decrease is shown by the category Private Domestic Service which had a peak employment of 1,539,000 in 1931 but which by 1971 had fallen to 240,000. This decline may be attributed to the relative fall in the income of the wealthy and middle classes, the rise in the cost of labour, and the availability of labour saving devices in the home. Not surprisingly the regional distribution of such employment reflected the geographical pattern of wealth, with more jobs per head in the South East, South West and East Anglia, where there were approximately one and a half times more jobs than could be expected from population. In contrast the industrial regions of the North West and Yorkshire had considerably fewer jobs than could be expected from population. The rate of decrease in jobs was fairly even across the country with regions maintaining their relative position. The South East lost over half a million jobs in this category. The consequences of the fall in jobs in this category may not be as great as the numbers suggest since 80 per cent of the employment is female. Today Private Domestic Service provides only one per cent of all jobs, and many of these are part time, compared to 7.5 per cent in 1931 and 10 per cent in the eighteenth century.

Two transport industries have shown a significant loss. The railway industry has lost 400,000 jobs since 1921, or nearly two-thirds of the total for that year. This is partly a reflection of the run down of the system and the closure of many lines, particularly following the Beeching Report of the early 1960s. The change from steam to diesel and electric locomotion and the modernisation of the signalling systems has also caused a large loss of jobs. The decrease in employment has affected all regions, but rural regions have probably been the most affected while the South East, where railway commuting remains important, has been least affected.

The other transport industry to lose jobs is water transport, principally in shipping and at ports but also including canals. Since 1921 over 210,000 jobs have been lost and this decline continues. The main cause is the introduction of bigger ships and modern methods of cargo handling such as containerisation and greater mechanisation. Moreover the quicker turn-round of ships and their greater size has made many of the older docks, particularly in London and Liverpool, obsolete. These two are the main ports of Britain and, together with Southampton and the cross-channel trade of south coast ports, this accounts for the reason why nearly two thirds of employment in this category is found in the South East and North West. The decline of employment has been even across all regions of Britain, but inevitably the South East and North West have suffered most.

In this chapter we have been concerned to examine how service employment is distributed amongst the regions and how the changes since 1921 have affected the balance. It is obvious that, arising from London's role in the life of the country, the South East has a greater share of service employment than could be expected from its share of the population. By multiplying the South East's share of the population and the total for service employment we can gain some indication of the extra jobs the South East has gained in Services. Surprisingly the figure has remained at about the same level, just below one million jobs, for the fifty year period. In 1921 it was 966,000 and in 1971 it was 930,000. However, the composition of this figure has changed in some ways. The surplus created by greater wealth in such categories as private domestic service has been replaced by a greater surplus in those categories which reflect London's role as the business and financial capital of the country. Meanwhile the government's role remains important in accounting for extra service sector jobs in the region.

CHAPTER EIGHT

The Role of New, Existing and Foreign Firms in Regional Development

In an earlier chapter it was emphasised that every regional economy constantly needs to renew itself through growing forms of employment or else it will find that existing jobs have disappeared or been reduced through automation. The processes of change and growth can be described in various ways. In the previous three chapters these changes have been discussed in terms of the industrial classification. Another way of discussing these changes is in terms of the organisation which makes the decisions and which in the end produces or does not produce an increase in jobs. This study of corporate behaviour is referred to as the 'components of change' approach and can be divided into three main sections concerned with new, existing and foreign firms. The following discussion will be mainly concerned with manufacturing industry, although some of the comments will also be relevant to the service sector.

The Development of New Firms

The significance of new firms in the economy is that they provide an industrial seed-bed from which a few successful companies emerge to replenish the existing industrial structure and provide for growth. Some will merely replace existing firms which have proved inefficient, whilst others will be innovative, introducing new products or production methods. This has certainly been true of the past, including the period under review, but some commentators doubt the potential, scale and significance of their role in the future, since the economy is now much more dominated by large firms.

The successful emergence of a new firm depends on certain economic conditions being present. Generally new firms only emerge in those industries where the barriers to entry are low because economies of scale, whether of production or organisation, are limited and there are thus no advantages to the existing large firms. Production economies of scale are limited when it is difficult or expensive to introduce machinery which occurs when the total production is small or fluctuates widely or where personal attention to the customer is important (Davies and Kelly, 1971, Chapter 4). Economies of scale may be limited in the early stages of a new product before demand has developed: for example, at the beginning of the century it was possible for many new firms to enter motor car production but later this became almost impossible as demand increased and economies of scale developed. In the clothing industry the multiplicity of styles and fashion changes has traditionally hindered mass production, although the concentration of selling in chain stores has modified this. In other industries, new firms producing short runs of components in metal, wood or plastic may find entry relatively easy. Short runs are also typical of the printing industries where jobbing printers are common. Economies of scale are also impossible in those industries producing one-off products such as specialised machinery or prototypes. Entry rates for new firms will thus vary between industries (Gudgin, 1978, 138), and where there are high entry rates there are often high closure rates as well.

A second condition for the successful emergence of a new firm is a growing demand situation (Johnson, 1978). New firms usually develop in growing sectors of the economy and when the national economy is expanding. In such a situation new firms are able to find a place in the market and there may also be a greater demand for contract work. Paradoxically more new firms may be established in hard times by displaced managers, but their chances of success are less.

To these economic characteristics of the new firm should

be added the personal qualities of the founder. Opportunities must be perceived and taken and this requires a fair amount of drive and determination. Whilst it is easy to exaggerate the qualities of the founder and look for the ruthless ambition of the archetypal entrepreneur, the founders of a new firm must be sufficiently individualistic to work on their own and wish to be master of their own house. Such persons are always a minority of the population, although their numbers may vary from time to time and area to area according to economic and social conditions. The new firm will also require adequate capital but in many cases they have started with surprisingly little, using rented equipment and premises and gaining credit for materials used.

Most entrepreneurs are already involved in the general line of business in which they decide to establish themselves independently. In a survey of new firms established in the East Midlands, Gudgin (1978, 113) found that 85 per cent of the founders had experience in the same trade. Often potential entrepreneurs feel that they could make and sell a product more efficiently than the firm they work for or perhaps just want to work for themselves. In other cases they see a line of product development which is not being exploited by the existing firm and leave to set up a new enterprise. Sometimes such entrepreneurs have been working in research, whether in industry, government or university. In yet other cases the founder of a new firm has seen from inside an existing one a need for components, special contract work or services which are not being met and establishes himself with the advantage of market contacts. Finally there are those involved in distribution, either wholesale or retail, who perceive a market demand for a product which is not being adequately met by existing producers and who move into manufacturing to supply this need.

When we turn to spatial variations in the formation of new firms we find the traditional approach to industrial location less helpful. This is because, even in dealing with the location of new firms, it has assumed perfect rationality of behaviour with least-cost sites being determinedly sought out by the entrepreneur. In practice the limited resources of time and money of the new entrepreneur make such an approach invalid. Of necessity he generally seeks cheap suitable premises near to where he is living. Since the new firm is likely to be small, finding premises and labour is not usually a problem. In his survey of new firms in the East Midlands, Gudgin (1978, 109) found that 81 per cent of the founders were previously resident in the area and, overwhelmingly, that no alternative location outside the home area had been considered. Another reason for the entrepreneur staying where he is arises from his local contacts in buying and selling. One consequence of this method of formation of new firms is the clustering of similar activities in particular areas. Often a pioneering firm has spawned many independent offshoots founded by previous workers of the company.

The Regional Distribution of New Firms in the United Kingdom

There are no comprehensive statistics on the role of new firms in regional development in the United Kingdom since World War I, so that any comments are somewhat speculative. Over the whole period it is likely that the rates of new firm formation have varied, and that certain periods such as the late 1940s have been more important than others. At the same time there will have been regional variations, but these differences will have varied over time.

The industrial structure of the regions will have been an important factor determining the rate of formation of new firms. By the early twentieth century the coalfield regions of Wales, Northern England and Scotland were dominated by large-scale activities like coal-mining, shipbuilding, iron and steel, and heavy chemicals which offered little scope for the would-be entrepreneur either in the main line or as a supplier of components (Manners, 1964, 37). In addition, the industries of the peripheral regions were in decline and did not provide the right kind of growth environment for the formation of new firms. Until recently it could be expected that the rates of formation of new firms in these regions would be low (Johnson, 1978). In contrast, the environment of the South East and Midlands was more conducive to the formation of new firms. In the earlier part of the period there were many new industries still small in scale but growing, which provided opportunities for the entrepreneur. Many of these industries required components, thus providing another source market for new firms. The works of Beesley (1955) and Gudgin (1978) provide evidence for high formation rates of new firms in the West and East Midlands. However, even within a growing region like the East Midlands, Gudgin noted that where a town was dominated by, for example, large-scale engineering works, this appeared to act as a damper and the formation of new firms was lower (Gudgin, 1978, 211).

More recently the industrial structure of the assisted areas has been changing and is becoming more diversified. This could have the effect of increasing opportunities for the formation of new firms. Since many of the new factories are branches this may reduce the opportunities, but where divisions have been moved this may help the situation. The example of Ferranti, which moved to Edinburgh in 1943, is an oft-quoted example of the possible effects. The firm now employs 6,000 people in Scotland with additional factories at Dalkeith and Dundee. The Scottish section of Ferranti have their own product line and research section and it is from the latter that several persons have left to establish new electronics firms. There can be no doubt that the rate of the formation of new firms in the assisted areas has increased, whereas the lack of growth in the West Midlands since the mid-1960s has slowed it down. This at least could be the interpretation of a study of the Clydeside and West Midlands conurbations for the 1960s by Firn and Swales (1978) which found that the rate of new independent firm formation was higher in the former than latter.

Several aspects of the economic structure of the South East have made it very favourable for the formation of new firms. As will be discussed later, the region is very important for research and development activities and although there are no science parks (areas reserved for companies requiring access to laboratories) of the kind found in the United States, this has provided a source for founders. London is also a very important wholesale centre and many trading companies have later moved into manufacturing: in particular, the raising of tariffs in the inter-war period persuaded a number of importers to go into manufacturing to the benefit of this region. The close relationship between government and defence suppliers may have benefited the South East, at least up to World War II. An early example was the establishment of the radio valve firm of Mullards by a former Admiralty research worker who was able to supply a government need for radio communication equipment. The South East has probably always been a more market orientated economy than some of the older industrial areas and it is from this vantage point at the centre of the largest and richest consumer market in the country that many new firms have been launched.

The individualism necessary for entrepreneurship may be less likely to be found in the assisted areas than in other regions of the country. The large-scale industries of the older industrial areas involving much manual work have given rise to a working class solidarity amongst the labour force which creates a poor social climate for entrepreneurs (Northern Region Strategy Team, 1977, 2, 54). Moreover, in such large-scale organisations the specialised role of the individual employee does not provide a wide enough background for entrepreneurship. These adverse factors in the assisted regions have almost certainly had a negative cumulative effect on new firm formation. In contrast the numerous small firms of the South East and Midlands provide an environment in which many individuals learn about the possibilities of establishing new firms and this has a positive cumulative effect (Gudgin, 1978, 227).

The effects of government policy on the formation of new firms and their location have been erratic but increasing in recent years. In the 1930s foreign refugees from Europe with industrial backgrounds were given permission to establish firms if they settled in the Special Areas, which several did to the benefit of these regions. At Treforest in South Wales half of the 66 firms established by September 1939 were of refugee origin (Davies, 1951). In the post-war period new firms were able to get cheap premises and grants for equipment if they moved to the assisted areas. Such a move would take them away from their preferred local environment and not surprisingly the number of such moves has been small. Further, since they often used small existing premises they would not have been much affected by IDC controls, at least until they sought to expand. However, the availability of assistance may have encouraged more entrepreneurs in the assisted regions to start than would otherwise have been the case.

During the 1970s governments have been more interventionist in helping new firms to establish themselves and have been willing to provide share capital. In 1971 the Northern Ireland government established the Local Enterprise Development Board which has since created about 1,000 new jobs a year in manufacturing firms. In Britain the National Enterprise Board, Scottish Development Agency and Welsh Development Agency have been established with a brief that includes helping new firms. These initiatives are potentially important new methods of encouraging indigenous industrial growth in the assisted areas, but it is too early to evaluate their success.

The quantitative effect of new firms is difficult to estimate. For any short period the number of new jobs provided is bound to be small, but will increase in time as a few firms grow to become large. In his study of the East Midlands, Gudgin (1978, 59) found that nearly 3,000 firms had been created in the period 1947–67, creating 65,000 jobs or 11 per cent of the total employment of the region in 1967. More recently the Department of Industry record 456 firms new to manufacturing for the period 1966–71 creating 18,500 jobs. Significantly, the North, Wales, Scotland and Northern Ireland all did better than could be expected from their share of the population.

The general conclusions from these comments is that, in

the period up to the end of the 1950s, new firm formation was much more likely in the South East and Midlands than in the assisted areas, but that since then the opportunities in the latter areas have increased and regional differences have been reduced.

The Role of Existing Firms

The possibilities for a new manufacturing company are varied. It may fail in business after a few years, as many do. It may remain small, in the same location and with the same product: or it may grow, develop new plants, new products and become a very large company. As we have seen in Chapter 2 the growth of large firms to an important place in the economy has been a significant feature of the twentieth century and therefore in this section we shall be concerned with their growth and organisation and with effects on regional development. The large firm is usually the result of a combination of processes, of internal growth, takeovers and mergers. In Britain the merger movements of 1890–1930 and of the 1960s have often resulted in several or very many firms coming together to produce a large firm almost out of the blue with consequential rapid changes in organisation and structure. These changes will be considered in a later section: here attention is focused on the large firm which evolves more slowly.

The goals of a firm are sometimes elaborated at length or may be undefined, but essentially they revolve around the need to survive, to grow and produce profits. To survive a firm must adapt to changing business conditions which may produce varying responses. Frequently firms enter a trade where a new product is being manufactured. There may be a limited market and limited economies of scale resulting in many entrants. As demand grows so will the economies of scale leaving room for only a few large firms. The survivors will be those that have been technically and commercially efficient and have been able to increase their share of the market either by internal growth or takeovers. The less efficient firms will either be taken over, go out of business or concentrate on some specialised aspect of production. The successful firm usually continues to grow since it has resources which through further growth can be made even more profitable (Penrose, 1959). Having secured a prominent position in the marketing of a particular product, the firm will often become involved in some forward or backward integration to secure markets or materials. Frequently the firm finds itself manufacturing products outside its original range as a result of technical and material linkages. Such diversification may be accidental or planned, but in the latter case it is generally the result of a desire to spread risks and not be too dependent on one product. The firm by now will be multi-product, multi-plant and it will usually not be too long before it is multi-national, exploiting its expertise in other countries.

The expansion of the firm often requires increased production capacity, and this may be met where there is no room on an existing site by the development of branches. Except where material supplies or regional markets are important the company will usually seek to have its branches near the parent plant as this facilitates management oversight and the transfer of labour. Government policy often prevents this, and the topic of industrial movement will be considered more fully in the next chapter.

The motives for acquiring other firms include the need for extra production capacity and skilled labour, gaining increased market share (including local markets), gaining access to new products and technology, securing forward markets and securing supplies of materials and components. The acquired firm will be the one that meets these requirements and is available for takeover. Such firms will possibly be up for sale (on the death of their owner), bankrupt or susceptible to takeover. In the case of small firms it is likely that the search for an acquisition will begin in the local area and move outwards, whilst the larger firm is able to take a more national or international viewpoint. The distance between acquiring and acquired firms will also be affected by the density of available firms. A further variable may be the dynamism of certain areas which have been more active in the takeover business.

Putting these ideas together, a model of corporate growth in Britain may be described (Taylor, 1975). A new firm is established usually by the founder leaving an existing firm. In the early stages its local area is all important in terms of markets and possibly supplies. The successful and growing company will gradually extend its market to cover other regions. Initially extra production capacity will be met by either extensions, branch plants in the home region, or possibly by the takeover of a local firm. Further growth will lead to more remote branch plants and more remote takeovers. At a certain stage in its growth the company may decide to move its head office to London as it is now a national company. This may coincide with a large take-over which may be described as a merger. The company will diversify by moving away from one product and will be involved in forward and backward integration aided by further acquisitions. The next step will be for the company to look overseas.

The study of such spatial aspects of acquisition behaviour has only recently attracted attention so that it is impossible to describe regional variations for firms in the UK in the period under study. Leigh and North (1978a) in a pioneering study studied only four industries and only for the period 1973–4. As might be expected they showed that in regionally concentrated industries like textiles and clothing there were strong neighbourhood effects in the pattern of acquisitions but that overall the acquisitions of firms in the South East were far greater than might be expected. This could be mainly explained on the basis of having larger firms who were more active in acquisition activity and operated at the national scale. This result was confirmed by Goddard and Smith's (1978) study of the acquisition activity within the top 1,000 companies where out of 160 examples, 116 had headquarters in the South East.

Over the whole period the South East and Midlands have had most of the growing industries, so it would not be surprising if some of the companies in these regions had not actively expanded. Further, as mentioned already the South East benefits by the fact that when companies reach the national scale they move their headquarters there.

The Rationalisation Process

The creation of most large firms, as we have seen, has involved mergers and acquisitions. In some cases the new large firm has merely been a holding company allowing the individual units to continue their separate existence as before. This may happen when the interests of the component parts are strong or the holding company is merely a tax saving or capital sharing device. More generally, and particularly recently, the purpose of forming large organisations has been to gain the benefits of scale, and consequently the existing interests have had to be reorganised to create a more efficient structure. In this section we shall consider the regional effects of this rationalisation process which also occurs during business recessions, when there is over capacity, and in declining industries. The rationalisation process involves functional specialisation and includes the development of head offices and research facilities. These two topics will be dealt with in later sections.

Functional specialisation in the multi-product company will result in a divisional structure. In some cases these divisions will be referred to as subsidiaries and carry the names of pre-merger or acquired companies. The divisions of very large companies like ICI would rank among the larger companies in the country if they were independent. Each division or subsidiary will be allocated a product specialisation and will acquire activities from a number of sites belonging to the pre-merger companies. In the case of horizontal mergers such divisions may not be necessary as there is only one product and all activities can be organised from head office. The new horizontally integrated firm or division will seek to plan production on the most efficient basis and this may involve the concentration of production at specific sites. Plants where production costs are high, where the factory is badly laid out, where there is no room for expansion, where labour is difficult or in short supply, or perhaps where the capital value of the site is high, will be closed and production concentrated at those sites which offer the most efficient production possibilities in the long term. Another possibility is to close most or all existing sites and develop a new plant where the most efficient production methods can be introduced. The results of firm rationalisation may thus be various: plant specialisation, plant closure, plant expansion and the development of new sites (Watts, 1974).

Within Britain there have been great fears that the development of large firms and the accompanying rationalisation process would adversely affect the peripheral regions in two ways: firstly, firms with head offices in the London region, a very common occurrence as we shall see, would discriminate in favour of plants near to them; secondly, newly opened branches in the assisted regions, to which they had gone because of government policy, would be the first to suffer in any post-recession rationalisation process. Given the many variables in the situation, now added to by government policy, there is unlikely to be any simple answer to these questions. The process of change and rationalisation is not a once and for all affair, but is continuous; regions which benefit in one period may lose in another and vice versa. In the case of vertical integration, whether backward or forward, closure is unlikely and expansion more common since acquisitions have usually been made by a growing firm with the aim of either aiding expansion or securing materials or markets (Leigh and North, 1978a).

Nationally it is the horizontal rationalisation process which has concerned most people. Before 1930 many mergers were in regionally concentrated industries like textiles and brewing and it is unlikely that there were noticeable inter-regional effects. Where parent plants can be identified and where expansion was possible on site it would not be surprising if rationalisation benefited such factories. The only comprehensive test of these ideas has been carried out by Atkins (1973) studying employment changes between 1966 and 1971 of branches opened between 1945 and 1961 and of their parent plants. Overall there was a loss of employment in both categories but this was greater among parent plants. In the case of branches opened in assisted areas by parents from non-assisted areas there was a greater chance of closure among branches than parents, but overall employment declined faster in parents than branches, so that there was a net redistribution towards the latter. In the case where both branches and their parents were in non-assisted areas there was a much greater chance of closure among parent plants, and employment decreased in the latter but increased in the branches: possibly the shorter distance between parents and branches leads in the long run to a transfer of activity. In a study of rationalisation within the electrical engineering industry in the late 1960s Massey (1979) found that firms favoured Development Area plants where there were labour subsidies and where investment grants encouraged the introduction of new machinery which reduced manning levels and the need for skilled labour. The conclusion to be drawn is that whilst the opening of branch plants in assisted areas is risky the overall effect is an increase in jobs. The assisted areas benefit by subsidies, whilst the planning restrictions in the London region force up property values and make firms consider the opportunity costs of remaining within the area.

So far we have only considered the growth and rationalisation process of large corporations in terms of the regions within Britain, but increasingly this is taking place at the international scale, particularly with falling tariffs since the late 1960s. In particular the growth of the EEC has persuaded many companies to plan their operations on a European rather than British scale. An oft-quoted example is Ford which in 1967 established Ford of Europe to coordinate the activities of its British and West German companies and rationalise both model lines and components. Many multinational companies are planning at world level and often moving labour intensive operations to developing countries. This trend is likely to grow making regional prosperity dependent not just on their national economy but on the world capitalist order (See Chapter 12).

The Location of Head Offices

The development of a separate head office has been one of the results of the growth of the large corporation and the accompanying structure and role specialisation. In the early history of the company the head office will be at the parent and/or largest manufacturing plant, but later this may be regarded as a disadvantage since it may become too closely involved with one activity. The larger the company the more likely it is to have a detached head office (Crum and Gudgin, 1976), and for this to be located in a large city centre close to business services.

Historical information about the location of head offices of large companies is difficult to acquire, but Hannah (1976) provides a list of the fifty leading firms in 1919 and 1930 and using directories an analysis can be made. In 1919 about one-third of the companies had their head office in London or the South East, whilst by 1930 this proportion had risen to over half. According to Evans' (1973) list, reproduced in Table 29, 86 per cent of the top fifty companies had their head offices in London. The table also shows that the larger the company the more likely it is to have its head office in London, and this equally applies if the companies are ranked by employment size (Crum and Gudgin, 1976). Westaway's (1974) comparison of the location of the head offices of the top 500 industrial companies for 1969 and 1971 suggested that London was gaining whilst the provincial capitals were losing. Goddard and Smith (1978) in a study of change in the top 1,000 companies between 1972 and 1977 confirmed the growth of corporate control in the South East, but found that there was some decentralisation from Greater London to the rest of the region. By 1977 62 per cent of the leading 1,000 companies had their headquarters in the South East and the increase of 3 per cent since 1972 was mainly due to London firms acquiring regional companies. In another survey of head and divisional

TABLE 29 Location of the Headquarters of Large Industrial Companies in the United Kingdom 1971

Rank of Company Based on Turnover	*Central London*		*Rest of London Region*		*Rest of UK*	
	No	*%*	*No*	*%*	*No.*	*%*
1–25	22	88	1	4	2	8
26–50	17	68	3	12	5	20
51–100	31	62	14	28	5	10
101–200	60	60	12	12	28	28
201–300	49	49	17	17	34	34
301–400	34	34	29	29	37	37
401–500	29	29	20	20	51	51
501–600	30	30	20	20	50	50
601–800	44	22	44	22	112	56
801–1000	44	22	36	18	120	60

Source: A. Evans *Urban Studies* 1973, 387 based on *The Times 1000* (1971)

offices Parsons (1972) found that the only other region to have more than its expected share was the West Midlands, particularly of divisional offices. All the other regions had fewer head offices, fewer divisional offices and fewer central services than could be expected from their share of the population. Finally Crum and Gudgin (1976) and Goddard and Smith (1978) divided the top 1,000 companies into home and foreign, concluding that the foreign companies were much more likely to have their head offices in London than the UK companies.

The evolution of London as a centre for head offices parallels the evolution of large firms. The first large firms were often the result of horizontal mergers creating single product companies. When these industries were geographically concentrated it was natural that the head office should be in the largest city of that region. More recently many of the larger companies have become multi-product and their activities show no such geographical concentration. Although apparently foot loose, the head offices of these large companies have been drawn almost irresistibly towards London. The advantages of London arise from its concentration of business and government activity and its good communications both for home and overseas travel. The large companies are multi-national and need to keep in contact with their overseas subsidiaries, whilst foreign-owned firms need to keep in touch with their parent. The large firm needs contact with many national organisations, most of which function from London, and in particular it may need the services of the headquarters of the large banks (Crum and Gudgin, 1976).

The concentration of corporate control functions in the South East has aroused much hostility with the suggestion that the region is thereby favoured in terms of investment. Such as bias would be difficult to test in the post-war period owing to industrial location controls. Leigh and North in their study of four industries in 1973–4 could find no such bias. The growth of head offices in the South East has obviously created many extra jobs both directly and indirectly. Crum and Gudgin (1976) suggested that in 1976 there were 50,000 jobs in detached head offices compared to only 13,000 in the rest of the United Kingdom. These offices boost the demand for business services and enable a widening range to be offered which makes London more attractive in comparison with the provincial capitals.

This concentration of highly skilled and highly paid jobs at the head office is allied with another concern that the quality of labour and thus its remuneration decreases with distance from the head office. Some evidence for this assertion will be considered in Chapter 10.

Research and Development

A feature of the twentieth century has been the increased importance of highly organised research and development programmes seeking to increase and direct the rate of technical change rather than rely on the haphazard inspiration of individual inventors and developers. Such programmes, which have been increasing throughout the century, are based on government laboratories, cooperative research associations, the laboratories of industrial firms and the activities of universities, polytechnics and colleges. In 1972 over 260,000 people were employed in research and development (excluding those in universities and colleges), two-thirds in private industry and one-third in government (Central Statistical Office, 1976). In terms of expenditure industry spent just over half, the government between one-quarter and one-third and the rest was in research associations and universities. Within industry the importance of research varied considerably, being high in chemicals, metals and electronics, and low in textiles, clothing and timber. Nevertheless throughout the period activity has been increasing and spreading to all sectors.

The government has played an initiating role in the development of research in Britain. In 1900 the National Physical Laboratory was established and its premises opened in 1902 at Teddington (London). Shortly afterwards, in 1905, the predecessor of the present Royal Aircraft Establishment at Farnborough was opened, while in 1909 the Post Office Research Station was established in London. The National Physical Laboratory was the parent of many other research stations and these likewise have shown a preference for the South East. The only effort to steer an establishment away from this region was the removal of the National Engineering Laboratory to East Kilbride near Glasgow in 1948. Although Buswell and Lewis (1970) found that 55 per cent of government research stations were in the South East it is probable that the percentage of employment is higher. In addition to their own laboratories the government often sponsor work in private industry and close liaison is often necessary.

In 1916 the government established the Department of Scientific and Industrial Research with the object of encouraging research in industry. This was to be partly achieved through financial support for cooperative research associations which were intended to help smaller firms unable to support their own activities. Within a few years there were twenty research associations (RAs) and there was a similar expansion after World War II. By 1968 there were 46 RAs of which 43 per cent were in the South East (Buswell and Lewis,

1970). According to a survey of 1963, a similar percentage of employment was found in this region, whilst the West Midlands, East Midlands and Yorkshire also each had over 12 per cent (OECD, 1967).

The development of research in industry is more difficult to date. Many firms were born as the result of scientific or technological discovery, usually by their founder, but thereafter research was often a minor or sporadic activity. Often a room was set aside next to the factory for product development or in chemicals and metallurgy for quality control. Gradually, from being a part-time activity, full-time research scientists were appointed and eventually proper research departments established. In Britain before World War I there were only a few such research departments. The war showed the need for research and with government propaganda many firms were encouraged to begin or formalise their research activities. By 1928 there were 400 firms carrying out research and by 1938 this had risen to nearly 600 (Sanderson, 1972). World War II had a similar effect on the expansion of research and after the war many new laboratories were established and existing ones extended.

The larger a company, the more likely it is to be involved in research and, as we have seen, these large companies have often been the result of amalgamations and subsequent rationalisation of activities including research. Frequently these large multi-product companies have a two-fold structure of research involving a central research laboratory where basic research is carried out and smaller laboratories concerned with product development. The location of these activities will depend a great deal upon the history of research in the group, but the larger the laboratory the more likely it is to be detached and separated from production sites. In contrast, the smaller product development laboratories are most likely to be at a production site, often the plant where the product was first made. The large central research laboratories are usually on separate sites and were often established as a new institution at an important point in the evolution of the firm. Although theoretically footloose, they have shown a great tendency to favour the South East where they are usually accessible to head office, to other researchers and research institutions and to good communications for home and foreign travel. This region is also favoured because its good environment facilitates the attraction of scientists and research workers. In the inter-war period there were only a few such central research facilities, but there has been a considerable growth in the post-war period. In the mid-1970s Crum and Gudgin (1976) estimated that there were about 60 detached research and development laboratories employing 27,500 of whom 20,000 were in the South East, 3,500 in the other southern and midland regions and only 4,000 in the assisted regions.

Two surveys, one by Buswell and Lewis (1970) and the other by Parsons (1972), have shown that nearly half the industrial research establishments are in the South East, compared to less than one-third of the population. The West Midlands was the only other region with more than its expected share of establishments. Of the research establishments of the 100 leading manufacturing companies, 47 per cent were in the South East. Only the West Midlands and East Anglia had more than their expected share and, in the case of the latter, many sites were near Cambridge with its heavy concentration of scientific expertise. Figure 27 maps nearly 200 large industrial research establishments, defined here as employing more than 100 workers, of which just over half were in the South East. These figures suggest that even allowing for the central laboratories a large number of companies have preferred to locate their research facilities in the South East, partly reflecting the industrial structure of the region, but also the other advantages mentioned.

Increasingly research is organised and carried out at the international level. The large multi-national company concentrates its research activity, usually in its home territory. Many foreign companies in Britain have hardly any research activities at all, relying on their parent companies. In other cases laboratories are spread across several countries, each specialising in certain areas of research. Clearly the latter is prefer-

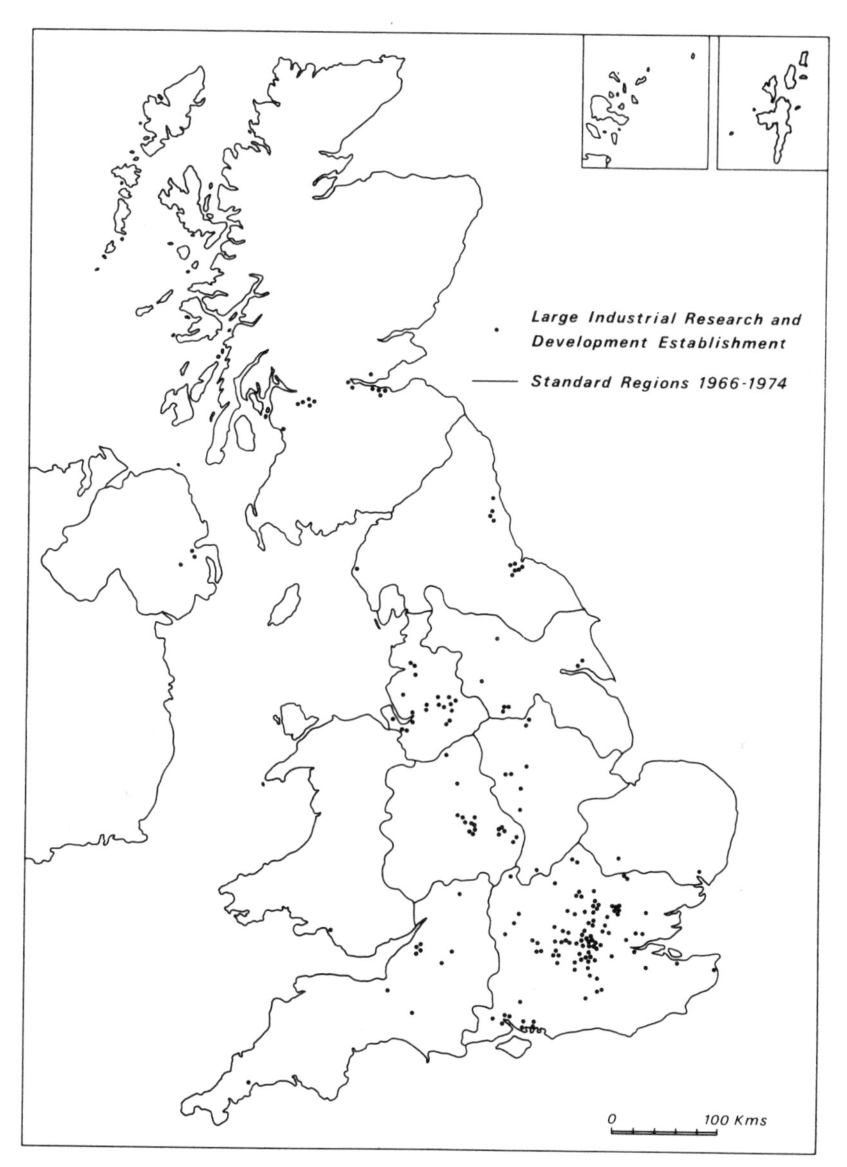

Fig. 27 The Location of Large Industrial Research and Development Establishments

TABLE 30 Employment in Research and Development 1971

	Employment	%	*LQ*
South East	53,620	60.1	1.94
East Anglia	3,460	3.9	1.30
South West	7,860	8.9	1.31
West Midlands	2,490	2.8	0.30
East Midlands	3,770	4.3	0.70
Yorkshire & Humberside	2,120	2.4	0.28
North West	4,580	5.2	0.43
Northern	1,760	2.0	0.34
Wales	1,100	1.2	0.24
Scotland	6,760	7.6	0.81
N. Ireland	1,135	1.3	0.46
Total	88,655	100.0	

Source: 1971 Census (MLH 876) Standard Regions (1966–74). Employment in separated establishments

able to the former with its attendant danger of Britain becoming peripheral to the world centres of innovation with its consequences for income levels and a perpetual drain of skilled scientific manpower to these centres.

Employment figures for workers in both government and industry's research establishments are given in the 1971 Census and are shown in Table 30. Only the three southern regions had a location quotient above 1 and the South East was clearly the most important. The poverty of research establishments in the North, Wales and Northern Ireland should also be noted.

Whilst there is a clear bias of research activity towards the South East, its effect on industrial growth is more speculative. It is suggested that firms will wish to manufacture new products in factories near to the laboratories in which they were developed, and that this would clearly favour the South East. However, it is difficult to find conclusive evidence in support of this idea: one example is the case of the Beecham pharmaceutical company which developed antibiotics in their Surrey laboratories and, in spite of government pressure, insisted on building a factory nearby at Worthing in 1959 for its manufacture (Lazell, 1975, 145) although later they were persuaded to build a factory at Irvine in Scotland in 1972. Another example is the 1967 Havant factory of IBM built to be near the Hursley laboratories established in 1957. The strength of regional policy in the post-war period has probably hindered a tendency which would have been much more common otherwise.

A second result of the concentration of research in the South East is the greater likelihood of new firms being established by research workers in this region. One of the earliest examples of this was Mullard who worked for Edison-Swan and the Admiralty before establishing his own firm in London. Whilst there are other examples we have not seen the development of science parks such as found along Route 121 in Boston (USA). A third result will be to encourage the development of ancillary industries in the region, such as the manufacture of scientific instruments. Finally, the concentration of laboratories adds to the number of highly paid and highly qualified people living in the South East, which may give it further advantages for attracting new activities.

The Branch Plant Economy

The previous discussion has shown that the increasing concentration of business activity into ever larger firms has resulted in the movement of the highest level of decision making into head offices most likely situated in the London region. The corollary is that more and more factories in the rest of Britain are becoming mere branch plants almost solely concerned with production processes with their future dependent on decisions made elsewhere. In the branch plant economy there is likely to be a high degree of external control amongst the larger plants whilst local control will be more important in the small factories, which belong to single-plant enterprises. There may also be structural factors involved, so that the older and declining activities in a region are more likely to be locally controlled whilst the newer and growing industries are externally controlled. This reflects both the organisational concentration in these modern industries and the role they have played in industrial movement.

In an interesting and pioneering study by Firn (1975), covering 92 per cent of Scottish manufacturing industry, it was shown that whilst 72 per cent of all plants were Scottish controlled they accounted for only 41 per cent of employment and had an average size of just over half the Scottish figure (Table 31). The study also confirmed the relationship between size and the degree of external control showing that only in plants employing less than 500 did Scottish control predominate (Table 32). As would be expected, Scottish control was greatest in the slow-growing trades like shipbuilding, leather, furniture, paper and printing but low in the growing industries like electrical engineering, chemicals and vehicles.

A comparative study of the Northern Region for the period 1963–73 by I.J. Smith (1978) for plants employing more than 100 found that in 1963 52 per cent of the plants and 54 per cent of the employment was externally controlled, whilst by 1973 the figures had risen to 73 per cent and 79 per cent respectively. These latter figures can be compared to Firn's Scottish figures for plants employing more than 100 of 51 per cent and 59 per cent respectively. Smith estimated that the increase in external control during the decade was accounted for equally by takeovers of local firms and the establishment of branches by firms outside the region. A similar study of manufacturing plants in Wales in 1969 found that 60 per cent of the plants employing more than 25 were controlled from outside Wales and for plants employing more than 100 this proportion rose to 72 per cent (Tomkins & Lovering, 1973, Table 15).

Information for other regions is mainly lacking, but what evidence there is suggests a high degree of external control and one that was increasing. Dicken and Lloyd (1978) found that local control of firms in Inner Merseyside fell from 49 per cent in 1966 to 30 per cent in 1975 while for Inner Manchester the figures were 72 per cent to 62 per cent, the higher levels reflecting the importance of the clothing industry.

A summary of the evidence available would therefore sug-

TABLE 31 Ownership of Scottish Manufacturing Plants and Employment 1973

Ownership	*Plants*		*Employees*		*Average Size*
	No.	*%*	*No.*	*%*	*(employees)*
Scotland	2176	71.6	243,440	41.2	111.9
Rest of UK	644	21.2	235,150	39.8	365.1
Europe	44	1.4	12,560	1.6	270.3
North America	148	4.9	87,730	14.9	592.8
Other (incl. joint)	29	1.0	11,820	2.0	407.6
Total	3041	100.0	590,700	100.0	194.2

Source: Firn (1975)

TABLE 32 Ownership of Scottish Manufacturing Plants by Size Number of employees

Ownership	*1–50*	*51–100*	*101–500*	*501–1000*	*1001–5000*	*5000+*
Scotland	85.6	72.8	54.6	37.3	26.0	21.4
Rest of UK	11.0	21.5	34.4	40.2	47.9	50.0
European	0.8	1.7	1.9	5.4	3.1	—
North American	2.0	3.8	7.6	14.3	19.9	28.6
Other	0.6	0.2	1.5	2.6	3.1	—
Total	100.0	100.0	100.0	100.0	100.0	100.0
No. of Plants	1526	520	773	111	96	14

Source: Firn (1975)

gest that in 1919 most manufacturing industries were locally controlled. Since then the decline of old activities, increasing business concentration and the development of widely spread branches has created a situation where in most areas outside the London region the majority of plants, and particularly the larger ones, are in the last resort controlled from outside the region. Variations in the degree of external control probably reflect the mix of large and small plants and the size of the traditional sector. High degrees of external control have also spread into the private sector outside manufacturing, such as distribution.

Controversy surrounds the question as to the significance of external control for regional development (Townroe, 1975). The small local firm appears to determine its destiny and control investment decisions, but this freedom may be more apparent than real and it may fall a victim to the larger firm. Whilst the branch plant can be quickly closed down by its parent in a period of rationalisation, equally the parent has more power to move the manufacture of new products to the plant when existing lines are no longer in demand and so ensure its survival. This produces the paradox that large firms are simultaneously opening new branches, developing the product lines of branches and closing them down. At different times and in different regions the overall net effect may either be positive or negative. Since the 1960s the incentives which the assisted regions receive have almost certainly enabled them to be a net beneficiary of the branch plant economy but some intermediate regions, like the Manchester area, close to but not receiving assistance until 1972, may well have lost out (Crompton, 1976).

Another concern about the branch plant economy relates to the multiplier effect on the region. Indigenous companies are hypothesised to have greater linkages, whether of inputs, outputs or use of business services, with the local economy, whilst the branch plant will be more integrated at the national and international level. Studies by Hoare (1978), Lever (1974) and Marshall (1978), using a limited sample of firms, have produced conflicting results. For inputs and outputs Hoare and Lever did find that indigenous firms had greater regional linkages, but Marshall could find no such evidence. However, Marshall did find that indigenous firms were more dependent on local business services than branch plants, which either bought their requirements from organisations outside the region or from inside their firm at its headquarters location. Greater integration of firms with the national and international economy is not necessarily harmful to the region unless, as with business services, an activity is highly concentrated in one region.

Organic Diversification

It has already been suggested that as firms grow they tend to become more diversified, sometimes by acquisition but more often by a natural growth of the original firm. The motives for diversification include the desire to use existing resources more fully, the desire to spread risks at a time of rapid change, and the desire to move out of declining industries (Penrose, 1959, Chapter 8). Frequently diversification builds on existing production and technical resources, and at other times exploits market outlets already developed. The ability of firms to diversify, which has played an important role in the evolution of local economies, is considered in this section from British examples since World War I.

The classic example of this process, begun before this period, is the evolution of Coventry's major industry from textiles to textile engineering, to cycles, to cars and aircraft. In this case engineering skills were transferred to newly developing and, in some cases, allied products. A similar evolution has been found in agricultural engineering, with firms in towns such as Lincoln, Stamford and Dursley moving into diesel engine manufacture, and with similar diversification at Lincoln and Ipswich into construction machinery. Engineering firms associated with the textile industry managed to change markets when making products like chains and gears, but firms more directly involved in machinery were less successful. Likewise in other declining engineering trades like railway and marine engineering there was little diversification except for the manufacture of engines, turbines and scientific instruments. Meanwhile in the South East and Midlands craftsmen were adapting to new products. In London, as we have seen (p. 122), clock makers like Smith turned to supply the motor industry whilst scientific glass makers like Cossor were drawn into valve manufacture and thence electrical goods.

The chemical and food industries also provide some interesting examples of adaptation. William Lever was able to use the vegetable oils processed in his soap-making complex at Port Sunlight for the manufacture of margarine and animal food. Similar groups at Hull and Liverpool were later eliminated by Lever competition. The soap industry also shows parallel developments, for example its move into the production of toilet goods. The milling of wheat for flour diversified into the manufacture of animal foods, whilst Distillers, the whisky company, moved into the manufacture of industrial alcohol and thence chemicals. Similarly Reckitts at Hull moved from the manufacture of starch derived from grain processing into colouring materials, pharmaceuticals and household chemicals.

During the two world wars, firms were often forced to diversify to help the military effort and sometimes the manufacture of such new products became permanent. During World War I, Rolls Royce turned to the manufacture of aircraft engines, which subsequently became the mainstay of the company. Likewise in World War II, English Electric at Preston began aircraft manufacture which continues to this day. In the same war the government asked ICI (Dyestuffs), Distillers (Chemicals) and Glaxo (Baby Foods) to use their manufacturing and technical resources to produce the new penicillin drugs and in this way these companies entered the pharmaceutical industry.

Whilst there are examples of diversification in all parts of the country, the tendency does appear to have been greatest in the South and Midlands and least in the peripheral regions where the need was most urgent. One explanation is that many of the newer industries were developing in the South and Midlands and the close juxtaposition of old and new trades encouraged diversification. Another factor was that many of the newer industries were consumer-orientated and similar industries with a similar marketing outlook were found principally in the South and to a lesser extent in the Midlands. In the peripheral regions goods were produced for other industries, in small quantities and often one-off. The smaller firms were often satellites dependent on one or two firms for sales with no general marketing organisation capable of developing new outlets. These factors, coupled with a pessimistic economic environment, and shaped by decline, help explain the lack of diversification in the industries of the peripheral regions.

The Role of Foreign Investment

Foreign companies investing in Britain play an important role in the growth process, introducing new products, new production processes and new management techniques. In this section we shall examine the environment in which this investment takes place and the resulting spatial patterns.

The foreign company which considers investing in Britain is usually one which has already established a good position in its home market as a result of a combination of good management, marketing, research and development on product lines, and improved production processes. In seeking to capitalise on these resources it is led to consider markets outside its home territory which may be approached in a number of ways. One well-worn path is to begin by importing goods into Britain via a sales subsidiary which, if successful, is followed by manufacturing operations. Alternatively a British firm may be licenced to make the product, or a new manufacturing company may be established jointly with a British company, or a British company may be taken over and its manufacturing and selling organisation used. The policy adopted will depend on a number of factors such as the resources of the parent company, the nature of the product, including transport costs, fragility and perishability, and tariff duties. In order to preserve patent rights, foreign companies are often forced into local manufacture or licensing, whilst many firms believe that local manufacture is important giving customers confidence and thus increasing sales. The distinctive spatial aspects of foreign investment can best be seen where companies establish their own manufacturing facilities rather than in a joint company or through takeover.

The foreign company establishing manufacturing facilities in Britain is in a very different situation from a new company and this may affect its choice of a location. In the first place it has all the resources of a large company behind it. Often it will have built up a significant sales base so that manufacture can begin in quantity assuring the company of economies of scale. Using the company's other overseas markets it may even be able to begin by exporting. The experience of its home operation should also mean that its plant can commence with a high level of production efficiency. All these factors suggest that foreign firms should be able to establish relatively efficient manufacturing plants which in Smith's terminology have wide spatial margins of profitability. The second distinctive aspect of the foreign company's evolution is that it has often begun as a selling organisation and this could influence its choice of a manufacturing location. Usually a company will locate its selling organisation in London, which is the obvious centre for trans-national connections. Occasionally, where firms are selling to industries which are geographically concentrated, the sales office will be in the main commercial centre of that industry. Following the commencement of sales a warehouse will be established, usually near the sales office, but sometimes at a port. In the case of engineering companies this warehouse may also act as a service and repair centre, and from here it is only a short step to assembly of imported parts and then to complete manufacture. In the case of food and chemical companies, a similar transition may be seen, with the intermediate stage involving the packing of imported materials. This pattern of evolution was very common in the inter-war period but has been prevented in the post-war period by various planning controls, notably those which prevent change of use to manufacturing without an IDC.

The spatial pattern of initial foreign manufacturing investment in Britain is shown in Table 33. Information for the post-1945 period is available from the Howard Report (Board of Trade 1968) and the Department of Industry, but for the earlier period the author has had to make his own, ine-

TABLE 33 The Location of Initial Foreign Manufacturing Investment in Britain

A Firms			*Period*			
	1918–44	*1945–51*	*1952–9*	*1960–5*	*1966–71*	*1972–5*
No. of factories	*162*	*55*	*77*	*126*	*174*	*106*
			Per cent of total			
South East	70.3	16.4	20.1	18.3	36.2	26.4
East Anglia	0.6	—	3.9	3.2	2.9	0.9
South West	0.6	1.8	3.9	6.3	2.9	—
West Midlands	6.8	—	2.6	0.8	1.7	—
East Midlands	1.2	3.6	5.2	2.4	3.4	8.5
Yorkshire & Humberside	3.7	—	1.3	4.0	1.7	2.8
North West	11.7	14.5	13.0	11.1	7.5	8.5
North	0.6	5.4	7.8	7.9	9.2	10.4
Wales	0.6	20.0	9.1	4.8	7.5	11.3
Scotland	3.7	36.4	24.7	29.4	20.1	26.4
N. Ireland	—	1.8	7.8	11.9	6.8	4.7

B Jobs						
Employment (000)	*100.0*	*44.7*	*40.5*	*23.3*	*14.0*	*10.3*
			Per cent of total			
South East	65.2	4.7	27.2	16.3	21.6	*
East Anglia	2.0	—	2.5	1.7	1.3	*
South West	—	*	3.7	7.3	3.5	—
West Midlands	18.4	—	*	*	*	—
East Midlands	0.5	*	9.9	0.4	1.3	*
Yorkshire & Humberside	3.8	—	*	4.3	*	*
North West	8.2	8.3	10.9	6.0	8.4	3.9
North	0.1	2.7	5.4	8.2	18.5	*
Wales	1.2	14.3	5.2	1.7	*	9.7
Scotland	0.7	65.8	25.9	27.0	23.8	50.5
N. Ireland	—	2.5	4.0	27.0	*	5.8

Source: Post-1945 Howard Report (Board of Trade 1968) and Regional Statistics 1979. Pre-1945 Author's estimates

* No figures available

vitably incomplete, estimates. In addition to contemporary directories which list surviving firms, Dunning's (1958) study of American investment is particularly useful.

The inter-war years were very important for the entry of foreign firms into manufacturing in Britain owing to the raising of tariffs. This process began in 1915 for strategic goods, was made permanent in the mid-1920s for goods like motor cars, and became general for most goods in 1931. Most foreign firms selling goods in Britain were forced into local manufacture if they wished to continue selling in Britain. One report suggested that in the eighteen months from the introduction of the Tariff in 1931, 275 foreign firms established factories in Britain which were expected to employ 17,000 (House of Commons, 1932–3). Not all of these production plans may have been successful. The Surveys of Industrial Development by the Board of Trade found that 266 foreign firms established factories between 1932 and 1938, whilst for the 225 moves between 1932 and 1936, 21,200 jobs were expected. Of the 156 firms starting manufacture between 1933 and 1938, one-third came from Germany, one-sixth from the USA and the rest mainly from Europe: just over half of these firms located in the South East, one-sixth in the North West and the rest mainly in the Midlands and North East.

The author has been able to trace 162 of these firms, probably representing about half of all the foreign companies moving into Britain in the inter-war period, of which two-thirds came from the United States and the rest mainly from Europe with a few from Australasia. There are only 6 from Germany, compared to 52 in the Board of Trade list, which shows the difficulty of tracing these firms, all of which were taken over by the Custodian of Enemy Property during the war and often sold to British companies.

The South East attracted three-quarters of these foreign companies and nearly two-thirds of the jobs (Table 33). Most of these firms were located in north and west London, including Park Royal, the Great West Road, Slough and Welwyn Garden City. At least 47 of the 114 firms establishing in the

South East had a London selling organisation prior to manufacture, and doubtless more work using directories would produce evidence to raise this figure. Besides such development from a selling organisation, the London region possessed another advantage for American firms in being near the continent where it was believed, in the event falsely, that goods made in Britain could be sold. The West Midlands attracted 7 per cent of the firms but 18 per cent of the jobs, with important contributions from a few large rubber tyre companies. The North West attracted 12 per cent of the firms and 8 per cent of the jobs, including several firms in the traditional textile and clothing sections. In all about 95 per cent of the firms and jobs were located in the core region of Britain stretching from the South East to Lancashire–Yorkshire.

The impact of foreign firms on the economy of the South East was more significant than the mere creation of jobs: many introduced new industries to Britain and, by locating in the South East, reinforced that region's capacity for innovation. At the same time many of these firms needed materials and industrial services which stimulated these other activities in the London region. Finally, many of these firms introduced new production and management processes which diffused to other firms in the region and gave valuable new experience to potential entrepreneurs who later established their own firms in the region.

The pattern of incoming firms in the post-war period has been completely different. Since 1945 the Board of Trade and its successor the Department of Industry has been able to steer incoming firms to Development Areas (Steuer *et. al.* 1973), causing a reversal of inter-war trends with the peripheral regions gaining a major share of firms and jobs (Table 33). As a result of the efforts of the Scottish Council many American firms have been attracted to Scotland, introducing new industries and giving Scotland a significant share of the electronics industry. Northern Ireland, which has its own promotion agency, also did well in the period up to 1971. Whilst these firms have provided many jobs their total impact has not been as great as was hoped. Many firms have not been able to buy components from local firms and have had to buy from other regions and in some cases from abroad (Forsyth, 1972). Many foreign firms in these peripheral regions still have sales offices in the London region and many have their head offices and, where relevant, their research and development in the South East as well. Of 60 firms traced which had established plants in the assisted regions between 1945 and 1965, 18, or 30 per cent, had their head offices in the South East and these tended to be the larger companies. This behaviour is thus similar to the tendency, already discussed, within British industry as a whole.

The influence of foreign companies in the British economy has been growing, not only through the establishment of manufacturing plant, but also through the takeover of British firms. The greater this influence the more Britain as a whole will tend to become a branch plant economy divorced from the ultimate centres of decision making and often, but by no means always, of research and development. Whilst every advanced country has foreign firms, the degree of importance of such investment is usually low. Should it rise to a high level then the country could become peripheral to the western economy just as some British regions have become peripheral to the South East.

From the inter-war period to the early 1970s foreign companies were attracted to Britain because of the size of the market and the fact that it was protected by tariffs. Since the early 1970s falling tariffs and Britain's entry into the EEC have made this country just one part of the West European market. As British companies choose their location between British regions, so multi-national companies choose between countries, with levels of productivity, wages and incentives offered playing a crucial role in their decisions. In the future foreign companies may only need one plant (for each product) to serve Western Europe, and whether this is in Britain or not will depend on the factors mentioned above.

CHAPTER NINE

The Movement of Economic Activities

Whilst many firms stay in the same location for a long period there is no reason why this should be the norm and many reasons why firms might consider a new site. Expansion or contraction and changes in technology may make the existing plant unsuitable whilst changing locational factors of access to materials, markets, labour and capital may cause the firm to re-evaluate its location. These changes may operate in both a push or pull manner. Thus a shortage of labour may encourage a firm to consider other areas or, alternatively, knowledge of cheaper labour elsewhere may attract the firm to that place. Imbalances in regional development will tend to enhance the possibility of movement. This, as we have seen, agrees with the equilibrium theory of regional development in which it is suggested that capital will move to the poorer regions with high unemployment in order to gain lower labour costs and greater return on capital. Movement may also be encouraged by government regional policy for, as we have seen, the main solution proposed for the problem regions since 1937 has been the injection of new activities. In this chapter we shall review the British experience of movement of economic activity and assess its significance for regional development.

The greatest amount of movement is over short distances, such as from the inner areas of large cities to the outskirts, but in this chapter we shall be mainly concerned with long-distance movement between the principal British regions. Of course wherever regional boundaries are drawn there are bound to be a few cases where firms have just moved a few miles over the border and been counted, but in the main inter-regional movement involves longer distances. International movement will be excluded as this has already been considered in the section dealing with foreign firms.

Official statistics about movement relate to the opening of new premises by a firm, whether this be a branch or a transfer of the company. As such it omits the movement of activities between different plants belonging to the same company. This would include the situation where manufacture of a product with declining demand in a branch is replaced by one with greater prospects. It also excludes the situation where a company takes over another firm and closes its plant and transfers its product manufacture to one of its other factories. It is likely therefore that official statistics underestimate the amount of movement that is taking place.

Industrial Migration

Throughout the period the movement of manufacturing industry has been regarded as of the greatest importance to the solution of the regional problem since this activity is both basic to a regional economy and potentially the most footloose form of employment. Over the whole period the rate of inter-regional industrial movement has varied considerably and so it can best be described in terms of sub-periods.

1918–1936

There are very few statistics for this period and therefore any discussion is somewhat tentative. The only official statistics are for the years 1932–8 and are found in the Board of Trade's annual Surveys of Industrial Development. It is likely that the definition of movement in these surveys covers only transfers (and not the opening of branches) and on this basis the number of inter-regional moves varied from 4 to 19 a year. These moves were not all in one direction as illustrated by the year 1935 when there were 12 moves, 6 from north to south and 6 from south to north. The total numbers of moves were small, as probably also was the number of jobs, although no details are given. The conclusions drawn by the authors of these surveys and other commentators was that the transfer of industrial activities from north to south could in no way account for the prosperity of the London region. Similarly it could be suggested that there was no evidence of capital seeking out cheap labour in the declining industrial areas.

These views are confirmed by an analysis of 48 moves which have been discovered by the author for the sub-period and which include branches. The South East region was the origin for 15 moves and the destination for 10. The outward moves were often by expanding firms like Smith's Crisps establishing market-orientated factories whether serving consumers or industries. Although there was no dominant bias in the direction of moves, some of the most significant in terms of jobs were towards the South East and West Midlands. Ford moved its motor vehicle works from Manchester to Dagenham in 1933 and by the 1960s was employing between 35–40,000 in the South East. Coventry also attracted at least three important firms in this period; a telephone manufacturing plant from Manchester, an aircraft firm from Newcastle and motor car firm from Blackpool, which at their peak employed 26,000 workers. The redevelopment of the Corby works by the tube firm of Stewart and Lloyds, which involved the physical transference of plant from Clydeside, was also significant although not strictly classifiable as a move.

1937–1944

The two years before World War II have been added to the war period since the government was beginning to attempt to steer firms to the Special Areas and strategic factors were affecting the siting of plants in the rearmament programme. The vulnerability of the eastern side of the country to German attack prompted the government to designate a 'safe zone' covering the western side of the country where preference would be given for new industrial building and for industrial movement. That this policy was not always strictly adhered to is seen in the building of shadow factories in Birmingham and Coventry. To allow essential war industries to expand, other industries were grouped and concentrated and often transferred to other regions. The demand for factories was increased by a policy of duplicating plants so that the effects of bombing could be mitigated. One result was a wide search for premises and labour involving many isolated and remote areas. During this time the government had complete control over the location of all plants resulting in a very large amount of inter-regional industrial movement. Much of this was merely temporary. When the war ended most of these factories were no longer needed either because they were making war goods or because the dispersed tenants could return to their pre-war location. However, in other cases the firms stayed on, converting a plant that had become an efficient production unit to peace-time uses. The long-lasting effects of wartime movement were therefore considerable. Even where firms closed down at the end of the war they often left premises and a labour force that had been trained in new skills which later became an important factor in attracting industries. It is not an overestimate to say that the experience of industrial movement during World War II proved a turning point for many depressed areas enabling them to commence the process of rebuilding their economy on a different economic base.

There are no official statistics of either temporary or permanent moves for this period but the author has traced 116 moves which survived until at least the late 1950s and which involved 141,000 jobs (Table 34). As could be expected the main source of moves was the South East and West Midlands whilst the main recipients were Wales, the North West, South West and Scotland. In the Northern region many of the moves went to the strategically located Cumbria area. Many of the industries that moved not unnaturally had wartime significance, such as in the aircraft and electrical industries.

TABLE 34   Inter-regional Industrial Movement 1937–1944. Number of Moves and Jobs (1960)

Destination	*SE*	*EA*	*SW*	*WM*	*EM*	*Y & H*	*NW*	*N*	*W*	*Sc*	*N.I*	*Total Moves*	*Jobs*
Origin													
SE	—	3	14	4	8	3	14	7	12	4	1	70	
		3,600	18,280	2,600	1,550	2,600	19,270	5,840	15,970	5,660	6,000		81,370
EA				1								1	
				3,500									3,500
SW												—	—
WM	1	1			4	1	5		4	2		18	
	200	2,000			4,300	3,000	5,000		10,000	530			25,030
EM								1	1	2		4	
								100	3,000	6,100			9,200
Y & H							3	3		1		7	
							2,600	2,000		2,000			6,600
NW									3	2		5	
									1,900	5,000			6,900
N	1						2		1	1		5	
	800						1,100		500	300			2,700
W												—	—
Sc							3		3			6	
							3,000		2,600				5,600
N.I.													
Total Moves	2	4	14	5	12	4	27	11	24	12	1	116	
Jobs	1,000	5,600	18,280	6,100	5,850	5,600	30,970	7,940	33,790	19,590	6,000		140,900

Source: Author's Estimates. Top row – moves; bottom row – jobs

1945–1951

The immediate post-war period was distinctive for several reasons. There was a production boom fuelled by the need to replace war damage which resulted in severe shortages of labour and premises. Manufacturers were prepared to move in a way not seen before or since. In addition the government had just introduced powers to control industry through Industrial Development Certificates and still retained the wartime system of building controls. As a result there was great success in steering firms to the assisted areas. The Board of Trade, the department responsible for industrial location policy, began to monitor the success of its policy and later reports (Board of Trade, 1968) provide invaluable information on post-1945 industrial movement. By 1966, 552 moves survived from the period 1945–51 (Table 35). In that year they provided 228,000 jobs with 81 per cent going to the assisted areas. Wales and the North both received over one-quarter of the total. The main source region was the South East supplying 45 per cent of the jobs followed by the West Midlands providing 20 per cent. The Yorkshire and Humberside region also supplied many moves, most of which went to the adjacent Northern region. The average size of the move was 41 jobs but this conceals wide variations with a few large moves being very significant.

1952–1959

Around 1950 the controls on industrial location began to be lessened (see Chapter 2). The result was that during the 1950s firms had much greater freedom in location with less pressure and less incentive to go to the assisted regions. The figures of inter-regional industrial movement show a dramatic change for 1952–9 when compared to the previous period. By 1966 there were 323 surviving moves from this sub-period providing 100,000 jobs. (Table 36). The South East continued to supply most of the moves, but the number of jobs moving to the assisted regions fell and they received only 53 per cent of all inter-regional jobs. The North and Wales received less whilst the North West and South West became the main receiving areas. The 41,000 jobs moved out of the South East during this period also need to be compared to 100,000 jobs involved in intra-regional movement within the region, many of which went to the new towns. The rise of the North West which received over 40 per cent of the jobs going to the assisted regions was connected with the designation of two new Development Areas, Merseyside (1949) and North-East Lancashire (1953).

1960–1965

Towards the end of the 1950s unemployment began to increase, causing the Conservative government to reactivate regional policy as discussed in an earlier chapter. The number of inter-regional moves increased and the share of jobs going to the assisted areas rose to 75 per cent (Table 37), with the North West receiving the largest share. Part of this region's success was due to the movement of three car plants to Merseyside employing about 25,000 in all. In addition to the assisted regions, the South West and East Anglia also received significant inflows partly reflecting increased overspill from the South East as well as the favourable image of the regions. Once again the South East and West Midlands were forced to provide most of the jobs, and the tightness of IDC control caused intra-regional movement in these regions to fall compared to the 1950s.

1966–1971

Under a Labour government, the late 1960s was one of the strongest periods of regional policy, with tight IDC control and high levels of incentives. In the six years 1966–71 over 1,000 inter-regional moves were recorded providing nearly 125,000 jobs at the end of 1975 (Table 38). The average size of firm moving was small, although there could often have been subsequent expansion. The South East provided over

TABLE 35 Inter-regional Industrial Movement 1945–51. Number of Moves and Jobs (1966)

Destination	*SE*	*EA*	*SW*	*WM*	*EM*	*Y & H*	*NW*	*N*	*W*	*Sc*	*N.I.*	*Moves*	*Jobs (000)*
Origin													
SE		19	22	4	6	7	24	49	74	29	17	251	
		3.2	7.7	0.8	4.0	1.5	8.8	28.4	35.1	5.9	6.5		101.3
EA	1		—	—	—	1	—	2	2	—	1	7	8.1
	*		—	—	—	*	—	*	*	—	*		
SW	2	—		—	—	—	1	1	2	—	1	7	
	*	—		—	—	—	*	*	*	—	*		3.7
WM	3	—	7		5	4	11	2	34	5	5	76	
	1.3	—	0.6		1.8	4.5	18.3	1.5	11.9	0.9	3.7		44.4
EM	—	—	—	5		15	2	8	9	4	5	48	
	—	—	—	0.5		3.7	*	6.3	5.3	1.4	0.4		18.0
Y & H	2	—	1	1	8		13	31	2	6	2	66	
	*	—	*	*	1.1		2.8	20.9	*	0.6	*		27.9
NW	2	1	2	4	3	10		7	19	9	7	64	
	*	*	*	0.7	0.5	1.9		1.5	3.7	3.2	1.3		14.2
N	—	—	—	1	1	1	1		—	—	—	4	
	—	—	—	*	*	*	*		—	—	—		3.1
W	1	—	—	2	—	1	—	—		—	—	4	
	*	—	—	*	—	*	—	—		—	—		1.2
Sc	1	—	—	1	—	1	1	4			1	9	
	*	—	—	*	—	*	*	0.6			*		1.2
N.I.	—	—	—	—	—	—	—	—	—	—			
	—	—	—	—	—	—	—	—	—	—		—	—
Moves	12	20	32	18	23	49	55	104	143	57	39	552	
Jobs (000)	3.6	3.6	9.1	2.9	8.9	14.8	32.9	61.5	63.0	14.9	13.1		227.5

Source: Howard Report (Board of Trade 1968). Old Standard Regions

Destination	*SE*	*EA*	*SW*	*WM*	*EM*	*Y & H*	*NW*	*N*	*W*	*Sc*	*N.I.*	*Moves*	*Jobs (000)*
Origin													
SE		17	22	9	12	3	17	12	14	14	9	129	
		2.4	11.4	1.5	2.8	1.9	12.4	3.0	2.2	2.3	1.7		41.7
EA	2		—	—	—	—	1	—	—	1	—	4	
	*		—	—	—	—	*	—	—	*	—		3.4
SW	4	—		2	—	—	1	1	3	2	1	14	
	0.4	—		*	—	—	*	*	0.8	*	*		5.6
WM	5	—	9		3	3	7	2	4	4	4	41	
	0.5	—	0.8		2.8	2.3	5.4	*	0.5	0.5	1.9		15.8
EM	3	2	—	2		12	4	3	2	2		30	
	0.1	*	—	*		2.7	0.9	2.5	*	*			7.8
Y & H	2	—	—	1	12		8	7	3	2	1	36	
	*	—	—	*	2.5		0.9	3.1	0.3	*	*		8.2
NW	11	—	—	3	1	8		1	11	4	4	43	
	3.3	—	—	1.4	*	0.7		*	1.8	0.8	0.6		9.4
N	1	—	—	—	—	1	2		—	—	1	5	
	*	—	—	—	—	*	*		—	—	*		1.2
W	3	—	—	—	1	2	—	—		1		7	
	0.6	—	—	—	*	*	—	—		*			4.3
Sc	—	—	2	—	—	—	1	2	—		2	7	
	—	—	*	—	—	—	*	*	—		*		1.0
N.I.	—	—	—	—	—	—	—	—	—	—		—	—
	—	—	—	—	—	—	—	—	—	—			
Moves	32	20	33	17	30	30	42	28	38	31	22	323	
Jobs (000)	6.7	3.2	12.4	4.1	9.2	13.6	23.1	11.0	6.3	7.9	5.5		100.7

Source: Howard Report (Board of Trade 1968). Old Standard Regions
* No figures available. Top row – moves; bottom row – jobs (000). Unallocated moves included in totals

TABLE 37 Inter-regional Industrial Movement 1960–6. Number of Moves and Jobs (1966)

Destination	*SE*	*EA*	*SW*	*WM*	*EM*	*Y & H*	*NW*	*N*	*W*	*Sc*	*N.I.*	*Moves*	*Jobs (000)*
Origin													
SE		69	60	9	22	9	45	33	29	54	22	352	
		7.3	6.0	0.9	1.9	0.5	25.4	4.5	5.9	16.9	8.7		77.9
EA	—		—	—	1	1	2	1	3	2	—	10	
	—		—	—	*	*	*	*	0.4	*	—		1.0
SW	—	—		2	3	1	4	—	4	3	—	17	
	—	—		*	0.3	*	0.7	—	0.4	0.1	—		1.8
WM	5	2	19		6	3	17	6	21	17	2	98	
	3.0	*	2.8		0.5	0.3	10.0	2.3	6.0	7.3	*		32.3
EM	1	4	2	5		9	6	6	4	9	4	50	
	*	0.3	*	0.3		0.9	0.7	0.7	0.4	0.6	0.9		5.3
Y & H	1	1	1	—	10		6	13	—	1	3	36	
	*	*	*	—	1.0		1.1	2.8	—	*	1.7		6.9
NW	2	3	3	2	—	1		6	16	7	4	44	
	*	0.6	0.2	*	—	*		0.9	1.7	0.5	0.6		4.6
N	2	—	—	—	—	2	1		1	1	1	8	
	*	—	—	—	—	*	*		*	*	*		1.8
W	—	—	1	1	—	—	2	—		1	—	5	
	—	—	*	*	—	—	*	—		*	—		3.0
Sc	1	1	—	—	2	1	2	3	1		1	12	
	*	*	—	—	*	*	*	0.1	*		*		2.8
N.I.	—	—	—	—	—	—	—	—	—	—		—	—
	—	—	—	—	—	—	—	—	—	—			
Moves	12	80	87	20	44	27	86	69	80	95	37	637	
Jobs (000)	4.4	8.6	12.2	1.6	4.7	1.9	39.2	11.8	15.5	25.6	12.3		137.9

Source: Howard Report (Board of Trade 1968). Old Standard Regions.

Destination	SE	EA	SW	WM	EM	Y & H	NW	N	W	Sc	N.I.	Moves	Jobs (000)
Origin													
SE		140	124	4	52	12	35	53	68	55	28	571	
		10.7	12.0	*	4.3	*	5.8	11.9	14.2	8.7	5.0		73.5
EA	8		1	2	—	1	1	2	2	2	—	19	
	0.4		*	*	—	*	*	*	*	*	—		1.4
SW	10	2		1	1	—	2	2	8	1	—	27	
	*	*		*	*	—	*	*	*	*	—		1.1
WM	18	2	12		10	—	17	12	49	8	2	130	
	1.2	*	*		0.8	—	6.4	1.5	3.9	*	*		17.1
EM	17	4	9	4		11	5	14	14	8	7	93	
	0.8	*	0.6	*		2.1	*	3.8	*	0.8	1.6		12.6
Y & H	10	3	1	2	16		4	17	2	2	5	65	
	0.3	*	*	*	1.0		*	3.6	*	*	0.6		6.2
NW	10	—	4	3	3	1		23	18	9	6	77	
	0.8	—	*	*	*	*		2.7	3.4	1.0	0.6		9.2
N	4	2	—	—	2	1	1		—	6	1	17	
	*	*	—	—	*	*	*		—	*	*		1.9
W	4	—	1	—	1	—	3	3		—	—	12	
	*	—	*	—	*	—	*	*		—	—		0.9
Sc	3	—	1	—	1	—	1	4	2		1	13	
	*	—	*	—	*	—	*	*	*		*		*
N.I.	1	—	—	—	—	—	1	—	—	—		2	
	*	—	—	—	—	—	*	—	—	—			*
Moves	85	153	153	16	86	26	70	130	163	94	50	1,026	
Jobs (000)	4.5	11.2	13.5	1.0	6.7	4.0 (E)	14.0	24.7	22.9 (E)	12.9	9.5 (E)		124.9

Source: *Regional Statistics* 1979. New Standard Regions.
* No figures available. Top row – moves; bottom row – jobs (000). E – Estimate (author)

half the jobs with the East and West Midland regions being the other main source areas (Table 38). The five assisted regions received over two-thirds of inter-regional moves, slightly less than in the early 1960s, whilst the South West and East Anglia maintained their share.

1972–1975

The most recently available figures for industrial movement are shown in Table 39. The South East continued to provide the majority of mobile jobs, its share increasing to two-thirds, while the importance of the West Midlands declined. In terms of destination, the share of moves and jobs going to the five assisted regions declined to a half, with the Northern region experiencing the greatest fall, while the share of jobs going to the South West, East Anglia and East Midlands increased to well over one-third.

Since 1975 no figures have been made available from the Department of Industry (successor to the Board of Trade in dealing with industrial location policy) so it is impossible to continue the analysis to the present. However, it is known that the world recession which followed the 1973 rise in oil prices has slowed down industrial investment and consequently industrial movement also. This is confirmed by the promotional bodies in the assisted regions which all report difficulty in attracting industry.

The scale of inter-regional industrial movement in the post-war period, and particularly that to the assisted regions, has clearly been affected by the strength of government regional policy. Comparing the weak policy period of the 1950s with the strong policy period of the 1960s, several commentators have suggested that the strengthening of policy resulted in between 60 and 80 extra moves a year to the assisted regions. (Ashcroft and Taylor, 1977; Moore and Rhodes, 1976; and McKay, 1978). Allowing for subsequent expansion of these moves, Moore and Rhodes have estimated that policy-induced moves to the Development Areas over the period created 165,000 jobs in manufacturing. Given the low

Destination	SE	EA	SW	WM	EM	Y & H	NW	N	W	Sc	N.I	Moves	Jobs (000)
Origin													
SE		84	64	4	57	30	35	28	48	25	1	376	
		4.7	4.7	*	4.9	3.0	*	4.5	3.4	*	*		28.9
EA	3		—	—	4	1	1	3	2	4	—	18	
	*		—	—	*	*	*	*	*	*	—		0.9
SW	6	—		2	—	2	1	3	16	6	1	37	
	0.2	—		*	—	*	*	*	1.2	*	*		1.9
WM	7	1	1		6	3	11	3	17	8	—	57	
	0.2	*	*		0.2	*	0.8	*	1.2	1.6	—		4.4
EM	2	7	1	—		11	3	4	3	1	—	32	
	*	0.3	*	—		0.8	*	*	*	*	—		2.3
Y & H	2	—	1	—	4		3	4	1	6	1	22	
	*	—	*	—	*		*	*	*	0.3	*		1.1
NW	1	—	6	1	4	9		4	3	3	4	35	
	*	—	0.2	*	*	0.6		*	*	*	*		2.1
N	—	—	—	—	1	1	3		1	4	—	10	
	—	—	—	—	*	*	*		*	*	—		0.5
W	2	1	1	1	—	—	—	—		1	—	6	
	*	*	*	*	—	—	—	—		*	—		0.3
Sc	—	—	1	—	1	1	1	3	1		—	8	
	—	—	*	—	*	*	*	*	*		—		0.3
N.I.	—	—	1	—	—	—	1	—	1	—		3	
	—	—	*	—	—	—	*	—	*	—			0.5
Moves	23	93	76	8	77	58	59	52	93	58	7	604	
Jobs (000)	1.1 (E)	4.8 (E)	5.3	0.4	5.5 (E)	4.4 (E)	4.0	5.6 (E)	6.5	4.5	1.1 (E)		43.2

Source: *Regional Statistics* 1979. New Standard Regions
* No figures available. Top row – moves; bottom row – jobs (000). E – Estimate (author)

level of movement in the inter-war period towards the depressed areas and the fact that some regional policies were still operating in the 1950s, these figures may underestimate the true effect of regional policies (see Chapter 4).

The Impact of Inter-regional Industrial Movement

The impact of these moves can be assessed from a number of viewpoints. In the first place the total number of jobs involved in moves since the late 1930s can be compared to the total number of manufacturing jobs now present. Since employment in migrant firms is rarely stationary, this provides only a crude indication of the quantity of jobs involved.

The South East has been the main exporting region, being responsible for at least 1,700 outward moves since the late 1930s involving over 400,000 jobs equivalent to 17 per cent of its manufacturing labour force in 1971. Wales and the North West have each received over 70,000 jobs, the South West and North about 60,000 each, Scotland and East Anglia between 30 and 40,000, with Northern Ireland receiving over 26,000 jobs. In contrast only about 21,000 jobs have been moved into the South East.

The West Midlands has contributed at least 420 outward moves involving 139,000 jobs, equivalent to 12 per cent of its manufacturing labour force in 1971. The main receiving areas have been the North West with 45,000 jobs, Wales with 33,000 jobs followed by Scotland, the East Midlands, and Yorkshire each receiving 10,000 jobs. Like the South East, there were relatively few inward moves—only 16,000 jobs.

The five assisted regions have been intentionally made the main recipients of this movement. The North West received at least 144,000 jobs equivalent to 12 per cent of its manufacturing labour force in 1971, and for the other regions the respective figures were: Wales 148,000 jobs and 44 per cent; the North 121,000 jobs and 26 per cent; Scotland 85,000 jobs and 12 per cent, and Northern Ireland 48,000 jobs and 28 per cent. With the exception of the North West, which lost 46,000 jobs, these regions exported few jobs.

The South West and East Anglia have also benefited from the inward movement of firms. The former has gained at least 71,000 jobs equivalent to 17 per cent of its manufacturing labour force in 1971 whilst the latter gained 37,000 jobs equal to 18 per cent of its manufacturing labour force. Both regions are adjacent to the South East and have received overspill in expanded towns, though not all movement was of this type nor was it to localities immediately peripheral to that region. The out movement of jobs, 14,000 jobs from the South West and 18,000 from East Anglia was much smaller than the inflow in both cases.

Finally the East Midlands and Yorkshire/Humberside regions have each received about 40,000 jobs and lost about 55,000 jobs. The outward movement represents a creaming off of growth whilst the inward movement in the East Midlands represents an overspill from the adjacent South East and West Midlands.

Such direct impact in terms of job gains and losses may be only part of the effect of industrial movement. Sometimes a branch plant may spawn further local branch plants or feeder plants which will not appear in the industrial movement statistics. An industry moving into a region may purchase local services, materials and components as well as selling to firms in the region and thus producing multiplier effects. In practice these hoped for spin-off effects have not materialised as surveys have shown (Townroe, 1975). In the first place migrant firms usually have their input-output linkages already well developed before the move and see no point in changing them (Moseley and Townroe, 1973). Uniform prices are usually charged across the United Kingdom regions for most materials at least where quantity is involved, so movement, even if to a region where new suppliers are available, will not produce any changes. Again most firms involved in movement have already established national and even international markets for their products so that an increase in local sales is not likely to occur because of a move. The only exceptions are likely to be firms engaged in non-routine product manufacture, such as contract engineering firms, where a move may herald more involvement with the receiving region. There are also a small number of cases where the industry has market-orientated plants and develops by establishing new plants in growing markets.

The low level of local impact of migrant plants may reflect organisational characteristics. Many branch plants are concerned purely with production, and functions such as buying and selling are dealt with from head office which cannot be expected to show much favour to any particular region. In some cases branches are established purely as feeder plants to other factories belonging to the company, so that right from the start there is little opportunity for local impact. In other cases branches are more self-contained, with their own product line and purchasing and selling functions. In this they are similar to transferred companies and in both cases the opportunity for and likelihood of local linkages is greater (Northern Region Strategy Team, 1977b).

In some cases the low level of impact of branch plants may reflect the narrowness of the economy of the receiving region which has both few firms capable of supplying materials (James, 1964) or of using the products made by the migrant firms. In such a situation only those firms which do not need local linkages or can be self-contained will be prepared to move to such regions. In time this situation may change and as the economy becomes more diversified potential linkages will appear. It may also take time for firms to develop possible linkages so that the full impact of industrial movement may take many years to appear.

Factors in Industrial Movement

One of the most important factors causing industrial movement is the expansion of the firm resulting in shortage of space on an existing site (Keeble, 1968; Expenditure Committee, 1973b; Northcott, 1977). Expansion may also result in a shortage of labour which encourages movement. Given this latter factor it is not surprising that the rate of industrial movement reflects the growth rate of the national economy with recessions revealing low rates of movement. Had Britain had a faster rate of national economic growth in the recent past there would have been more industrial movement and the possibility of more movement to the assisted regions. Not surprisingly the bulk of the firms involved in industrial movement are drawn from the so-called growth industries including mechanical and electrical engineering, vehicles and chemicals (Board of Trade, 1968). However, even slow-growing or declining industries may be forced to move by a shortage of labour as has been seen in the hosiery and clothing industries of the East Midlands, Yorkshire and London regions, which have moved to areas with a supply of women workers.

Normally firms that have to move will look for a site as near as possible to their existing one. This will facilitate the transfer of labour and where a branch is envisaged it will enable management to oversee both parent and branch. This type of local movement, particularly from the inner city to the suburbs, has always been very common, but since 1945 government policies have resulted in much more longer-distance industrial movement. IDC policies severely limited the possibilities of firms obtaining suburban or nearby sites, whilst the incentives offered have encouraged firms to consider long-distance movement. As we have seen, the rate of inter-regional movement has considerably increased during periods of strong regional policy. Although firms have been persuaded to move over longer distances, this does not mean that distance is irrelevant. Keeble (1972) has attempted to model movement from London and the West Midlands, the two principal exporting areas and, for the period 1945–65, he found that flow was proportional to number unemployed and inversely related to distance. This may explain why Wales and the North West (including Merseyside), the two nearest DAs to the West Midlands and London, have been the most successful in attracting migrant industry jobs.

In spite of incentives, long-distance migration to the assisted areas has not been popular with industrial firms and various attempts have been made to circumvent controls.

Before 1960 when controls were tightened up, it was sometimes possible to convert buildings such as warehouses to manufacturing whilst applications for factory extensions in the South East nearly always underestimated the increase in employment expected (Holmans, 1964). Although the South East and Midlands have been regarded as congested regions where controls would be tight, there have always been areas within them where development was possible: these areas have included new towns, expanded towns and other towns, like the naval bases, where actual or potential unemployment was a threat to the local economy. Accordingly, both these areas and the South West and East Anglia regions have become popular destinations for industrial migration since the 1950s, combining proximity to core areas with what are perceived as environmentally attractive locations. The effect of post-war planning controls in conjunction with improved transport would appear to have been to push industrial development away from close proximity to London and outwards to the remoter parts of south and east England.

The Cost of Industrial Movement

Critics of regional policy have argued that forcing firms to move long distances against their better judgement will raise costs and make firms less efficient than would be the case than if they had had a free choice. To test this assertion a number of studies have been made. Luttrell (1962) compared production costs in the new location with the old one and found that, whilst there were settling-in costs, after a short period, usually not more than three years, costs in both locations were about the same. Hague and Newman (1952) and Hague and Dunning (1954) carried out a similar enquiry but by comparing the costs at the new plant with what they would have been at the old location had expansion occurred: they too found that after a period there was on average little difference. Luttrell also considered management costs and experience and found that in the case of small branches which relied on management from the parent, close proximity was advisable, whereas the larger plant, with its own management, could function satisfactorily at a distance from its parent. These studies suggested that for most industries and for most areas of Britain, carefully planned long-distance industrial migration was both feasible and without additional costs. Later studies have also come to the same conclusion (Cameron and Clark, 1966; Trotman-Dickenson, 1961 and Expenditure Committee, 1973b). The only contrary evidence has come from the motor car manufacturers who claim additional costs from moving to Development Areas, although admitting that part of the explanation may lie in lower than planned productivity in these plants (Expenditure Committee, 1973).

Movement in the Service Sector

Until the early 1960s efforts to steer jobs to the assisted regions were confined almost entirely to the manufacturing sector, still considered the basis of local employment. By then it was realised that employment in the service sector was growing more rapidly and that not all parts of it were necessarily market orientated. In particular, the office sector, then showing rapid expansion in London, was considered a possible source of mobile jobs. The government took a lead in dispersing its own activities and encouraged the private sector to do the same by setting up the location of Offices Bureau, though with much less success.

The first government dispersal of offices took place in 1940 in anticipation of enemy air attack on London and resulted in moves to places like Bath, Blackpool, Colwyn Bay and Harrogate where accommodation was readily available in large hotels (Hammond, 1967). At the end of the war most of the offices returned to London, but some stayed including part of the Admiralty at Bath and some National Savings offices at Lytham St Annes. After the war a programme for the dispersal of government offices was prepared but the only significant move to materialise was a large new office for the then Ministry of Pensions and National Insurance located at Newcastle in 1946. By the mid-1970s this was employing over 10,000.

The renewed interest in office dispersal of the early 1960s resulted in a 1963 report to the government by Sir Gilbert Flemming which suggested that 20,000 jobs should be dispersed from the London area. Later it was decided that wherever possible government offices should be established outside London and that preference should be given to the assisted areas. As a result of these initiatives it was estimated that by 1973 33,000 posts had been dispersed and that a further 17,000 were in the pipeline for dispersal (Hardman Report, 1973). Among the larger moves were those of the National Savings Bank to Durham and Glasgow, of the Inland Revenue to Bootle and Manchester and of the establishment of the Vehicle Licensing Centre at Swansea. Whilst the assisted areas did well in this exercise, the outer parts of the South East, including places like Basingstoke and Southend, also benefited while Yorkshire and the two midland regions received only a few dispersed posts.

Another review by Sir Henry Hardman in 1973 considered headquarters staff and recommended a further dispersal of 31,000 posts (Hardman Report, 1973). However only just over half of these were to be moved to the assisted areas, a proportion which the Labour government of 1974 considered was too low. Consequently a revised scheme was proposed in 1977 in which nearly 87 per cent of the dispersed posts were to be moved to the assisted areas. The new Conservative government of 1979 immediately reviewed these plans and announced a massive cut in dispersed posts to only 5,000 and an expected saving of over £200 million out of a forecast cost of £250 million. Only two large moves survive: the Ministry of Defence to Glasgow (1,400 posts) and the Manpower Services Agency to Sheffield (1,500 posts). Apart from the desire to save public money, the rationale for the decision was the new planned fall in the number of civil servants and consequent lack of a need for extra office space. However, for the assisted areas (as defined in 1978) it meant approximately 18,000 fewer government jobs by the late 1980s.

TABLE 40 Destination of Offices Relocating from London, 1963–77

	Jobs Decentralised		*Annual Rate*		*Decentralised Jobs*	
	1963–71	*1971–77*	*1963–71*	*1971–77*	*1963–71*	*1971–77*
					Per Cent of Total	
South East (excl Gt London)	23,798	38,048	2975	7610	33.6	51.3
Greater London	32,988	16,004	4123	3201	46.5	21.6
South East	56,786	54,052	7098	10810	80.1	72.9
East Anglia	1,126	4,380	141	876	1.6	5.9
South West	3,561	8,087	445	1617	5.0	10.9
West Midlands	148	849	19	170	0.2	1.1
East Midlands	2,845	1,443	356	289	4.0	1.9
Yorkshire and Humberside	3,373	753	422	151	4.8	1.0
North West	1,656	3,385	207	677	2.3	4.6
North	1,201	526	150	105	1.7	0.7
Wales	73	344	9	69	0.1	0.5
Scotland	216	330	27	66	0.3	0.4
N. Ireland	21	0	3	0	—	—
Total	70,921	74,194	8865	14839	100.0	100.0

Source: Location of Offices Bureau (quoted in Marquand, 1978)
Note: These are only of moves known to the LOB

There are no comprehensive records of private office movement, but the previous discussion of business concentration and the development of head offices (p. 159) would suggest that over the whole period there was some movement of activity towards London. Coupled with the growth of activity in London this encouraged the government to establish the Location of Offices Bureau in 1963 with the object of encouraging movement out of the capital and particularly its central area. (The Location of Offices Bureau was axed by the new Conservative Government in the Summer of 1979). Their records provide evidence of movement from what is undoubtedly the most important originating centre (Table

40). These movements show a strong distance decay factor with a large number of short-distance moves and only a few long-distance movements (Daniels, 1969). Three-quarters of the moves have been inside the South East either to outer London or the rest of the South East. Just outside the South East towns like Bournemouth, Poole, Swindon, Bristol, Cheltenham, Ipswich and Peterborough have proved very attractive to office firms. Beyond this South East periphery zone there have been few moves although interesting ones include Barclays Bank to Knutsford (near Manchester) and the Midland Bank to Sheffield. The four remotest regions have received few jobs.

The explanation for this pattern is to be found in terms of labour, accommodation and communication costs. Office rents, rates and salaries all decrease from central London up to a distance of about forty miles from the capital. Thereafter these costs remain about the same in all regions, although they may rise in the centres of the provincial capitals (Rhodes and Kan, 1971). However decentralised offices usually need to maintain contact with London either via telephone or, where face-to-face contact is necessary, by travel (Goddard, 1975). These costs will increase with distance from London and the extent of these costs will vary from one company to another. Bringing these two factors together it can be seen that the greatest advantage to a firm often lies in moving to the outer parts of the South East or to adjacent regions. To encourage firms to move further would need some form of incentive. Since 1973 the government has provided building, removal and training grants but it is too early to evaluate the results.

The main private office movements have taken place in insurance and banking. Frequently a company is faced with a choice of either moving a whole section including senior personnel or merely moving routine office work. The choice will be partly determined by the nature of the activity and partly by company preference (Rhodes and Kan, 1971, 29). Both policies have been pursued, but the combination ensures that the areas outside London tend to have a higher proportion of routine and clerical jobs whilst London retains a higher proportion of senior management.

Since the late 1930s there has been a considerable policy-assisted movement of jobs to the assisted regions without which these regions would be considerably worse off. However, there has been insufficient movement to reduce unemployment and income inequalities between the regions or to give the regions a self-sustaining economy. Further, the movement has helped the trend to a branch plant economy in these regions involving much low level routine work, whilst the higher level work and decision making remains in the London area.

CHAPTER TEN

Location Factors in Regional Development

In Chapter 1 it was suggested that one of the main themes of regional development studies was the role played by economic advantage including the traditional location factors of access to materials, markets, labour and capital. Although it is sometimes suggested that these factors are no longer important since the spatial margins of profitability are now so wide that many firms have a choice of several regions, such conclusions need to be critically examined and it is the aim of this chapter to consider the available evidence. Even if the traditional location factors are found not to be very important it would be surprising if they had not played some role, albeit a small one, in the process of regional development.

Transport Costs

Transport costs can be expected to be decisive in industrial location when they vary significantly according to the location of the firm and when they form a large component of the cost structure of the firm. Transport costs have been found to be most important for those industries dealing with one or two raw materials, often resulting in location at source or at a port, and in those industries where the relative cost of transport of the final product is great, as occurs when it is of low value and bulky, resulting in location at or near market. Over time it is thought that both the real and relative cost of transport has been falling, freeing many industries from the constraints imposed by transport costs. At the same time many new industries are of the type least affected by transport costs since they use many different materials, most of which are already at least partially processed, so that there is little pull to material sources. These ideas would suggest that an increasing majority of industries are not fundamentally affected by considerations of transport costs. Although these ideas are widely held (Brown, 1969, 778) conclusive evidence is not easily available. Information from the Censuses of Production has to be interpreted carefully, but one estimate for 1963 suggested that transport costs represented 3.5 per cent of the value of sales (Edwards, 1970). Gudgin (1978) estimated that in 1968 for 75 per cent of British industry the transport element formed less than 3 per cent and for 95 per cent less than 5 per cent of the total costs. Most of these costs are likely to be concerned with the distribution of the finished product rather than with procurement of the materials, many of which, particularly those which come from other manufacturing companies, are delivered at uniform prices throughout the country (Cook, 1967). Further, within this figure a high proportion of the total is fixed cost, and less than half varies according to the distance over which goods are carried (Chisholm, 1972). Consequently, for most industries extra transport costs for peripheral locations are unlikely to add more than one per cent to total costs (Gudgin, 1978, 23). Using the iron foundry as an example, and assuming that firms were aiming for at least 10 per cent profit, Taylor (1970) has shown that firms could serve the West Midland market from a distance of up to 644 miles. Firms in the core market area stretching from the London region to Lancashire/Yorkshire and including the Severn estuary (Clark, 1966) will therefore only have a small advantage over more peripheral regions and this may be offset by other lower costs such as labour. Edwards (1975) has shown that peripheral regions such as Scotland, the North and East Anglia do have slightly higher transport costs, but that this is generally unlikely to add more than 1 per cent of sales value. (See also Chisholm and O'Sullivan, 1973.) The increase in energy prices at the end of the 1970s could reverse the trend, but it is too early to make a precise assessment.

Location by raw material source is confined to a relatively

few industries which are mainly concerned with processing materials such as metal ores, rocks for chemicals, clays and foods often involving a considerable loss of weight in manufacture. Most of these industries are of long standing and have experienced few locational changes since World War I. The growth of iron and steel manufacture at Corby and Scunthorpe in the inter-war period reflects the pull of low-grade iron ores, whilst the development of food processing industries such as sugar beet (Watts, 1971), canning and freezing in the eastern counties also reflects the pull of materials (Moseley and Sant, 1977, 72). More recently in the 1950s and 1960s there has been a movement of the animal foodstuffs industry away from ports to a more scattered locational pattern responding both to the increased use of home grown materials and the need to be closer to the market. These examples may be extended to include those industries located at ports to process imported raw materials, although in many cases such industries are also near markets. One of the most spectacular developments has been the growth of oil refining at Milford Haven, although being a capital intensive industry the total number employed is small (John, B.S., 1976). Elsewhere there has been some growth of the iron and steel industry (Llanwern works in South Wales) and the fertiliser industry at ports though this may not reflect inter-regional movement of the industry.

Market Orientation

In a few industries where distribution costs vary significantly, factories are located near the market: among traditional industries in this category are bread and flour, confectionery, brewing and soft drinks; other industries near markets include clothing and printing, where contact between producer and consumer are necessary. In the past such industries as soap, paint and biscuit manufacture were close to the market, but falling transport costs and economies of scale have enabled firms to serve national markets. Among growing industries since World War I printing, packaging (paper, glass, wood or plastic), and products for the building industry have tended to be market orientated.

Firms in the core area of Britain have only a slight advantage in serving the national market, but it has been suggested that for consumer goods the national distribution of population may not always be a good guide to market location. In particular the South East with its high per capita incomes will have a significantly greater pull in the luxury goods market. Since many present-day consumer goods industries started as luxury articles it is suggested that many new industries will develop in the South East because of market orientation, thus accounting for the vitality of the region in the twentieth century. Since this proposition has received much emphasis in studies of British regional development it is desirable to examine it in more detail.

The wealth and cultural role of London in British life has been reflected in its industry for many centuries (Hall, P., 1962; Martin, 1966): among traditional industries attracted by the market have been fashion clothing, furs, watches and clocks, musical instruments, jewellery, precious metals and printing. Only the latter, which is also linked with London's commercial and administrative roles, has been a twentieth-century growth industry. More recently industries like pharmaceuticals, cosmetics, radio/TV, gramophone, domestic appliances, stationers' goods, and cars have become important in the South East and it is suggested that they are here because of the market. Whilst it would be true to say that the market has been one factor in their location, there are other factors which may also explain their location. Many of the firms in these trades were established by foreign companies which, as we have seen, showed a preference for the South East in the inter-war period. The electrical trades evolved out of pre-1914 activities, the location of which in the South East was connected with the role of government, which may here be considered as a special market of the region. Finally, the motor vehicle trades were obviously drawn to the London market, though this was by no means essential as is shown by the strength of the West Midlands industry. The wealth of the

London region has clearly acted as a stimulus for local entrepreneurs and for the immigration of firms, but it would be too simple to see this as the sole factor in the location of these industries, rather than one of several factors which gives the South East a competitive edge over the rest of the country.

Outside such consumer industries there are many firms supplying other industries. Frequently they are located near to their markets, although it is unlikely that transport cost factors are the cause. Proximity to a need has often prompted the establishment of the firm, while industrial purchasers often prefer the convenience of a nearby supplier. In the nineteenth century agricultural engineering, textile engineering and mining engineering all developed close to their markets, although firms in these trades later came to serve world-wide markets. The growth of industry in the Midlands and the South East since World War I has inevitably meant the simultaneous development of many ancillary industries supplying goods like components, machine tools and packaging.

Finally under market orientation should be mentioned the growth of services. As has been seen in Chapter 6 these have been the biggest growth industries of the twentieth century and a significant proportion of them are market orientated.

The Attraction of Labour

The location of economic activities is often affected by spatial variations in the cost and supply of labour. Since these two factors are clearly related, it would be expected that where labour demand is high, and unemployment is low, wages will also be high and vice-versa. This correlation is found to be broadly but not exactly correct as is shown in Table 41.

The South East and West Midlands have the highest wages, and Northern Ireland the lowest, as could be expected, but regions like the South West and Yorkshire are ranked lower whilst Wales is higher than would be predicted on the basis of unemployment levels. The discrepancies are

TABLE 41 Average weekly wages (£) for full-time manual workers over 21 in 1973

	All Trades	*Manufacturing*	*Mining & Quarrying*
South East	42.30	43.21	39.04
East Anglia	39.05	39.30	42.93
South West	38.85	40.24	38.02
West Midlands	42.03	42.70	44.18
East Midlands	39.38	39.47	46.08
Yorkshire and Humberside	39.06	39.37	37.98
North West	40.28	40.61	42.48
North	40.05	40.08	39.66
Wales	40.05	41.76	38.52
Scotland	40.35	41.14	39.74
Northern Ireland	36.37	36.90	34.33
UK	40.92	41.52	39.86

Source: Regional Statistics 1975, Standard Regions

partly explained on the basis of the structure of industries, so that where a high-paying industry is important in the structure of the regional economy the average wage level is raised (Brown, 1972, 233). The remainder of the discrepancy can be explained on the basis of the relative strength of trade unionism in different regions. In Yorkshire (outside coal-mining), the South West and East Anglia trade unions are generally weak and consequently wages not as high as in regions of similar labour demand, whereas in Wales manual wages are above what could be expected. Both aspects illustrate the effects of trade unions since in the first case trade unions are able to obtain national rates of pay for industries even though labour demand conditions vary in different regions. The consequence of these actions is to reduce any advantage which an industry may have in seeking peripheral regions. This may apply even more so within industries and within firms, since often firms are bound to pay the same rates, at least for well unionised grades, throughout the country. During the 1970s percentage differentials between regions have fallen further reflecting the factors discussed above and possibly the influence of incomes policy (Department of Employment Gazette, April 1979).

Employers are not only interested in the wage levels in a region but also the productivity of labour, since together they combine to give 'efficiency wages'. The productivity of labour is difficult to measure, being much affected by the capital equipment employed, so that a region dominated by capital intensive industry is likely to have a high output per head (Leser, 1950). The incidence of strikes clearly affects productivity and, since this aspect often receives press publicity, it may play an important role in determining how employers perceive different regions. Strikes are more common in certain industries, such as coal-mining and the motor vehicle industry, and also in large plants but when the statistics are adjusted for these factors certain areas such as Merseyside and Clydeside still appear to have a higher incidence of strikes (Department of Employment Gazette, November 1976). Regional differences in the incidence of strikes extend back many years as revealed in the clear contrast in the 1920s and 1930s between the older industrial areas and the South East and Midlands (Daly and Atkinson, 1940). More recently it has been suggested that significant differences in the incidence of strikes have arisen between the large cities and small towns (Massey, 1979). Although these differences may have arisen through the understandable insecurity felt by workers in depressed urban environments, they clearly make them less attractive for investment.

The fact that wage rates imperfectly reflected labour market conditions, coupled with the government's desire to create jobs in the Development Areas, was one reason for the introduction by the Labour Government of the Regional Employment Premium in 1967, which remained in operation, albeit declining in real terms, until the end of 1976. This gave a labour subsidy to all manufacturing jobs in the Development Areas. Moore and Rhodes (1973, 1976a and 1977, 76) calculated that between 1967 and 1976 REP diverted between 30,000 and 60,000 jobs to the Development Areas, half of which were created by immigrant firms to the areas and half by indigenous firms, including those jobs which would have been lost without a subsidy. Some of these latter jobs were in plants involved in company rationalisation proposals where the REP subsidy helped to tilt the balance in favour of the plant's retention (Massey, 1979). The removal of the subsidy at the end of 1976 could result in between 17,000 and 35,000 jobs being lost over a four year period plus additional indirect employment effects.

The importance of the availability of labour arises from its relative immobility. It might be thought that labour is mobile and so can move to where jobs are available; as we have seen this migration has been an important feature of regional development. However, the mobility of labour varies from one segment of the labour force to another, and so particular types of labour may have had greater influence on the location of employment than others.

Married women workers are particularly immobile and as we have seen this is a major reason why female activity rates vary significantly from area to area. Cheap female labour is important in a number of industries in which labour costs are important in the cost structure so, not surprisingly, these industries have shown a relative shift towards the peripheral regions with labour surpluses. This shift can be understood by reference to local labour markets where female labour has become fully utilised, necessitating the opening of branches in areas, such as coal-mining and heavy industry districts, where reserves are available. Examples can be seen in the clothing industry with movements from Yorkshire to the North West and North, in hosiery from the main East Midland urban centres to coal-mining and rural areas (Rake, 1974), in footwear from Street in Somerset to many other small towns in the South West (Spooner, 1972; Rake, 1975), and in electrical consumer goods from Cambridge to other towns in East Anglia (Moseley and Sant, 1977).

Skilled manual labour has generally been in short supply throughout the period and it might be thought that its availability would have had an influence on industrial development. This might have been so in the growing engineering industries where, particularly in the pre-World War II period, such skills were also limited to certain geographical areas. However, the necessities of war broke down some of the traditional demarcation lines, simplified many tasks and led to a dispersal of industries, as already described, with the consequence that engineering skills became more spatially widespread. The continued mechanisation of manufacturing has resulted in fewer skilled manual workers being required, thus lessening this factor's importance in regional development.

In theory this de-skilling process might have been expected to affect all regions equally but in practice it has re-emphasised the divisions of the country. When firms have opened branches in the assisted areas they have taken the opportunity to move the manufacture of those products where the production processes have been de-skilled. In part this was necessary as often skilled labour was not available, but it had the additional advantage to the firm in that low-skilled labour received low pay (Townsend, Smith and Johnson, 1978). Meanwhile the firm kept its skilled labour at the parent plant where newer products were developed. Ernest (later Lord) Hives, managing director of Rolls Royce was one of the first to describe this process in 1939 (Lloyd, 1978, 189). He described the parent Derby plant as a 'development factory' where aero-engines were designed and developed with prototype production. Skilled men were employed as modifications were constantly being made as the 'engineering bugs' were cleared. In contrast the new shadow works at Crewe and Glasgow were described as 'production factories' employing mass production techniques and less skilled labour. This differentiation has often been recognised when firm rationalisation has taken place following mergers with plants being retained for low and high skilled work (Massey, 1979, Massey and Morgan, 1978 and 1979). The results of this process is a spatial dichotomisation of skills with highly skilled work being found in the South East and to a lesser extent in the East and West Midlands and semi-skilled and unskilled work dominating the assisted areas in the north and west.

Although the evidence is limited it does provide some confirmation for Wilbur Thompson's (1969) filter-down process of industrial location discussed in Chapter 1.

At the same time industry has become more dependent on the skills of managers and scientists, and although in theory these groups are mobile they appear to have a distinct preference for the southern parts of the country, similar to the pattern revealed by sixth formers' preferences (Gould and White, 1974, 82). This is clearly seen in research and development establishments where it has often been stated by firms that their laboratories were located with a view to attracting the necessary skilled scientists. It also applies to management in general where it has sometimes been reported that firms have had difficulty in persuading their senior personnel to move to Development Area branches.

Overall there is little evidence to suggest that the supplies of labour in the Development Areas and the lower wage rates have on their own proved a great attraction to employers, the only exception to this statement relating to female labour. If this is due to the labour market imperfectly reflecting demand conditions then the attempt at regional devaluation through the introduction of REP in 1967 suggests that even if there was no difficulty here, the number of jobs attracted to the Development Areas would be small. Although employers often claim that one of the attractions responsible for movement to the assisted areas is labour availability, we have seen that in the absence of government regional policy there have been few such moves.

The Availability of Capital

Opinion about the effect of the availability of capital on regional development is divided. On the one hand there are those who suggest that since there has been a national banking system since the end of World War I capital must be equally mobile and available at the same cost in all parts of the country and therefore has had no influence on regional development. Against this argument others see the sinister hand of London stockbrokers who would prefer to put money into factories within the South East rather than into works or mills in other parts of the country. Not unexpectedly it is difficult to find evidence to support such a proposition. In the nineteenth and early twentieth century, local investment was important and it was not uncommon for the successful industrialist to invest his profits in some promising nearby company. The depression of the older industrial areas in the north and west of the country would naturally have had repercussions on such local investment whilst in the South East and Midlands the process would have continued to the benefit of these regions. These processes would probably still have operated in the inter-war period though less likely in the post-war period when death duties and wider share ownership have reduced the influence of local wealth.

Whether capital was available in some regions more than others or not, regional policy in the post-war period has attempted to make it more accessible in the assisted areas, as our discussion on the evolution of regional policy has shown. Since 1945 loans have been available in the Development Areas, whilst since 1963 cash grants or investment allowances have been offered (Bird and Thirlwall, 1967 and Thomas, 1971). There are two effects of this capital assistance; firstly indigenous firms are encouraged to invest since marginal projects are now made profitable, and secondly firms in other parts of the country are encouraged to move to the assisted areas to obtain the incentives. Moore and Rhodes (1976a) calculate that capital incentives are the second most important tool of regional policy, after IDC controls, accounting for one-quarter of the jobs diverted to these areas. The use of capital incentives has led to some criticism, suggesting that capital intensive industry provides few jobs, which is what the assisted areas need. In some recent cases the cost per job provided has been exceedingly high, one example of a pharmaceutical plant in Scotland (Roche) quoted in 1978 being £100,000 per job; and inevitably there has been the suggestion that there should be a limit on the capital per job provided. Given the advantage for capital intensive industries in moving to assisted areas, a shift of such industries might well be noticed. This is difficult to test since the industry most affected, chemicals, was already well established in these areas before the incentives were introduced (Chisholm, 1970). One clear example of such a shift has been the man-made fibres industry. In 1931 Northern Ireland, Scotland, Wales and the North had 21 per cent of the employment but by 1971 this had risen to 44 per cent, the shift to Northern Ireland being particularly important. In the chemical industry the effect of capital incentives is seen in the continued growth of the industry of Teesside and Grangemouth, and also in the development of the Baglan Bay complex in South Wales. Outside the Development Areas there are few such complexes and those that exist, such as at Fawley and Severnside, have grown slowly (ICI, 1973).

The Availability of Industrial Sites and Premises

Usually it might be expected that the supply of industrial sites and premises in any area would reflect demand in that locality and therefore that adequate facilities would be available in all areas. Further, since the cost of premises is only a small part of the cost structure of the firm it might be thought that geographical variations in price would not be sufficient to influence decisions. Where premises are not available for renting a firm could construct its own factory and so choose the locality for its plant. However, it could be that the market mechanism for the supply of industrial sites and premises does not work perfectly and that some areas are better provided for than others. Industries which are relatively footloose may be influenced in their location by the supply of these facilities. Even though the cost of premises in the cost structure of a firm may be small, the convenience of finding premises easily may draw firms to certain areas. The Board of Trade Surveys of Industrial Development for 1935, 1936 and 1937 asked industrialists the main reason for their location and it is perhaps significant that in half the cases the reply was convenience of premises. Many new firms wish to rent premises to save capital, so that their ready availability may be a significant factor in location.

Today the provision of rented industrial sites and premises whether by private or public bodies is taken for granted, but this is very much a feature of the post-World War II period. In the inter-war period there were only a few private industrial estate companies, and these were mainly in the South East. The pioneer industrial estate established at Trafford Park, Manchester, in 1896 provided sites beside the recently completed Manchester Ship Canal. Shortly afterwards, in 1903, the first garden city was established at Letchworth, north of London, featuring industrial estates in a planned town. In the 1920s Welwyn Garden City and the Slough Industrial Estates were developed and at the same time new arterial roads were being built around London: the Great West Road, Western Avenue, North Circular Road, Great Cambridge Road, Eastern Avenue, Sidcup bypass, Purley Way and Kingston bypass, which provided good industrial sites and quickly attracted numerous firms. Close to these roads new industrial estates were developed, one of the most important being at Park Royal. The great activity of the London region at this time contrasted with the lack of activity elsewhere in the country, but to what extent this was the cause of London's dynamism or merely reflected it, is difficult to say. By the late 1930s the need for industrial estates was widely recognised and the larger municipal authorities like Liverpool and Manchester began to develop such estates. In the Special Areas the government began the development of the Team Valley (Gateshead), Treforest (Wales) and Hillington (Glasgow) estates, which became a feature of the post-war period.

Since 1945, local authorities have been active zoning land for industry and in some cases developing estates. The government has sponsored many industrial estates in the Development Areas and the ready availability of advance factories with their subsidised rents have attracted many firms to them. Elsewhere the government has developed New Towns, particularly in the South East which contain well-planned industrial estates. There have also been several large private firms active in developing industrial estates in many parts of the country. There has certainly been an adequate supply of premises in the peripheral regions whilst in the South East and Midlands the supply has deliberately been limited by IDC controls.

Vacant factories provide another source of supply for the industrialist. Traditionally the inner areas of large cities have provided many old premises where new small firms could obtain cheap premises. The redevelopment of these areas since the late 1950s has reduced the supply, but often larger premises farther out are being subdivided for letting. Another major source of old premises has been in regions like the North West and Yorkshire where the declining textile industry has left vacant mills at low prices. One disadvantage of these premises is that they are multi-storied, whereas modern industrialists prefer a horizontal layout. In the case of the North West nearly one half of the jobs provided in industrial movement in the period 1945–64 were in existing premises (Board of Trade, 1969), although it cannot be necessarily concluded from this that vacant premises were either the sole or major factor for jobs coming to the region.

The role of changing technology is important in determining the value of industrial sites and premises. Thus even when a firm is maintaining its output levels it may find that its site and premises are no longer adequate, and a move to a new site is necessary where new methods can be introduced. At this point regional policy may intervene and ensure that at least some plants are diverted from regions where development is tightly controlled. Old plants may be reoccupied by new firms, but in other cases may be demolished. Individual moves may have no noticeable effect on the regional economy but cumulatively over many years the effects may be considerable. Within these regions the effects will be most clearly experienced in the older industrial districts such as the inner areas of large cities, but may well be beginning to affect the inter-war industrial suburbs. The decline of industrial employment in Greater London and the West Midlands conurbation are examples of this process and illustrate the delayed effect on regional economies of control measures (Dennis, 1978; Stone, 1977).

The supply of new and vacant premises, demand conditions and government restrictions are responsible for geographical variations in industrial rents. The highest rents are found in London, followed by the rest of southern England. The gradient away from London is continued, the lowest rents being found in Wales and northern England. As with office rents, there is a clear advantage in moving away from the South East but no great advantage in long-distance movement.

The Role of Local Promotion

Local promotion is not a location factor as such but is considered here since one of its main functions is publicity and provision of information about the advantages possessed by particular areas. It may also involve the provision of facilities including industrial estates which have been referred to earlier in the chapter.

Examples of local promotion can be found at least as early as the beginning of the century but in general it did not become important until the inter-war period when legislation enabled local authority expenditure on such activities to be increased. The depression heightened the need to attract industry encouraging local authorities either individually or jointly to start local promotion (Fogarty, 1947). Increasing unemployment in the 1960s caused a renewal of interest in this field with many local authorities establishing their own industrial development office. Not unexpectedly, both in the 1930s and more recently, the greatest activity has been in the areas most affected by industrial change—the north and west of the country (Camina, 1974).

The achievements of local promotion are difficult to evaluate. Promotional bodies naturally like to advertise new industrial investment in their areas, but it is difficult to distinguish between those developments which would have occurred anyway and those resulting from their efforts. Inevitably local promotion appears most successful in an expanding economy and in the assisted areas when regional policy has been strong. It is unlikely that on their own the inter-regional moves attracted merely through publicity would be large. However, within regions, and perhaps within the assisted areas group, it is possible that the direction of investment has been affected by the scale of local promotion and the helpfulness of local authorities.

Conclusion

The factors discussed in this chapter have individually played a minor role in the process of regional development, but they are not without significance. In the inter-war period the South East and Midland regions have benefited from centrality and proximity to the wealthiest markets of the country. They also benefited from resources of skilled labour and a ready supply of premises, while economic success was no doubt self-perpetuating through the further supply of capital. Some advantages, such as centrality, remain whilst the ease of attracting highly qualified personnel has become a significant advantage today. In contrast the peripheral regions appear to have had few advantages except those given by regional policy. The one expected advantage of an adequate supply of relatively low-cost labour has proved less effective than thought, largely as a result of trade union activity, but even without them labour would not have been the equilibrating mechanism that theory suggests. In the inter-war period, industrial decline was self-perpetuating through reduced capital supplies and the poor psychological climate for investment failing to produce modern industrial premises and sites, but in the post-war period regional policy has turned these factors to the advantage of the assisted regions.

CHAPTER ELEVEN

An Interpretation of Regional Development

In previous chapters the various aspects of regional development have been considered and in this chapter an attempt will be made to bring these different strands together. This interpretation will be made first on the basis of historical development, secondly on the basis of present spatial characteristics, thirdly on the basis of theory and fourthly from the viewpoint of government intervention which has been a powerful force for much of the period.

The Evolution of Regions

By World War I the regions of the United Kingdom exhibited a considerable variety in their development. The industrial areas forming the cores of many of the regions of the north and west had experienced rapid growth in the previous fifty years whilst the rural zones of every region had experienced decline. Nevertheless, the London area also experienced rapid growth and remained, as always, the richest and most prosperous region of the country, a position derived from its role as the social, economic and administrative capital not only of the country but also of a vast empire and global trading system. It had a varied industrial base but excluded the heavier industries like iron and steel and also textiles. Because of the wealth of the region consumer-orientated industries were well developed. The role of government including defence created many jobs in London and the rest of the South East region. Already the beginnings of concentration of business were beginning to result in more head offices being found in London. Another trend, to become important later, was the establishment of research facilities, which, directed by the government, were already concentrated in the region and which were affecting the development of the aircraft and radio industries.

The London region thus entered the inter-war period with structure and trends in its favour. During this period the continued growth of consumer-based industries, of the radio and aircraft industries, of the concentration of head offices in London and of the emergence of research, all enabled the region to add to previous prosperity. Further the raising of tariffs on imported goods encouraged foreign firms to establish manufacturing plants in Britain and these were heavily concentrated in the South East. All these trends produced a spiral of growth which encouraged more growth through the process of cumulative causation. The growing infrastructure of roads, industrial estates and the provision of capital all favoured this whilst the regional prosperity of industry provided the right psychological climate to encourage more new company formation. Employment growth attracted labour from all over the country and particularly from Wales. Although much of this labour was unskilled it was probably young and able and ready to be trained for the new industries of the twentieth century. Industrial movement to the South East was not important although the movement of Ford from Manchester to London was not without significance. This, like the growth of foreign firms, may have partly been encouraged by the region's proximity to Europe, an advantage which has been of enduring importance to the region.

The industrial core of the West Midlands region also entered the inter-war period with a structure favourable for growth. In the previous thirty years its industries had made an important evolution from the manufacture of metal parts to the production of engineering goods (Allen, 1927). These included cycles, motor vehicles and electrical goods for which there was a growing demand. Its old metal working industries continued to supply components to firms both inside and outside the region. This growth environment encouraged the formation of many new companies drawing on the existing entrepreneurial talent of the region.

The economy of the East Midlands at the end of World War I superficially looked less favourable for growth containing both coal-mining and textiles. However the coalfields were not highly dependent on exports and the mining conditions were favourable for low-cost production so that during the 1920s expansion in the Nottinghamshire concealed coalfield continued. Similarly hosiery and knitwear in the region differed from other textile industries like cotton not being dependent on exports and actually experiencing growth in this period. Existing activities, including the footwear industry, therefore remained buoyant and encouraged related industries including engineering. Additionally, and once again apparently against the trends, the region attracted some new activities including the expansion of the iron and steel industry on the Jurassic iron ore fields at Corby (Northamptonshire) and Scunthorpe (Lincolnshire).

The Yorkshire region shared some of the characteristics of the East Midlands with an expanding coalfield and a textile industry only slightly affected by decline. Outside these regions most of the rest of the country suffered from the run down of industries which reached its nadir in the depression of 1929–1932. This decline was caused by the loss of exports which had been very important for areas like South Wales, the North West, the North East and west central Scotland. The economies of these regions had been very much dominated by these activities, and although there were some growth points, these could do little to offset the effects of large-scale decline. Further the multiplier effects of decline affected other sectors providing locally produced goods and services. The effects of the loss of exports and the depression were most severely felt in Wales, the North, Scotland and Northern Ireland. Growth came to a halt and many communities experienced absolute decline with large-scale out-migration of the younger and more able to the more prosperous regions of the country. In spite of high unemployment there was hardly any industrial movement to these areas (before 1937), either from other parts of Britain or abroad. There was also a lack of indigenous growth in new activities. This was partly a result of the narrow base of many of the economies coupled with the fact that there were often no technological or marketing links with newer products. The depression also had an effect in limiting the amount of capital available for investment and a psychological one in discouraging new enterprise.

In contrast, while East Anglia and the South West were affected by the decline in agriculture and its multiplier effects, the South West benefited by the inflow of defence activity and also by the growth of engineering in the Bristol area.

During this period from 1919 to 1936 the basic spatial division of the country became established with a prosperous zone focused in the South East and the East and West Midlands contrasting with the rest of the country. Within the latter there were only a few points of growth such as Manchester, West Yorkshire and Teesside hardly compensating for the overall picture of stagnation and decline in these regions. In the absence of full employment and any government regional policy, the only equilibrating mechanism was the movement of people which did not solve the problems of the depressed regions and only exaggerated and emphasised their weaknesses.

As in previous sections the period immediately before World War II will be considered with that period. The economy was picking up slowly and this helped to revive the economy of the depressed regions and reduce unemployment. The beginnings of regional policies were also to be seen with the establishment of industrial estates and the direction of refugee European industrialists to these regions. The activities of the new regional promotional bodies may have also had some effect. At the same time the government was beginning to rearm, and in spite of some shadow factories being built in the West Midlands the emphasis was on the western half of the country, including many lagging regions.

World War II speeded up some of these trends including the revival of basic industries and the development of war industries, and added new features such as the direction of industries from London and the West Midlands to safer and more isolated communities generally in the western half of the country, but largely excluding Northern Ireland. The effect was to slow down the rate of growth in the core areas and raise the rate of growth in many of the assisted regions. Lasting results of such movements were the development of new labour skills, the introduction of women to employment and in some cases the permanent introduction of new industries. Whilst most of eastern England was unaffected by these trends, the establishment of airfields helped to broaden the economy and again introduce some lasting employment.

In the immediate post-war period, boom conditions and the new regional policy operated to the advantage of the assisted regions. A shortage of labour, housing and industrial premises (caused by war damage) in the London and West Midland urban areas coupled with the new industrial controls in these areas encouraged industrial movement to the assisted regions on a large scale and continued the process of diversifying their economies. The boom also benefited the basic industries of these regions which were kept working at a high level.

The 1950s was a period when some of the inter-war trends re-emerged. The new Conservative government relaxed regional policies so that industrial growth in the South East and Midlands forged ahead aided by favourable structure. In the South East there was also a revival of growth in business activities and overall the region benefited from the further growth in head offices and research and development. By contrast the older industrial regions of the north and west experienced slow growth. By the late 1950s, the staple industries were once again beginning to decline, but the effect of diversification of industry during the 1940s, with some continuing expansion, was to provide a cushion against absolute decline. Meanwhile the South West and East Anglia regions were showing further signs of being caught up in the outward moving prosperity of the South East.

Compared with the 1950s, the 1960s appear as a dynamic period with rapid changes in industrial structure and many other facets of economic life. The older industrial regions were threatened with growing unemployment by the renewed decline of their basic industries but the reactivation of regional policies under both Conservative and Labour governments increased industrial movement to these regions and stemmed both unemployment and out-migration. All the assisted regions benefited from these movements with Wales being the most successful. As before, growth was diverted from the South East and West Midlands, but the former region was able to maintain its growth through the continued expansion of services which benefited from the continued trend towards business concentration. Efforts to disperse offices began in 1963 but met with only limited success, and as with industrial dispersal many of the benefits went to the South West and East Anglia which proved far more attractive to businessmen than the assisted areas. At a time when the remoteness of many regions was being broken down by the improved roads and motorways and increased car ownership, this preference was perhaps a significant pointer to the future of regional development.

Since the mid-1960s a dispersal of activities has been noted (Keeble, 1976). The London and West Midland conurbations have been in decline whilst the metropolitan region, the area immediately around London, has been stagnating in employment terms. This is probably a consequence of the physical and industrial controls applied to these areas, plus the continued automation of industries found here resulting in reduced labour demands. Meanwhile there has been a decentralisation to the environmentally attractive and less controlled areas of East Anglia, the South West and parts of the East Midlands, where the countryside is being repopulated, made possible as a result of the improved forms of communication. At the same time the assisted regions have attracted industrial employment benefiting from the incentives offered by regional policies. These trends appear a reversal of previous ones which showed a concentration of growth in what were termed the core areas. The dispersal of growth in southern England is seen by some as part of a wider movement described in the United States as the 'sun belt' phenomenon in which footloose activities often employing highly paid workers are attracted to the environmentally favoured southern and western states. This movement, it is suggested, is symptomatic of the post-industrial society with its emphasis on highly skilled white collar jobs, on service employment, on increased leisure and the pursuit of consumption and amenity. The vanguard of this movement, the highly skilled, as suggested in Chapter 9, have already begun to exert an influence on the location of certain activities, accounting for the growth of the favoured areas. An alternative, but possibly complementary view, suggests that dispersal represents positive discrimination by firms against the large city and conurbation where labour costs are high and labour productivity low (including the consequences of trade union activity) towards more profitable locations.

The Spatial Division of the United Kingdom

The terms 'centre', or 'core', and 'periphery' have been widely used in describing major differences between the regions of Britain. These terms were introduced in the first chapter but without precise definition. Only now, when the various facets of regional development have been described and discussed, is it possible to attempt a definition of their meaning and use with respect to the regions of the United Kingdom. It will be obvious that the terms centre and core are not used in any simple geographical way to refer to those regions which are in the areal or population centre of the country. Rather they relate to a particular conception of spatial structure in which these regions play a central or core role. This may be understood in three ways: firstly the centre region or regions is where power, control, decision making and the ability to initiate change are concentrated; secondly the centre region is the area of greatest prosperity, highest incomes and where work earns the highest rewards; and thirdly it is the area of greatest growth whether of people, jobs or other activities (Friedmann, 1966 and 1972). The characteristics of peripheral regions are the opposite of these, and they are described as being in a colonial or dependent relationship with the centre. Using the three criteria suggested, it might be possible to derive three different sets of regions but clearly the intention is that they are merely three facets of the same process.

In addition to defining the centre/core periphery regions it is of interest to notice how they are changing in time. Are the differences between the core and periphery being reduced and/or is the core area expanding through a spread and trickling down process? As stated the model is relatively simple postulating only a two-category classification of regions. In reality we should expect some shading between these two positions which represent extremes on a continuum.

The term centre or core can only really be applied to the London region, which may be defined as the zone within a radius of about seventy miles from the capital. Here is the area of the country where control and decison making, whether in government or business, are concentrated. London has always been important in this respect but the evidence that has been presented in the earlier chapters suggests that this control has been increasing. This growth of power is a result of particular changes in society, which some might regard as inevitable, in which the government assumes ever increasing functions and business becomes more concentrated. This growing power over decision making has led to some reaction over what is regarded as over-centralisation most noticeably seen in the rise of nationalism in Scotland and Wales and in some, although perhaps exaggerated, demand for devolution. As the core area of the country the London region also has the greatest wealth, the widest economic structure, the highest skills, the greatest ability to innovate—as shown by the concentration of research and development—and the best facilities whether cultural, entertainment or educational.

Outside this core region may be seen a core-fringe zone divided into four parts. Of these parts the West Midlands has for most of this century appeared as the second most prosperous region in the country. Over a period of two hundred years it made a successful evolution from basic metal manufacture to the making of metal goods and thence to engineering, in the process creating a resource of manual and managerial skills (Allen, 1927). For much of this century its prosperity has been based on the growth and success of the motor vehicle and its associated industries, and it is perhaps the faltering performance of this industry since the mid-1960s which has affected the overall performance of the regional economy and given rise to concern (West Midlands County Council, 1975). Perhaps because of regional policy it has remained an economy based on manufacturing, and a fairly narrow base within that sector (Wood, 1976). It has a low proportion of employment in services and significantly has hardly attracted any office dispersal from the South East. Although in the numbers of company head offices and research and development establishments it has been more successful than other regions outside the South East, it has still suffered in competition with that region. Yet for all the concern that is now expressed, the West Midlands still has a great potentiality for growth, being well placed near the geographical centre of the country, with labour skills of many types and an ability to supply components needed by many other industries. A weakening of industrial development control would allow the region to use these advantages to create growth.

The South West region has been steadily improving its performance throughout the century. In part this has been the result of overspill or dispersal from the South East as witnessed in the early development of Salisbury Plain by the army. Its proximity to London and the continent coupled with improving communications have helped and will continue to help this trend. But in part its growing prosperity is caused by its other advantages including a warmer climate and attractive unspoilt scenery, both inland and coastal. More people are willing to move to this region than any other (Harris and Clausen, 1966) and this is demonstrated by the inflow of industry, offices and the retired. Although the western part of the region, particularly Cornwall, has suffered from some of the problems of the other peripheral regions such as high unemployment and remoteness, improving communications are easing the situation. Overall the region is rapidly growing in population and prosperity and appears assured of this in the future.

East Anglia shares some of the characteristics of the South West. It too has moved away from a dependence on agriculture and has gained defence establishments, industry, offices and retired people from the South East. It also is close to the London region and the continent and has an attractive environment. Similarly it is growing rapidly in population and prosperity, which is likely to continue, although it may be marginally less popular and attractive than the South West.

The final region of the core-fringe zone is the East Midlands. As befits a region with three focal urban centres, its economy has never been narrowly based. Earlier it could have been said to have had three basic industries in coal, hosiery and footwear, but fortunately for the region these have either remained stable or declined slowly so that the region has been able to diversify its economy without the problems of high unemployment. Like the West Midlands it has the advantages of geographical centrality and labour skills and in recent years has been able to attract overspill industry from the South East. Past and present performance would suggest continuing growth.

The remaining regions, often loosely called peripheral, can also be divided into two types. In a periphery-transition zone can be identified Wales, the North West and Yorkshire and Humberside.

The development of Wales in the last forty years is without doubt one of the most successful happenings of regional development. At the beginning of the period its economy was narrowly based on coal, metallurgy and agriculture. In the inter-war period these activities suffered terribly from depression and decline resulting in high unemployment accompanied by out-migration and actual population decline. During this period it must have lost many of its most able people. However, since the late 1930s it has been the most successful region in attracting industrial employment benefiting from its position as the nearest assisted area to the South East and West Midlands. This in-migration of industry has cushioned the continuing decline of jobs in its basic industries and together with retirement migration has enabled the population to increase faster than in other assisted regions. Yet in spite of these beneficial trends the economy has certain weaknesses. It is very much a branch plant economy with hardly any large Welsh firms, hardly any research and development, and dependent on regional policy for the continued attraction of industry. Whilst these policies continue, Wales can expect to be moderately successful, but without them its prosperity could easily slip back.

The North West has likewise had its successes as well as its problems. The traditional textile areas have suffered from the run-down of that industry but high levels of unemployment have been prevented, except on Merseyside, by the long period over which the decline has been spread, the high proportion of women in the industry (who might not register as unemployed), and the steady rate of net outward migration. The Manchester area has successfully diversified its industrial structure and its growth might have been greater but for regional policy which until the early 1970s diverted growth elsewhere through the operation of tight IDC control and the value of incentives in areas relatively close by. In contrast to the rest of the region, Merseyside has its own distinctive problems. Its high rate of unemployment is a result of a past high birth rate unaccompanied by sufficient net outward migration and the run down of basic activities like the docks. Although the area has proved attractive to industrial movement helped through assisted area status and proximity to southern and midland regions, some of this success has been lost in recent years through the poor industrial relations which result in lower productivity, and this may deter further investment in the future. Overall the tremendous nineteenth-century vitality of the region, which continued well into the twentieth century, has been slipping away harmed by government regional policies, poor industrial relations and the growing concentration of power in the South East.

The last region of the periphery-transition zone is Yorkshire and Humberside, which for long has appeared on the boundary between core and periphery. Like more southerly regions its unemployment has been low, partly a result of the stability or slow decline of the basic industries of coal, metallurgy and wool. In part this is a result of steady net outward migration similar to more northerly regions with which it has also shared a slow rate of growth. Like parts of the North West, its proximity to assisted areas has probably resulted in the diversion of some of its own industries as well as the loss of some that might otherwise have come to the area. However, although there are weaknesses in its economy, including the low proportion of growing industries, its position is not as serious as the truly peripheral regions to which we now turn.

The real peripheral regions are Northern England, Scotland and Northern Ireland which also happen to be the most remote from London. As could be expected they have suffered from the run down of traditional industries, net outward migration and high unemployment. Their remoteness has made it less easy for them to attract industries from the rest of the country and this has only partly been compensated by the inflow of foreign investment. They have become increasingly dependent on government largesse whether to provide basic services, build infrastructure or attract new activities, and cut-backs here could have serious repercussions on their economies.

Following on from these comments, it can be seen that in the period since World War I the role of the core and periphery regions has altered. In terms of the first two criteria of our definition, power and prosperity, the role of the London region has been steadily growing. It has also been extending outwards through a process of decentralisation from a region with a radius of twenty miles in the inter-war period to one of about seventy miles today. In the inter-war period the third criterion of growth was also satisfied. However since then, and particularly since the early 1960s, economic and physical planning policies have slowed down the growth of employment and distributed it more widely. This has helped both the neighbouring regions as well as the more remote areas which have received government assistance. Although this has produced a more equitable result in terms of jobs it has not affected the basic spatial structure of the country. It will be apparent from the above discussion that the nature of the spatial division of Britain has been changing over the period which has been reviewed. In the earlier part of the period the difference was perceived as one of industrial structure which predisposed some regions for growth and others for decline. More recently the differences have been seen more in terms of power and occupational structure with certain regions predisposed towards high skills and high incomes and other regions always destined to be at the lower end of the hierarchy (Massey, 1979b).

British Regional Development and Theory

As predictors of British regional development, the theories discussed in the first chapter have not been very useful. The spatial equilibrium theory would have suggested the elimination of inequalities but in practice this has not happened. There has been very little voluntary movement of activities from the prosperous regions to the poorer regions. This may be because labour markets in the prosperous areas have never been sufficiently tight to force firms to move out, and this in turn may be due to the slow overall rate of economic growth in the British economy. In contrast there has been a considerable movement of people away from the less prosperous areas, but this has not been sufficient to close unemployment differences and bring income levels together. This may be because there was insufficient out-migration and, as discussed in Chapter 3, this could be because of unemployment benefits and insufficient differences in wages between regions inhibiting movement, as well as the British council house system making movement difficult. However, even if unemployment differences had been evened out it is apparent that income differences would have remained since there is an increasing occupational difference between core and periphery regions.

A rival theory would have suggested that regional inequalities would have increased through the operation of multiplier effects. This has not happened to any great extent and is partly due to the steady growth of population during much of the period, which has meant that actual population decline has been relatively rare. In addition the role of government has been important, subsidising services in the poorer regions so that the state of the economy is not totally reflected in the service sector.

As anticipated, theories of regional development ignore the role of government which in Britain, as elsewhere, has been growing in importance. Government, both through its general policies based on equity and its direct regional policies, has had a great effect on the fortunes of the regions. This was particularly seen in World War II, a shock event when normal market conditions were suspended, but the effects may be lasting. The growing role of government is part of a wider structural change in society which results in a concentration of power and benefits the capital city. These structural changes are ignored in theories of regional development with consequences for their predictive power. Finally, these theories have ignored the growing role of good environments, which however subjective, are exerting a growing influence on regional development.

The Success and Failure of Regional Policy

It is difficult to evaluate regional policy when the precise aims have never been defined, and only by making some assumptions can judgements be made. Most obviously the objectives of policy would appear to be the elimination of inter-regional disparities particularly with regard to unemployment, activity rates and net migration. On this basis, as we saw in

Chapter 3, there have been some successes and some failures. For activity rates there has been some convergence, notably with regard to female rates. For net migration, the outward movement has been successfully reduced for Wales, but remains high for Scotland, while for unemployment rates the general rankings of the regions have remained similar over a long period.

Moore and Rhodes (1974a) have attempted to quantify the success of regional policy by comparing the success in creating employment (see Chapter 10) with the needs of the assisted regions. They assumed that the aims of government policy were to equalise inter-regional unemployment and activity rates and eliminate net outward migration. On this basis it was estimated that between 800,000 and 1,000,000 jobs would have needed to be created in the Development Areas for the period 1960–70, whereas their figures suggested that the effects of policy were between 250,000 and 300,000 jobs. They believed that this 30 per cent success rate was moderately encouraging.

Regional policy has also failed at another level, namely that of recreating a self-sustaining economy in the assisted regions so that regional policies are unnecessary. The assisted regions are still dependent on the inflow of jobs from the more successful parts of the country and also abroad, and if movement policies were stopped their situation would deteriorate quickly. Their rate of indigenous job creation is low, and only now are policies being directed towards this aspect. The assisted regions are still poorly equipped to meet the future with the inevitable reduction of job opportunities in certain activities and the need for replacement jobs. Although their outworn physical environment has been considerably improved, they still often lack the cultural facilities which the higher skilled workers require. Perhaps more importantly, they lack skilled labour of all levels and the ability through research and development to adjust to future changes. In a situation where regions are in competition with one another those in the south and midlands have the greater advantage, and with or without regional policies are likely to attract the major share of new growth. The importance of this competitive view arises from Britain's low rate of economic growth. A higher rate of growth would have reduced national levels of unemployment, including that of the assisted regions and made the movement of jobs to them easier. Higher rates of growth have been prevented by balance of payments problems which have arisen after every short rush for growth. The fears of some regional economists that higher rates of growth would force higher wage rates in the congested regions followed by demand inflation when transferred to the national economy has rarely been put to the test. Given an economy with less than a full demand for labour, then the weakest regions will go to the wall and the regional problem will remain.

Given that regional policy has so far failed to solve the regional problem, is it possible to suggest with hindsight methods by which it might have been more successful? As with so many of Britain's problems any inadequacy of policy has arisen because of a concern with the present at the expense of the future and a shortsightness about the changes taking place. The 1950s, as in the rest of British life, could have been the period when the basis of more successful policies were laid, rather than waiting for the end of the decade and being caught off guard by the scale of changes taking place. The impetus of regional policy gained in the 1940s should have been continued into the 1950s so that the dependence of the assisted regions on declining activities was reduced. At the same time the policy should have been broadened not just to cover the production activities of manufacturing, but the non-production aspects and also office jobs in the service sector. Even if these policies had been applied earlier, more consistently and more selectively, it is arguable that Britain's regional problem would still remain. This is because of the national problems of obtaining growth and reducing unemployment discussed above, and of the preferences which are being expressed for the southern part of the country. In the long term this must mean some relative decline in the peripheral areas of the north and west.

CHAPTER TWELVE

The Future of Regional Development

At the beginning of this book, it was suggested that the early to mid-1970s might be a turning point for regional development, with new developments like North Sea Oil, devolution and entry into the EEC becoming important new factors. Only time will tell the significance of these factors and, as we have seen, the period since World War I has been marked by many sub-periods and the mid-1970s may be merely the beginning of another. In this chapter we shall examine possible future trends in regional development, mainly up to the turn of the century, beginning with the national situation which will affect all that takes place within the regions. We shall conclude on a comment on the regional policy necessary in the future.

National Changes

The falling birth rate from 1964 to 1977 has made population forecasting a hazardous task, but any significant changes in fertility in the next few years are unlikely to alter the basic statistics of the British population at the end of the century. A study of the ages at which women have children suggests that at least part of the fall in the birth rate may be accounted for by a delaying of the child-bearing period, and when allowance is made for this a slight increase in the birth rate may be forecast resulting in an increasing number of children in the 1990s. Nearly all of those who will be of working age in 2001 are now alive and so, barring sudden changes in mortality and net external migration, it is possible to estimate its size. Owing to a rise in the birth rate in the late 1950s and early

1960s, the population of working age is expected to continue increasing for the next thirty years which will require the economy to expand if these increasing numbers are to be employed. If the 1971 activity rate for the population over fifteen was to be maintained then 1,819,000 extra jobs would be required in the year 2001. Even allowing for some fall in male activity rates mainly caused by earlier retirement, and assuming no further increase in female activity rates there would still be required a large increase in jobs. The elderly population, which has been increasing rapidly in recent years, is likely to stabilise and fall slightly in the 1990s reflecting the low birth rate of the inter-war years. Overall, the Office of Population Censuses and Surveys (1978a) expects the population to increase by one and a half million between 1976 and 2001, a much smaller increase than in earlier periods. This assumes a continuing net external migration of up to 40,000 a year and a small decrease in mortality.

The rate of growth of the British economy during the rest of the twentieth century is very difficult to predict, in part being affected by the rate of world economic growth and in part by the competitiveness of the home economy. On neither count is the outlook at the moment particularly promising, with the world recession initiated by the late 1973 rise in oil prices continuing. Since the early 1970s the British economy has been more open to world trade, a consequence of the general lowering of tariffs as well as our entry into the EEC, and this has made our competitive position even more important. Unfortunately, there has been an increased penetration of imports without a corresponding increase in exports. In spite of the benefits of North Sea oil, the balance of trade continues to be a problem to the country, and for several years the trading position has only been maintained by continued devaluation, in some years made more necessary because of higher rates of inflation. The benefit of devaluation has not only been to make British goods competitive in export markets but also to make labour relatively cheap and thus attractive to foreign manufacturing investment. There is considerable competition in Western Europe for such mobile manufacturing investment with countries offering cash incentives and favourable tax policies. Also on the favourable side, Britain has a good environment for working and living, high quality labour, a favourable attitude to foreign investment and with the Irish Republic the advantage of the English language. Against this may be set the disadvantages of the 'British disease' which include the industrial unrest and restrictive working practices of trade unions, a slow rate of economic growth compared to other European countries, concern over inflation and with a Labour government fears over long-term policies on taxes and nationalisation. Dunning (1979) in a study of British and foreign investment has suggested that these latter factors are the cause of higher investment abroad by British firms since the late 1960s where they have found greater productivity and higher profits and also a decline in inward foreign investment to Britain with more firms preferring to serve Britain from the continent. The future attractiveness of Britain could also be affected by the activities of the EEC via its numerous harmonising policies. An EEC regional policy might be more successful in the future in harmonising the level of incentives offered which at present varies considerably from one part of the EEC to another with little regard to any common criteria of need. This could be advantageous to Britain's peripheral regions. On the other hand a European Monetary Scheme, if successful, would limit the possibility of devaluation and the increased competitiveness this has brought to the British economy, and might require some compensating increase from the Regional Fund. Overall the rate of economic growth in the future is unlikely to be faster than in recent years, with consequences for the growth of employment and unemployment.

Within the economy the greatest changes are likely to result from the introduction of micro-processors (the silicon chip revolution). These are likely to speed up the rate of change and affect every sector of the economy, bringing great cost advantages without any adverse health or safety effects. Already competitive pressure and the rising wage demands of the labour force have encouraged firms to automate as much as possible, and micro-processors will enable this trend to go much further. Although there will be some new jobs created in electronics manufacture and software services, overall there will be a large net reduction in the labour force affecting both the manufacturing and service sectors. This could result in higher unemployment, particularly if the existing labour force seeks to take the increased wealth for itself and refuses work-sharing schemes and the redistribution of wealth. International competition is so strong that it may be difficult to introduce work-sharing schemes without world-wide agreements which help to develop such arrangements in every country.

The manufacturing sector will also continue to be affected by the world redistribution of industries with continuing competition in textiles, and clothing from the low labour cost countries of the developing world. This type of competition has already spread to other industries such as electrical goods, and will increasingly affect other established industries. Other British industries like the manufacture of record players may be lost to advanced countries which have gained economies of scale in such activities. The international division of labour is continually being changed and Britain's industries will have to adjust to this, always seeking the higher skilled and higher value-added activities, or face extinction. The growth of public service sector employment, so important in the past, may be limited in the future by slow economic growth and the wish of the population to spend their own money. There may, however, be some increase in services catering for leisure pursuits.

The role of regional policy has been important in the past in directing growth to the assisted regions but at the moment is subject to conflicting tendencies. All governments are likely to remain committed in some form to regional policy and the idea of reducing inter-regional unemployment levels. This would certainly be true under a Labour government and the new Conservative government of 1979 has already pledged itself to keep the Scottish and Welsh Development

Agencies and a restricted regional policy. However, several adverse tendencies have appeared in the 1970s (Mackay, 1978). The general increase in unemployment which has affected every region has made it more difficult to apply a strict IDC control policy in the South East and Midlands, and thus help to divert activities to the assisted regions. The raising of the IDC exemption limit by the new Conservative government of 1979 will merely confirm the opportunity to develop in the South and Midlands. Secondly the competition with other EEC countries for mobile industrial investment has weakened the government's resolve to stop growth in the South East if this is likely to be at the expense of losing investment to another country. Thirdly, the increasing attention given to inner-city problems has detracted from inter-regional problems and diverted resources away. Fourthly, the development of sectoral policies has weakened the regional approach emphasising the need to strengthen competitive industries wherever they are located. Fifthly, the weakness of the economy has forced the abandonment of the Regional Employment Premium in 1976 and caused further cuts in 1979 and thus enacted a large overall reduction in the amount of aid to the regions. The slow growth of manufacturing employment in recent years and its expected slow growth is another adverse tendency, since the assisted areas depend on the diversion of this activity. Whilst service sector jobs, which are likely to grow, can be diverted, the potential is much less, so that traditional policy measures based on manufacturing are likely to be less successful. Against these adverse trends the only hope that the assisted areas can have is that the Regional Fund of the EEC will be increased and that more will be directed towards this country.

Regional Variations

In this section we shall discuss the regional incidence of some of the trends mentioned above. The slow decline of employment in Agriculture, Forestry and Fishing is expected to continue, affecting all regions. Already the collapse of part of the fishing industry in 1977 following the Icelandic ban has had severe repercussions on ports like Fleetwood, Hull and Grimsby. Likewise existing trends in the decline of employment in coal-mining will continue with particular consequences for areas like South Wales and Central Scotland. The development of new coal-fields at Selby (Yorkshire) and the Vale of Belvoir (East Midlands) only emphasises the contrast between the central Yorkshire–Nottinghamshire–Derbyshire coalfield and the rest. During the 1970s the North Sea oilfields have been exploited and there has been much speculation as to the effects on Scotland (Mackay and Mackay, 1975). According to a report on the impact of North Sea oil on Scotland, the direct employment effects are most significant in the exploratory and development stages, but relatively small in the production stages (Gaskin and Mackay, 1978). Indirect employment close by is mainly concerned with the building and servicing of rigs and this likewise is important in the first two stages and less thereafter. Other indirect employment, including the manufacture of equipment, usually does not have to be near the oilfields, and may be anywhere in the world. Gaskin and Mackay (1978) estimate that the employment effects of North Sea oil on Scotland rose from about zero in 1970 to reach 40,000 by 1976 and will most likely peak in 1979 at between 50–60,000, declining to about half this figure by 1986. About two-thirds of these jobs are north of the central belt of Scotland, with Aberdeen alone having 9,000 jobs in 1976. Downstream manufacturing jobs from oil production are likely to be small and not necessarily in Scotland.

In the manufacturing sector the traditional declining industries have continued their downward trend in the 1970s. Cheap imports from low-wage countries have affected the textile, clothing and footwear industries with employment consequences for the areas where these industries have traditionally been found (Mounfield, 1978). The world recession has hit the demand for new ships and badly affected the shipbuilding districts of the North East and Clydeside, which had already become less competitive in the world industry. Even with a world revival in orders only a slimmed down industry is likely to survive in these areas. Changing technology as well as surplus capacity is also affecting the iron and steel industry and the late 1970s have seen the run down and closure of many plants mainly in the north and west of the country, and these trends will continue into the 1980s. The effects of the micro-processor revolution in reducing labour requirements are likely to be more geographically widespread. This is because it will affect so many industries, both old and new, and because many of the latter have been scattered around the regions of the country as a result of regional policy. Already there have been large reductions in employment in telephone manufacture as a result of the new technology and these have included plant closures. Although the office activities of manufacturing firms will also be affected, the greatest relative effect will be on production, and thus the peripheral areas with branch plants solely concerned with production may be the most severely affected. Significantly this will include the more labour intensive and female employing activities which have been drawn to these areas. The new employment which will be created by the silicon chip revolution is already being keenly competed for by the regions. Almost certainly the functions requiring highly skilled labour will be located in southern England in order to attract the quality of labour required. The decision in 1978 by the NEB-backed Inmos company to locate its R & D activities in Bristol is indicative of this. However, it is likely that some of the more routine production will be sited in assisted areas.

As in the past, employment in the service sector will be less affected by automation and so its share of total employment will continue to increase. Once again most of the jobs will be market orientated and thus related to the distribution of population and any changes taking place. Retirement migration is likely to continue increasing and this will particularly affect the south coast, the South West and East Anglia with consequences for the growth of services in these areas (Law and Warnes, 1980 and Gordon, 1975). Another area of growth in recent years which is likely to continue is tourism, and particularly that by overseas visitors. All tourism favours the southern part of the country and the mecca of London is noticeably important for foreign tourists (Digest of Tourist Statistics). The latter are particularly important for regional development since they spend more and are more likely to stay in hotels than the home tourist, and this has employment consequences.

With a growing population of working age and increasing mechanisation, unemployment is likely to remain high for the rest of the country unless there is either dramatic economic growth or a massive redistribution of the available work. The attraction of labour is thus unlikely to be important, but, as we have seen, the highly skilled managers and scientists prefer the southern part of the country and so this will be a continuing influence on the location of industry and office activities. There is some evidence that industry prefers the small town to the large city, partly on account of its pleasanter environment, and partly because the work-force may be less strike prone (Keeble, 1976). This trend is likely to continue and benefit many parts of southern and eastern England.

The new regional policy of the 1979 Conservative government with its raising of the lower limit of IDC exemption, reduced incentives and restricted geographical coverage will inevitably reduce the employment created in the northern and western regions. This was likely to fall in any case owing to the effects of automation in the manufacturing sector and the consequences of the low rate of economic growth which is an adverse factor for industrial migration. Now there is likely to be even less diversion of jobs to these regions and less encouragement for the growth of indigenous industry. However, the residual incentives will ensure some flow of new jobs to the assisted regions and of these, South Wales with its proximity to the core areas of England and its good labour productivity record, will probably continue to gain most from regional policy.

The Regions

It is apparent from the foregoing discussion that unemployment is likely to remain high at perhaps up to and around two million, and that there is no sign that this unemployment is going to be evenly distributed across the regions. Further there is no sign that income differences are going to be removed or that without regional policies the assisted regions could attract employment growth on anything like the present scale. The regional problem appears as far away from a solution as ever. Fundamentally the regions are in competition with each other for economic and employment growth and those with the greatest attractions will enjoy the growth. Regional policies are only slowing down this rate of change, and making the transition more humane. In the nineteenth century the coalfields of the north and west proved an outstanding advantage to the industry of the time, but this advantage has now ceased to be, and it may be that this period was an aberration in the long-term development of the country. At the beginning of the twentieth century the labour skills of the Midlands coupled with centrality proved a key advantage. Throughout the nineteenth and twentieth centuries the attraction of London as capital and large market coupled with good communications to the rest of the country and Europe have proved important. As the century has progressed, ease and cost of transport has enabled a wider spread of activities and this has been to the advantage of southern and eastern areas. These regions benefit from better climates, the absence of nineteenth-century industrial environments as well as proximity to London. The core area of Britain in the late twentieth century will remain that area of England to the south of a line from Herefordshire to the Wash, within which are found the higher levels of decision making and higher levels of skills of all types.

North and west of this line the levels of prosperity will diminish and unemployment will tend to increase. Gradually with outward movement of people the population of these regions, except for environmentally favoured areas within them, will decline as is already happening and is forecast to continue to do so (OPCS 1978b). These regions will continue to be affected by the run-down of traditional industries and even the run-down of employment in newer industries resulting from new technologies.

A Regional Policy for the Future

The problem areas of the last quarter of the twentieth century, defined as those with relative high unemployment, are likely to be the traditional assisted areas and the inner areas of our large conurbations. This latter category covers not only London and Birmingham but also the conurbations of the assisted areas. Both types of area suffer from a poor environmental image and in the latter case there is the feeling, reported on numerous occasions, that these districts suffer from poor industrial relations which lowers productivity. In contrast small towns and rural areas are favoured by decision takers both because of good environment and good industrial relations, a version of 'small is beautiful' for regional development. It is inconceivable that Britain would abandon policies to help the areas of high unemployment, but perhaps these policies could be complemented by others which assist the more attractive and perhaps more profitable growth areas. The slow and planned run-down of our large conurbations, which many find increasingly dirty, dangerous, unsightly, unprofitable and expensive, could help in the effort to improve industrial performance which will remain a top priority for all governments during the rest of the century. Without success on this front the whole of Britain could become a peripheral problem region of Europe. The unemployed and their families moving out of such areas of high unemployment could be given financial assistance to help with the move, and also some preference for public housing. The growing areas of the south and east would need to be planned carefully. Dispersed settlement patterns could be both harmful to the landscape and expensive in the provision of services. With the fear of an energy crisis and the possibility of greater transport costs some form of concentration would appear desirable, preferably along Britain's remaining railway routes.

Within the northern and western parts of the country the areas of high unemployment will still have a strong case for some form of assistance. The new Conservative government has reduced the extensive assisted areas of the Labour administration, using once again relatively high employment as the criterion for designation. Whilst the limits of the new assisted areas are not as narrowly drawn as those of the early 1960s, it is still not clear that all of the areas are the most suitable in terms of regional growth strategies. This applies particularly to some of the coastal areas designated. Once again there is an argument for other considerations to be taken into account when designating assisted areas. For instance, assistance could also be given to areas with highly specialised economies where there is a long-term threat to employment unless new industries are introduced (Chisholm, 1976).

The aid given in these assisted areas could also be more selective. Long-term subsidies like the now abandoned Regional Employment Premium were justifiably criticised as supporting inefficient firms. Incentives should be seen as a bribe to attract economic activities to a region. Insofar as movement involves extra cost for a short period, some forms of aid like rent subsidies could be for up to three or four years, but after this firms should be expected to stand on their own feet. Likewise the high investment grants have been criticised as being expensive in terms of the number of jobs provided, which in some cases are negative. At the moment competition between European countries inhibits any one country from opting out of this Dutch auction, but agreement between EEC countries might eliminate waste on this front, with upper limits on grants per job provided.

It is impossible to specify the precise form which regional policy should take in the future since the nature of the regional problem cannot exactly be foreseen. The account of British regional development given in this book has shown that the nature of the regional problem has changed and that the precise parameters of regional change could not have been foreseen. There is a need for the continuing study of regional development in this country linking changes here to those in the rest of the EEC and even in the rest of the world. Past experience would suggest that neither regional equality nor the absence of regional problems is likely, and assuming the continuance of democratic governments concerned with the welfare of their citizens, there will be a need for some form of regional policy. Although there may be discussion on the details of this policy, such discussion should be based on a deep understanding of the regional development process and it is hoped that this work will have provided some historical input for such debate.

Appendix A

Sources of Employment Data

There are three sources of employment data for the period since World War I. Firstly there is the Census of Population covering the entire population and generally held every ten years except for the omission of 1941 and the addition of the Sample Census in 1966. In the case of Northern Ireland, the two inter-war censuses were held at different dates from the mainland, in 1926 and 1937, and the employment data from the second census was never processed and published. Secondly there is the annual count of insured employees made by the Department of Employment, formerly the Ministry of Labour. This count began in 1911 but for many years only covered the part of the working population affected by the unemployment insurance scheme. An extension of the scheme in 1920 and the adoption of an industrial classification scheme in 1923 made the statistics more useful but still less than comprehensive. It was not until 1948 that the scheme was extended to cover all insured employees and, though still omitting the self-employed, thus became of much greater use. From 1948 to 1971 the count was based partly on returns from major employers and partly on the exchange of insurance cards in the June quarter which was assumed to be a representative sample of the whole year. Included in these totals for insured employees were the unemployed and seasonal/occasional workers, such as students. At the local level there were often significant errors since not all insurance cards were exchanged at the place of work, important for multi-site firms, and so could only be added in at the regional level (Allen and Yuill, 1977). Since 1971 there has been an annual census of employment which is generally considered to be much more accurate. Although the Department of Employment's regional statistics before 1971 were more reliable than the local ones, any recalculation of the statistics to consistent regional boundaries would involve their use. The third and final source of data is the Censuses of Production and Distribution. The latter has only been held since 1950 and does not cover all services so that even combining both censuses for recent periods would not produce a complete coverage of all employment.

Several authors have made comparisons of these different sources of data revealing some significant differences even when allowance is made for the varying scope of each data set (Mackay and Buxton, 1965, and Fothergill and Gudgin, 1978). Of the three sources the Census of Population is the only one which is comprehensive and comparable for the period since World War I (Buxton and Mackay, 1977). It also has another advantage in that by using the building blocks of the counties it is possible to obtain a data set for a consistent set of regions. Its main drawback is its irregularity and invariability with respect to business cycles.

Appendix B

The Use of Census Employment Data

This work has made particular use of the employment data found in the industry tables of the census reports. There are several problems involved in the use of this data. The problems involved in using a consistent set of regions has been discussed in Chapter 1. In this appendix the problems of the 1921 and 1931 censuses and of industrial classification are discussed.

The 1921 census marked an advance in previous census reports by classifying people by both industry and occupation and also by place of work. However, it did not distinguish, as in later censuses, between the employed and unemployed, so affecting comparison forwards. One particular problem of the 1921 census is the large number of persons for whom no workplace was stated, totalling about 9 per cent. There are several possible explanations for this: such persons may have been unemployed, have no fixed workplace (i.e. be mobile in their job) or just have failed to state a workplace on the census questionnaire. Suspicion about the second possible reason is encouraged by a comparison of industries. For most industrial headings the unclassified by work place form only 1 or 2 per cent of the total for that industry, but in the case of fishing (as an example of an industry where the labour force is mobile) the figure was 75 per cent. To exclude those workers for which there is no stated workplace would result in a considerable underestimation of the regional employment figures, and this underestimation might vary between region depending on industrial composition. It was therefore decided to reallocate the unclassified across the regions in proportion to the classified figures for each industry. In most industries, as we have seen, the no workplace group formed only a small proportion of the total in the industry and this process, even if in error, would have made very little difference to the regional proportions. In a few industries, like fishing, where the unclassified formed a higher proportion much greater care was needed. In this and other cases recourse was made to the occupation tables which provided information by place of residence and enable regional proportions to be obtained for a much larger sample. This last method was also necessary in the case of the coal-mining industry where no geographical breakdown was given. Regional employment figures for this industry are also available from the Annual Abstract of Statistics.

The main problem about the 1931 Census Industry Tables arises from the fact that, unlike the 1921, 1951, 1961 and 1971 censuses, the results were classified by place of residence. This creates a great problem at the local level where there may be considerable inter-authority commuting. It is much less of a problem at the regional level since the main commuting flows are within the regions, but there may be difficulties where large towns are near the borders of regions.

The other main problem concerns the differences in industrial classification used at each census. In general the differences between any two censuses are small and it is possible by transfers or amalgamations of minimum list headings (MLH) to obtain comparable figures, but obviously there are more problems over longer periods. In the simplest case an MLH may have been transferred from one order to another between censuses and by simple transfer the orders can be made comparable. In other cases an MLH may have been divided into two and by combining at the later date comparison is again possible. A more complicated case is where part of an MLH has been moved to another MLH, but here again it is possible to combine MLHs to embrace the changes. Usually a table is provided in each census volume of Industry Tables showing such changes, but a comparative table has been assembled by Buxton and MacKay (1977).

References

Allen, G. C. *The Industrial Development of Birmingham and the Black Country, 1860–1927* (Allen and Unwin, 1927)

Allen, K. and Yuill, D. 'The accuracy of pre-1971 local employment data', *Regional Studies*, 11 (1977), 253–262

Andrews, H. P. 'Journey to work considerations in the labour force participation of married women'. *Regional Studies*, 12 (1978), 11–20

Armstrong, H. W. 'Community regional policy: a survey and critique', *Regional Studies*, 12 (1978), 511–28

Ashcroft, B. and Taylor, J. 'The movement of manufacturing industry and the effect of regional policy', *Oxford Economic Papers*, 29 (1977), 89–101

Ashworth, W. *The Genesis of Modern British Town Planning* (Routledge and Kegan Paul, 1954)

Atkins, D. H. W. 'Employment changes in branch and parent manufacturing plants in the U.K.: 1966–71', *Trade and Industry*, 30 Aug. 1973, 437–9

Beesley, M. 'The birth and death of industrial establishments: experience in the West Midlands conurbation'. *Journal of Industrial Economics*, 4 (1955), 45–61

Bird, P. A. and Thirlwall, A. P. 'The incentive to invest in the new development areas'. *District Bank Review*, June 1967, 24–45

Bloomfield, G. *The World Automotive Industry* (David and Charles, 1978)

Blunden, J. *The Mineral Resources of Britain* (Hutchinson, 1975)

Board of Trade *The Movement of Manufacturing Industry in the United Kingdom 1945–65* (1968, HMSO)

Board of Trade North West Research Section. *Study of Movement Affecting the North West Region* (1969, Manchester)

Bolton Report *Small Firms: Report of the Committee of Inquiry on Small Firms* (1971, HMSO)

Bowers, J. *The Anatomy of Regional Activity Rates* (Cambridge University Press, 1970)

Brown, A. J. 'Surveys of Applied Economics: Regional Economics with special reference to the United Kingdom'. *Economic Journal*, 89 (1969), 759–796

Brown, A. J. *The Framework of Regional Economics in the United Kingdom* (Cambridge University Press, 1972)
Buck, T. W. 'Shift and Share Analysis—a guide to regional policy', *Regional Studies*, 4 (1970) 445–50
Buck, T. W. and Atkins, M. H. 'The impact of British regional policies in employment growth', *Oxford Economic Papers*, 28 (1970), 118–32
Buswell, R. J. and Lewis, E. W. 'The geographical distribution of industrial research activity in the United Kingdom', *Regional Studies*, 4 (1970), 297–306
Buxton, N. K. and MacKay, D. I. *British Employment Statistics: A Guide to Sources and Methods* (Basil Blackwell, 1977)
Cameron, G. C. 'Regional economic policy in the United Kingdom', in M. Sant (Ed.) *Regional Policy and Planning for Europe* (Swan House, 1974)
Cameron, G. C. and Clark, B. D. *Industrial Movement and the Regional Problem* (Oliver and Boyd, 1966)
Camina, M. M. 'Local authorities and the attraction of industry', *Progress in Planning*, 3 (1974), 83–180
Carruthers, I. 'A classification of service centres in England and Wales', *Geographical Journal*, 123 (1957), 371–85
Central Statistical Office 'Research and development expenditure and employment', *Studies in Official Statistics* No. 27 (1976, HMSO)
Champion, A. G. 'Evolving patterns of population distribution in England and Wales, 1951–71', *Institute of British Geographers Transactions* N. S. 1 (1976), 401–20
Chapman, K. *North Sea Oil and Gas: a Geographical Perspective* (David and Charles, 1976)
Cherry, G. E. *The Evolution of British Town Planning* (Leonard Hill, 1974)
Chisholm, M. 'On the making of a myth? How capital intensive is industry investing in the development areas?', *Urban Studies*, 7 (1970), 289–293
Chisholm, M. Chapter 8, 'Freight costs, industrial location and regional development', in M. Chisholm and G. Manners (Ed.) *Spatial Policy Problems of the British Economy* (Cambridge, 1972)
Chisholm, M. 'Regional policies in an era of slow population growth and higher unemployment', *Regional Studies*, 10 (1976), 201–14
Chisholm, M. and Manners, G. (Eds.) *Spatial Policy Problems of the British Economy* (Cambridge University Press, 1971)
Chisholm, M. and O'Sullivan, P. O. *Freight Flows and Spatial Aspects of the British Economy* (C.U.P., 1973)

Christaller, W. *Central Places in Southern Germany*, translated by C. W. Baskin, Prentice Hall, New Jersey, 1966)
Clark, C. 'Industrial location and economic potential', *Lloyds Bank Review*, October 1966
Coates, B. E. and Rawstron, F. M. *Regional Variations in Britain* (Batsford, 1971)
Cook, W. R. 'Transport decisions of certain firms in the Black Country', *Journal of Transport Economics and Policy*, 1 (1967)
Coppock, J. T. *An Agricultural Geography of Great Britain* (G. Bell and Sons, 1971)
Crompton, D. *Employment Decline in the Engineering Industries of the Manchester Area* Unpublished M Sc thesis (1976), University of Salford
Crum, R. E. and Gudgin, G. *Non-production Activities in U.K. Manufacturing Industry*. Commission of the European Communities Regional Policy Series No 3 (1977)
Cullingworth, J. B. *Town and Country Planning in England and Wales: an Introduction* (Allen and Unwin, 1964)
Daly, M. and Atkinson, E. 'A regional analysis of strikes, 1921–1936', *Sociological Review*, 32 (1940), 216–223
Daniel, G. H. 'Labour migration and age composition', *Sociological Review*, 31 (1939), 281–308
Daniels, P. W. 'Office decentralisation from London—policy and practice', *Regional Studies*, 3 (1969), 171–8
Darwent, D. F. 'Growth poles and growth centres in regional planning: a review'. *Environment and Planning*, 1 (1969), 5–32
Davies, J. R. and Kelly, M. *Small Firms in the Manufacturing Sector* Committee of Inquiry on Small Firms Research Report No 3 (1971, HMSO)
Davies, W. 'The Nature and Significance of Trading Estates with Special Reference to Treforest and Slough Estates', unpublished University of Wales MA thesis (1951)
Dennis, R. 'The decline of manufacturing employment in Greater London, 1966–74'. *Urban Studies*, 15 (1978), 63–73
Department of Employment Gazette (1974) Female Activity Rates, 8–18
Department of Employment Gazette (November 1976) Distribution and Concentration of Industrial Stoppages in Great Britain, 19–21
Diamond, D. R. 'The Urban System' in J. W. House (Ed.) *U.K. Space* (Weidenfeld and Nicolson, 1979)
Dicken, P. and Lloyd, P. E. 'Geographical perspectives on United States investment in the United Kingdom', *Environment and Planning*, 8 (1976), 685–705
Dicken, P. and Lloyd, P. E. 'Inner metropolitan industrial change,

enterprise structures and policy issues: case studies of Manchester and Merseyside'. *Regional Studies*, 12 (1978), 181–198

Digest of Tourist Statistics (1978) No 8

Dunning, J. H. *American Investment in British Manufacturing Industry* (Allen and Unwin, 1958)

Dunning, J. H. 'The U.K.'s international direct investment position in the mid-1970s'. *Lloyds Bank Review*, 132 (1979), 1–22

Economic Trends 'Expenditure on Scientific Research and Development', (November 1970)

Edwards, S. L. 'Transport cost in British industry', *Journal of Transport Economics and Policy*, 4 (1970), 265–83

Edwards, S. L. 'Regional variations in freight cost', *Journal of Transport Economics and Policy*, 9 (1975), 115–26

Evans, A. W. 'The location of the headquarters of industrial companies', *Urban Studies*', 10 (1973), 387–96

Eversley, D. E. C. 'Population changes and regional policy since the war', *Regional Studies*, 5 (1971), 221–28

Expenditure Committee, Second Report, Minutes of Evidence, HC 327 of 1972–73 and HC 85–1 of 1973–4

Expenditure Committee (Trade and Industry Sub-Committee) *Regional Development Incentives* (1973, HMSO)

Fawcett, C. B. *Provinces of England: A Study of Some Geographical Aspects of Devolution* (Hutchinson, 1960)

Firn, J. R. 'External control and regional development: the case of Scotland'. *Environment and Planning*, A, 7 (1975), 393–414

Firn, J. R. and Swales, J. K. 'The formation of new manufacturing establishments in the central Clydeside and West Midlands conurbations 1963–1972: a comparative analysis'. *Regional Studies 12*, (1978), 199–213

Fogarty, M. P. *Plan Your Own Industries: A Study of Local and Regional Development Organisations* (Basil Blackwell, 1947)

Forsyth, D. D. *U.S. Investment in Scotland* (Praeger, New York, 1972)

Fothergill, S. and Gudgin, G. *Regional Employment Statistics on a Comparable Basis 1952–75* (1978, Centre for Environmental Studies)

Friedlander, D. and Roshier, J. 'A study of internal migration in England and Wales: Part I'. *Population Studies*, 19 (1966), 239–79

Friedmann, J. R. P. *Regional Development Policy* MIT Press, Cambridge, Massachusetts, 1966)

Friedmann, J. 'A general theory of polarised development' in N. M. Hansen (Ed.) *Growth Centres in Regional Economic Development* (Free Press, New York, 1972)

Gaskin, M. and MacKay, D. I. *The Economic Impact of North Sea*

Oil on Scotland: Final Report to the Scottish Economic Planning Department (1978, Edinburgh, HMSO)

Gober-Meyers, P. 'Employment motivated migration and economic growth in post-industrial market economies', *Progress in Human Geography*, 2 (1978), 207–29

Goddard, J. B. *Office Location in Urban and Regional Development.* (Oxford University Press, 1975)

Goddard, J. B. and Smith, I. J. 'Changes in corporate control in the British urban system, 1972–1977', *Environment and Planning*, (1978), 1073–84

Gordon, I. R. *Retirement to the South West*, (1975), South West Economic Planning Council, HMSO

Gould, P. and White, R. *Mental Maps* (Penguin, 1974)

Gudgin, G. *Industrial Location Processes and Regional Employment Growth* (Saxon House, 1978)

Hague, D. C. and Newmen, P. K. *Costs in Alternative Locations: the Clothing Industry* (1952, National Institute of Economic and Social Research, London)

Hague, D. C. and Dunning, J. H. 'Cost in alternative locations: the radio industry', *Review of Economic Studies*, 22 (1959), 203–13

Hall, C. B. and Smith, R. A. 'Socio-economic patterns of England and Wales', *Urban Studies*, 5 (1968), 59–66

Hall, P. G. *The Industries of London Since 1861* (Hutchinson, 1962)

Hall, P. *London 2000* (Faber and Faber, 1969)

Hall, P. 'The spatial structure of metropolitan England and Wales', in Chisholm and Manners (1971)

Hall, P. et al *The Containment of Urban England* 2 Vols (Allen and Unwin, 1973)

Hammond, E. 'Dispersal of government offices: a survey', *Urban Studies*, 4 (1967), 258–276

Hannah, L. *The Rise of the Corporate Economy* (Methuen, 1976)

Hardman Report *The Dispersal of Government Work from London*, (1973, HMSO)

Harris, A. I. and Clausen, R. *Labour Mobility in Great Britain 1953–1963*, (1966, HMSO)

Hart, R. A. 'Economic expectations and the decision to migrate: an analysis by socio-economic group', *Regional Studies*, 7 (1973), 271–75

Heal, D. W. *The Steel Industry in Post War Britain* (David and Charles, 1974)

Hirschman, A. O. *The Strategy of Economic Development* (Yale University Press, 1958)

Hoare, A. G. 'Industrial linkages and the dual economy: the case of Northern Ireland', *Regional Studies*, 12 (1978), 167–180

Holmans, A. E. 'Industrial development certificates and control of the growth of employment in South East England', *Urban Studies*, 1 (1964), 138–52

Holmans, A. E. 'Inter-regional differences in level of income: are there two nations or one?', in T. Wilson (Ed.) *Papers on Regional Development* (Basil Blackwell, 1965)

House of Commons (1932–3) Parliamentary Debates, Vol. 266

ICI Minutes of Evidence to Expenditure Committee (Trade and Industry), 31 January 1973, House of Commons Papers 42–6

James, B. G. S. 'The incompatability of industrial and trading cultures: A critical appraisal of the growth point concept', *Journal of Industrial Economics*, 13 90–4

James, V. Z. *Office Employment in the Northern Region: Its National, Regional and Organisational Context*, University of Newcastle Centre for Urban and Regional Development Studies, Discussion Paper No 14 (1978)

John, B. S. *Pembrokeshire* (1964), (David and Charles, 1976)

Johnson, P. S. *New Firms and Regional Development: Some Issues and Evidence*, Centre for Urban and Regional Development Studies, University of Newcastle-upon-Tyne, Discussion Paper No 11 (1978)

Jones, H. R. 'Rural migration in Central Wales', *Institute of British Geographers Transactions*, 37 (1965), 31–45

Keeble, D. *Industrial Location and Planning in the United Kingdom*, (Methuen, 1976)

Keeble, D. E. 'Industrial decentralisation on the metropolis: the North West London case', *Institute of British Geographers Transactions*, 44 (1968) 1–54

Keeble, D. E. 'Industrial movement and regional development in the United Kingdom', *Town Planning Review*, (1972), 3–25

Lausen, J. R. 'On growth poles', *Urban Studies*, 6 (1969), 137–161

Law, C. M. and Warnes, A. M. 'The changing geography of the elderly in England and Wales' *Institute of British Geographers Transactions*, New Series 1 (1976), 453–471

Law, C. M. and Warnes, A. M. 'The prospects for increasing retirement migration: an appraisal based on the characteristics of retired migrants', in D. T. Herbert and R. J. Johnston (Ed.) *Geography and the Urban Environment* (Wiley, 1980)

Lazell, H. G. *From Pills to Penicillin: The Beecham Story* (Heinemann, 1975)

Leigh, R. and North, D. J. (1978a) 'Regional aspects of acquisition activity in British manufacturing Industry', *Regional Studies*, 12 227–247

Leigh, R. and North, D. J. (1978b) 'The potential of the micro-behavioural approach to regional analysis' in P. W. J. Batey

(Ed.) *Theory and Method in Urban and Regional Analysis* (Pion, 1978)
Leser, C. E. V. 'Industrial specialisation in Scotland and in regions of England and Wales', *Yorkshire Bulletin of Economic and Social Research,* 1 (1948), 19–30
Leser, C. E. V. 'Changes in level and diversity of employment in regions of Great Britain, 1939–47', *Economic Journal,* (1948) 326–42
Leser, C. E. V. 'Output per head in different parts of the United Kingdom', *Journal of the Royal Statistical Society,* Series A (1950), 207–219
Lever, W. 'Manufacturing linkages and the search for supplies and markets' in F. E. Hamilton (Ed.) *Spatial Perspectives on Industrial Organisation and Decision Making* (Wiley, 1974)
Lind, H. 'Internal migration in Britain' in J. A. Jackson (Ed.) *Migration* (Cambridge University Press, 1969)
Lloyd, I. *Rolls Royce: The Years of Endeavour* (Macmillan, 1978)
Luttrell, W. F. *Factory Location and Industrial Movement: a Study of Recent Experience in Great Britain*, 2 Vols. (Cambridge University Press, 1962)
McCallum, J. D. 'The Development of British Regional Policy', Chapter 1 in Maclennan and Parr (1979)
McCrone, G. *Regional Policy in Britain* (Allen and Unwin, 1969)
McDermott, P. J. 'Overseas investment and the industrial geography of the United Kingdom', *Area,* 9 (1977), 203
Mackay, D. I. 'Industrial structure and regional growth: a methodological problem', *Scottish Journal of Political Economy,* 15 (1968), 129–43
Mackay, D. I. and Buxton, N. R. 'A view of regional labour statistics', *Journal of Royal Statistical Society,* Series A (1965), 267–84
Mackay, D. I. and Mackay, G. A. *The Political Economy of North Sea Oil* (Martin Robertson, 1975)
Mackay, R. R. *The Death of Regional Policy—or Resurrection Squared* Centre for Urban and Regional Development Studies, University of Newcastle, Discussion Paper No 10 (1978) and *Regional Studies,* 13 (1979), 281–95
Mackay, R. R. (1978b) *Planning for Balance: Regional Policy and Regional Employment: The U.K. Experience*, Centre for Urban and Regional Development Studies, University of Newcastle, Discussion Paper No 18 (1978)
Maclennan, D. and Parr, J. B. *Regional Policy: Past Experiences and New Directions* (Martin Robertson, 1979)
Makower, H., Marschak, J. and Robinson, H. W. 'Studies in the mobility of labour', *Oxford Economic Papers* No 2 (1939), 70–98

and No 4 (1940), 39–62
Manners, G. 'Some economic and spatial characteristics of the British energy market' in M. Chisholm and G. Manners (Ed.) *Spatial Problems of the British Economy* (Cambridge University Press, 1971)
Manners, G. (Ed.) *South Wales in the Sixties* (Pergamon, 1964)
Manners, G., Keeble, D., Rodgers, B., Wares, K. *Regional Development in Britain* (John Wiley, 1972)
Marquand, J. *The Service Sector and Regional Policy in the United Kingdom* (London, Centre for Environmental Studies, Research Series 29, 1979)
Marquand, J. *The Role of the Tertiary Sector in Regional Policy* Report to the EEC Commission Regional Policy Directorate (1978)
Marshall, J. N. *Ownership, Organisation and Industrial Linkage* Centre for Urban and Regional Development Studies, University of Newcastle Discussion Paper No 22 (1978)
Martin, J. E. *Greater London: an Industrial Geography* (Bell, 1966)
Massey, D. 'The U.K. electrical engineering and electronics industries: the implication of the crisis for the restructuring of capital and locational change', *Review of Radical Political Economy* (1979)
Massey, D. 'In what sense a regional problem?', *Regional Studies,* 13 (1979), 233–43
Massey, D. and Meegan, R. A. 'Industrial restructuring versus the cities', *Urban Studies,* 15 (1978), 273–288
Massey, D. and Meegan, R. A. 'The geography of industrial reorganisation', *Progress in Planning,* 10 (1979), 155–237
Mather, A. S. 'Patterns of afforestation in Britain since 1945', *Geography,* 63 (1978), 157–166
Moore, B. and Rhodes, J. 'Evaluating the effects of British regional policy', *Economic Journal,* (1973), 87–110
Moore, B. and Rhodes, J. 'The effects of regional economic policy in the United Kingdom', in M. Sant (Ed.) *Regional Policy and Planning for Europe* (Saxon House, 1974)
Moore, B. and Rhodes, J. 'Regional policy and the Scottish economy', *Scottish Journal of Political Economy,* 21 (1974), 215–35
Moore, B. and Rhodes, J. *Regional Policy and the Economy of Wales* (Welsh Office, Cardiff, 1975)
Moore, B. and Rhodes, J. 'Regional economic policy and the movement of manufacturing firms to development areas', *Economica,* 43 (1976), 12–31
Moore, B. and Rhodes, J. 'A quantitative analysis of the effects of regional employment premium and other regional policy instru-

ments', in A. Whiting (Ed.) *The Economics of Industrial Subsidies* (HMSO, 1976)

Moore, B., Rhodes, J., and Tyler, P. 'The impact of regional policies in the 1970s', *C. E. S. Review,* 1 (1977), 67–77

Moseley, M. J. and Darby, J. 'The determinants of female activity rates in rural areas', *Regional Studies,* 12 (1978), 297–310

Moseley, M. J. and Sant, M. *Industrial Development in East Anglia* (Geo Books, 1977)

Moseley, M. J. and Townroe 'Linkage adjustment following industrial movement', *Tijdschrift voor Econ and Soc. Geographie,* 69 (1973), 137–44

Mounfield, P. R. 'Industrial ablation in the East Midland footwear district', *East Midland Geographer,* (1978), 3–18

Musgrove, F. *The Migratory Elite* (Heinemann, 1963)

Musson, A. E. *The Growth of British Industry* (Batsford, 1978)

Myrdal, G. M. *Economic Theory and Underdeveloped Regions* (Duckworth, 1957)

National Health Service *A Hospital Plan for England and Wales* (HMSO, 1962)

Nockolds, H. *Lucas: The First One Hundred Years,* Vol. 1 (David and Charles, 1976)

Nockolds, H. *Lucas: The First One Hundred Years,* Vol. 2 (David and Charles, 1978)

North, D. C. 'Location theory and regional economic growth', *Journal of Political Economy,* 63 (1955), 243–258

North, J. and Spooner, D. 'The great U.K. coal rush', *Area,* 9 (1977), 15–27

North, J. and Spooner, D. 'The geography of the coal industry in the United Kingdom in the 1970s', *Geographical Journal,* 2 (1978), 255–72

Northcott, J. 'Industry in the development areas: the experience of firms opening new factories', *PEP Broadsheet* No 573 (1977)

Northern Region Strategy Team, *Office Activity in the Northern Region,* Technical Report No 8 (Newcastle, 1976)

Northern Region Strategy Team, *Strategic Plan for the Northern Region,* 5 Vols (Newcastle, 1977)

Northern Region Strategy Team, *Linkages in the Northern Region,* Working Paper No 6 (Newcastle, 1977)

O.E.C.D. *Industrial Research Associations in the United Kingdom* (Paris, O.E.C.D., 1967)

Office of Population Censuses and Surveys, *Population Projections 1976–2016* (HMSO, 1978)

Office of Population Censuses and Surveys, *Population Projections 1975–1991* (HMSO, PP3, 1978)

Oliver, F. R. 'Inter-regional migration and unemployment, 1951–

61', *Journal of the Royal Statistical Society*, Series A (1964), 42–68

Owen, A. D. K. 'The social consequences of industrial transference', *Sociological Review*, 29 (1937), 331–354

Payne, P. L. 'The emergence of the large-scale company in Great Britain, 1870–1914', *Economic History Review*, (1967), 519–41

Parsons, G. F. 'The giant manufacturing corporation and balanced regional growth in Britain', *Area*, 4 (1972), 99–103

Penrose, E. T. *The Theory of the Growth of the Firm* (Blackwell, 1959)

Perroux, F. 'Economic space, theory and applications', *Quarterly Journal of Economics*, 64 (1955), 89–104

Pitfield, D. E. 'The quest for an effective regional policy 1934–7', *Regional Studies*, 12 (1978), 429–444

Prais, S. J. *The Evolution of Giant Firms in Britain: A Study of the Growth of Concentration in Manufacturing Industry in Britain 1909–70* (Cambridge University Press, 1976)

Rake, D. J. 'Spatial changes in industrial activity in the East Midlands since 1945: the hosiery industry', *East Midland Geographer*, 6 (1974), 51–65

Rake, D. J. 'Spatial changes in industrial activity in the East Midlands since 1945: the footwear industry', *East Midland Geographer*, 6 (1975), 173–184

Rawstron, E. M. 'Industry' in Chapter 16 in J. W. Watson and J. B. Sissons (Ed.) *The British Isles: A Systematic Geography* (Nelson, 1964)

Rawstron, E. M. 'Electric power in Great Britain', *Geography*, 49 (1964), 304–9

Rhodes, J. and Kan, A. *Office Dispersal and Regional Policy* (Cambridge University Press, 1971)

Richardson, H. W. 'The development of the synthetic dyestuffs industry before 1939', *Scottish Journal of Political Economy*, 9 (1962), 110–29

Richardson, H. W. *Regional Growth Theory* (Macmillan, 1973)

Robson, B. T. *Urban Growth: An Approach* (Methuen, 1973)

Sanderson, M. 'Research and the firm in British industry, 1919–39', *Science Studies*, 2 (1972), 107–151

Sant, M. E. C. 'Inter-regional industrial movement: the case of the non-survivors' in Philips and Turton (Ed.) *Environment, Man and Economic Change* (Longman, 1975)

Simpson, E. S. *Coal and Power Industries in Post War Britain* (Longman, 1966)

Singer, H. W. *Transference and Age Structure of the Population of Special Areas*, Pilgrim Trust Unemployment Enquiry, Interim Report No 3 (1937)

Smith, B. C. *Regionalism in England*, London, Action Society Trust, 3 Vols (1965)

Smith, D. M. 'A theoretical framework for geographical studies of industrial location', *Economic Geography*, 42 (1966), 95–113

Smith, D. M. *Industrial Britain: The North West* (1966), (David and Charles, 1969)

Smith, I. J. *Ownership, Status and Employment Changes in Northern Region Manufacturing Industry 1963–1973*, Centre for Urban and Regional Development Studies, University of Newcastle, Discussion Paper No 7 (1978)

Spooner, D. J. 'Industrial movement and the rural periphery: the case of Devon and Cornwall', *Regional Studies*, 6 (1972), 197–215

Stamp, L. D. and Beaver, S. H. *The British Isles* (Longman, 1971)

Steuer, M. D. et al *The Impact of Foreign Direct Investment on the United Kingdom* (HMSO, 1973)

Stilwell, F. J. B. 'Regional growth and structural adaptation', *Urban Studies*, 6 (1969), 162–78

Stone, P. A. 'Policies for manufacturing industries in London', *Greater London Intelligence Journal*, No 37 (1977)

Taylor, M. J. 'Location decisions and the small firm', *Area*, 2 (1970), 51–4

Taylor, M. J. 'Organisational growth, spatial interaction and location decision making', *Regional Studies*, 9 (1975), 313–324

Thirlwall, A. P. 'A measure of the "proper distribution of industry"', *Oxford Economic Papers*, 19 (1967), 46–58

Thomas, B. 'The movement of labour into South East England, 1920–32', *Economica*, 1 (1934), 220–41

Thomas, B. 'The influx of labour into London and the South East, 1920–36', *Economica*, 4 (1937), 323–36

Thomas, R. 'The new investment incentives', *Bulletin of the Oxford Institute of Statistics*, 33 (1971), 93–105

Thompson, L. *Industrial Performance and Regional Policy, 1952–71* Centre for Urban and Regional Development Studies, University of Newcastle, Discussion Paper No 21 (1978)

Thompson, W. R. 'The economic base of urban problems' in N.W. Chamberlain (Ed.) *Contemporary Economic Issues* (1969)

Tomkins, C. and Lovering, J. *Location, Size, Ownership and Control Tables for Welsh Industry* (Welsh Council, 1973)

Townroe, P. M. 'Branch plants and regional development', *Town Planning Review*, 46 (1975), 47–62

Townroe, P. M. 'Settling-in costs of mobile plants', *Urban Studies*, 13 (1976), 67–70

Townsend, A. R. Smith, E. and Johnson, M. R. D. 'Employees experience of new factories in North East England', *Environment and Planning*, A 10 (1978), 1345–62

Trotman-Dickenson, D. I. 'The Scottish industrial estates', *Scottish Journal of Political Economy*, 8 (1961), 45–57

Watts, H. D. 'The location of the beet sugar industry, 1912–1936', *Institute of British Geographers Transactions*, 53 (1971), 95–116

Watts, H. D. 'Spatial rationalisation in multi-plant enterprises', *Geoforum* (1974), 69–76

Waugh, M. 'The changing distribution of professional and managerial manpower in England and Wales between 1961 and 1966', *Regional Studies*, 3 (1969), 157–169

Weir, I. *Regional Budgets, Regional Strategy and Devolution: an Inquiry Based on the Report of the Northern Regional Strategy Team*, Centre for Urban and Regional Development Studies, University of Newcastle, Discussion Paper No 8 (1977)

West Midlands County Council *A Time for Action: Economic and Social Trends in the West Midlands* (Birmingham, 1975)

Westaway, J. 'Contact potential and the occupational structure of the British urban system 1961–66: an empirical study', *Regional Studies*, 8 (1974), 57–73

Willats, E. C. and Newson, G. C. 'The geographical pattern of population changes in England and Wales, 1921–51', *Geographical Journal*, 119 (1953), 431–54.

Williams, J. L. 'Some social consequences of grammar school selection in a rural area in Wales', *British Journal of Sociology*, 10 (1959), 125–8

Wood, P. A. *Industrial Britain: The West Midlands* (David and Charles, 1976)

Wright, M. 'Provincial office development', *Urban Studies*, 4 (1967), 218–57

Index